by the same author

THE IMPROVISATION GAME
Discovering the Secrets of Spontaneous Performance

HOUSE OF GAMES

CHRIS JOHNSTON

Chris Johnston trained at the Drama Centre, London, before working in small-scale theatre as writer and director. He was Secretary of the Association of Community Theatres for several years. He has written shows for Greenwich Young People's Theatre, Word & Action (Dorset) and other companies. In 1987 he founded Insight Arts Trust, which creates arts programmes for prison and probation contexts. In 1998 he co-founded Rideout (Creative Arts for Rehabilitation) which has organised a range of innovative mixed-artform projects in prisons within the Midlands. He was a recipient of a Butler Trust Award in 2005 for work at HMYOI Swinfen Hall. Recently he has been exploring improvisation practice as part of a three-year fellowship awarded by the Arts and Humanities Research Board in 2003. One result of this work was his second book, *The Improvisation Game*, published in 2006.

HOUSE OF GAMES

MAKING THEATRE
FROM EVERYDAY LIFE

Chris Johnston

NICK HERN BOOKS
London
www.nickhernbooks.co.uk

A NICK HERN BOOK

House of Games
first published in Great Britain in 1998
as a paperback original by Nick Hern Books Limited,
14 Larden Road, London W3 7ST

This revised edition published in 2005

Front cover: www.energydesignstudio.com

Typeset by Country Setting, Kingsdown, Kent CT14 8ES
Printed and bound in Great Britain
by Cromwell Press, Trowbridge, Wilts

British Library Cataloguing data for this book
is available from the British Library

ISBN 978 1 85459 905 6

FOREWORD TO THE SECOND EDITION

The fact that we have a second edition of *House of Games*, following several reprints, is testimony to the increasing involvement of artists, performers and theatre directors with community-based projects as a core part of their practice. The field itself continues to expand in a variety of shape-shifting ways, with projects in schools, hospitals, prisons, youth clubs and outdoor spaces no longer regarded as the radical exceptions to the norm. It's been great to get feedback to the first edition from as far away as Holland, the USA and Cambodia. At the centre of this flux of activity remains the facilitator, that peculiar hybrid of artist, organiser and teacher who, typically in such projects, holds the various strings together. He or she is always trying to work a certain alchemy in unlikely situations. It's a matter of mixing idealism with pragmatism, courage with sensitivity, creativity with DIY, and the kind of determined inventiveness that can be repointed at a moment's notice. Underpinning all this will also be required a good sense of the social and political nexus within which the work is operating. To say it's a juggling act would be to accord jugglers a broader skill set than they would probably claim. What's more, this community-based work often takes place unheard and unrecognised, despite what for the participants is the experience of 'great reckonings in small rooms'.

This book is concerned with the exercise of this facilitator role, trying as best as possible to compute some of the different obligations and challenges involved. While many new projects have changed the contours on the map since the book was written, the essential tasks remain the same, and these are what I have tried to focus on, acknowledging at the same time the breadth of activity within which any facilitator might choose to place herself. We certainly haven't moved to a point where the role is redundant; far from it. As social institutions grow more complex, the need for the individual artist-facilitator to cut through the patina of consumerism to create some dynamic, creative and useful relationships with community groups has never been stronger. Inevitably, the art focus here is drama since that's my own background, but I hope those coming from other directions will find strategies of interest. As the last chapter suggests, artform boundaries are becoming increasingly blurred; however, the central notion of ineradicable, transformative, alchemical play remains as vital and constant as ever.

Chris Johnston, July 2005

FOR MY MOTHER

ELIZABETH JOHNSTON

CONTENTS

INTRODUCTION

PART ONE: FOUNDATIONS

PART TWO: FACILITATION

INTRODUCTION

NOTES ON THE AUTHOR

I was training to be a Stanislavskian method actor when a short, bearded man entered the rehearsal room and started throwing tennis balls around. Clive Barker had learned the value of theatre games during membership of Joan Littlewood's company where, I was amazed to learn, the actors made their own plays. The tennis balls changed everything. They made me realise that there might just be alternatives out there to my then classical, text-based curriculum. The idea of working within a community, ensemble tradition struck me as temptingly preferable to yet further exhausting analyses of Chekhovian super-objectives. What appeared so alluring about Clive's approach was its potential for reflecting chaos. Because that's what we experienced so profoundly just then: chaos, difficulty, insecurity, panic, the need for rebellion. Classical theatre, for all its power, seemed limited to adolescent eyes. It appeared to reflect these disturbing experiences only by means of cold mirrors. It didn't talk to working-class audiences. It offered no means to such audiences to express their own dilemmas. It was not open to be appropriated by those audiences for their own purposes.

Clive signposted a tradition which offered engagement with theatre through a different yet familiar language, that of games. Instead of elaborating a series of initiations, an elemental journey into the mysteries of Stanislavskian craft, he relied upon more immediate catalysts: physicality, fun and playfulness. Pleasure was the spring-board, lifting us into movement, dialogue, interaction. There was laughter. The work was accessible and lively, and the theoretical baggage light enough to carry. Most important of all, you could argue about it. There were no more inscrutable references to obscure methodologies that confused and generated anxiety. The teacher didn't necessarily have all the answers. Looking back, I think it had a lot to do with the role Clive played in the room. He played low status and argued that good practice depended more on playfulness than on private study. Not that other students agreed or saw things the same way. As my disenchantment with the classical idea was growing, a colleague arrived at a personal milestone on that journey. *'At a stroke, the mask that I had screwed onto my face fell away. I was free, easy, effortless . . . it was then, in that moment, that acting became second nature to me.'*[1] Simon Callow had arrived at the enlightenment of which the teachers had spoken, but this moment seemed to be about the self, about acting, about Being an Actor. Clive's work pointed obliquely in a different direction – although I subsequently realised how valuable it can be for enlivening a classical tradition – towards theatre rather than acting, towards an experience whose centre was less the individual actor than the shifting space between actors – and, by implication, between actors and audience. Following this, I speculated, if what was important was the science of collaboration, of ensemble, of complementarity, then all the shiny accessories of a young actor's assault into orbit: the interview with the agent, the audition pieces, the smiling, intense photographs – were no more useful to me than a high level of skill at bungee-jumping. More important clearly was learning about relationships that might be formed between actors, and about relationships that might be formed between actors and their potential or actual communities.

So on leaving drama school, I set about trying to discover where such an ensemble practice might be located. I sought a practice that was participatory and egalitarian while anchored in the lives of ordinary people. The search proved difficult in 1975. There was no consistent tradition of the kind Joan Littlewood, Ewan McColl, Clive Barker and others had worked to establish. But there was a fledgling community theatre movement and within it a range of new initiatives. Companies were moving out of theatres into youth clubs, prisons and schools, creating new constituencies. Theatre-in-education companies were receiving funding, and mixing and matching plays with participatory techniques. Visual and physical performance groups were carrying forward experimentation begun by the Living Theatre and the Open Theatre in the US, and by the People Show and others in this country. Their performances took place in unlikely venues: a pub, a telephone box, a swimming pool. Keith Johnstone's influence on improvisation was being felt. Augusto Boal's work with Theatre of the Oppressed was just reaching Europe. There was widespread decommissioning and deconstructing of old ideas about 'who theatre was for' and what the dialogue involved. Much of this involved real commitment to building relationships with working-class and disenfranchised communities; CAST, Red Ladder, Recreation Ground, Word & Action (Dorset) and Belt and Braces were among companies taking this route. In all this work, there was clearly scope for personal exploration.

But it was equally evident my collection of skills was inadequate. There were only so many uses for the Laban effort cube in Lambeth Day Centre where members' energies went primarily into holding their families together with dignity. Drama school had offered no classes in running improvisations with wheelchair users. My re-education was necessarily painful. It proceeded by virtue of the ancient science of making it up as you go along. Some argue this the best way but a sequence of howling errors did test the thesis. However, after a gruelling apprenticeship, I did emerge with some suspicions confirmed. I discovered that those coming to a devising process without formal training, can and often do make highly effective theatre. Coming from the community rather than the profession, these actors arrive with something to say rather than worrying overmuch about career priorities. They can project dramatic material effectively because they're less concerned with technical excellence than with whether or not that material is true to their own experience. Professional actors by contrast find it hard to generate improvised work which is so telling of their class and culture.

I saw how participatory drama can breathe life into formerly listless community centres. I saw how participants can break down personal barriers and grow visibly from the experience. They can bond in ways which day-to-day routines simply don't allow. Drama, I discovered, was clearly capable of generating real transformations at the centre of people's lives. So by the time I concluded this apprenticeship, I did feel confident to argue for a tradition I'd earlier only half-believed in. Evidently many community-based companies, despite their tenuous hold on funding, were having real impact within their areas. But what was frustrating was the absence of civic or governmental commitment to sustain this ongoing practice.

And if we use only statistics as an indicator, community theatre and theatre-in-education in Britain have suffered as cutbacks and shifting civic priorities have taken their toll. At the time of writing there are far fewer companies operative than in the peak period of the early eighties. Many early practitioners have been beaten by the struggle or have moved on to television or mainstream theatre. Nevertheless, others have perservered. Either working freelance or in small teams, these former students of Berman, Boal, Heathcote and Johnstone have created a body of practice that today appears as separate, distinct and influential. Many techniques are similar to those of earlier teachers and often there are hybrids and variations, but much of this new work is innovatory. It has a language which is varied but accessible, and its strategies are appropriate for a range of contexts and for people right across the social spectrum. The practice both acknowledges the potential creativity of disenfranchised groups, and has ideas and techniques for enfranchisement.

What most characterises current practice is its participatory, democratic nature: at best it avoids earlier mistakes and does not impose attitudes or programmes. Instead it places emphasis on innovative forms so the medium is better able to adapt to the priorities of differing groups; the elderly, offenders, the young, those having special needs or those who are disabled. One particular characteristic of the new momentum is the way drama is used as a learning tool in the study of social conflict. Acknowledging the needs of disadvantaged groups, theatre practitioners are developing techniques which engage directly with issues of personal development and group empowerment. At the same time, this work gives energy to the quiet voices of those who have often been silent. In youth clubs, day centres, prisons, clubs and hospitals, there are increasing opportunities for participants to challenge, through theatre, a status quo which would often rather not be listening.

In this book I hope to illuminate some of the strategies that make this drama practice so distinctive and wide-ranging. By drawing on my own and contemporaries' experiences I hope to feed back some insights that will help this tradition re-invent itself, as it must do consistently if drama is to be a successful catalyst to community development.

THE BOOK

The book is particularly intended for those running participatory drama or theatre work in community settings. Having said that, it's concerned more with drama than theatre. It deals with the drama workshop experience, how a group works together privately behind closed doors, rather than how it meets an audience. In particular it's concerned with the role of the drama facilitator. There are three sections:

FOUNDATIONS   The functions, hypotheses and polarities of drama. This looks at what practitioners generally conceive as the underlying assumptions behind their work – what gives the medium legitimacy in the sports hall or the old people's club? What assumptions underpin a marriage of the arts and social psychology?

FACILITATION   What does a drama facilitator do? What are the nuts and bolts of this role which is not quite a teacher nor a director? What are the potentials and limitations of the role?

ANIMATIONS   Games, exercises and techniques that can be used in drama workshops, with a commentary about the challenges and difficulties of applying them. Finally there are some pointers for devising plays for production.

The book is intended as a sourcebook, allowing readers to make their own journey around it. It might be read from first page to last, or raided for inspiration as necessary. Each of the three sections may be read separately or in a different order. The techniques and games come from a variety of sources. Some are standard drama games, others have come from practitioners like Augusto Boal, Ed Berman, Clive Barker or Keith Johnstone. The following generation of practitioners have often adapted these exercises. Consistently there's re-evaluation going on. As a result, games and exercises appear in different forms with different emphases and under different titles. No apologies are made for these changes. Doubtless earlier generations of practitioners themselves borrowed and adapted accordingly. Some of the exercises come directly from facilitators who are my contemporaries and where it's appropriate I've noted their authorship. My apologies if they're presented with an unfamiliar emphasis. Other exercises I invented myself.

Whatever their source or background, all these games and exercises are in the public domain. Theatre games by nature resist copyrighting. Whoever originates a particular exercise is likely to be echoing an earlier one, which itself may well be rooted in a children's game or folkloric ritual. Everyone has the option of inventing their own exercises; hopefully this book will make it easier for readers to do that. My contemporaries' contributions are invaluable; it would be very hard to write this kind of book without them. This is true not just for the exercises but for their insights into different working processes. Where possible, I've used their own words to describe these approaches, drawing from personal interviews. All the unreferenced quotations are from these interviews. Of course many of these practitioners have differing priorities and contexts for their work, but it's also possible to see common ground. All have an interest in two key questions which this book hopes to address: *How can a facilitator use the drama medium to enable a group to speak, learn and empower itself ?* And *How can a group, especially a non-professional group, collaborate to make performance which is rooted in the group members' experiences?*

TERMINOLOGIES

Some definitions may be useful, not to curtail debate but rather to encourage some consistency in an area where looseness is often a tactic to encourage participation. Between 'drama' and 'theatre', I follow a popular distinction which argues that drama is not dependent on the presence of an audience. It is rather a spontaneous, creative enactment of fiction within a private sphere. Theatre opens out the enactment process to include the presence of spectators, and aims to trigger a reflective process in them. Of course such a distinction can appear superficial. There are many theatre moments within a drama workshop. As with Russian dolls, we open the box marked drama only to find a theatre experience within. In a drama workshop, the group often divides to create an audience; at a theatre event, audiences can sometimes intervene and participate. But in a drama workshop, the audience is made up of participants while in the theatre, even spectators who intervene or Boalian 'spectactors' have turned up primarily to watch. So broadly the distinction holds.

The term 'drama workshop' is taken as a collaborative event which might have one of the following objectives: recreation, learning, experimentation, debate, confidence-building, research into social conflict or even devising a play. The only characteristics we do assume are that it uses the drama medium and tends not to involve the presence of an audience.

The term 'community' has become the king of polysemes. Raymond Williams notes its presence in our vocabulary since the fourteenth century and by the nineteenth it had already acquired a confection of different meanings. This has allowed politicians to attach it to banners and programmes of widely differing even opposite persuasions. Here, Baz Kershaw's use of the terms community of place and community of interest, best help to identify the contexts where community theatre can take a role.[2] What tends to characterise such communities today is their modes of relating, which may not always be the shared hostelry, church or street of the past but rather the conference, the festival or the demonstration – brief associations which signify felt identification.

While 'community' is problematic, terms such as 'fringe' and 'alternative' have floated to the surface during a more recent period of cultural gestation, and also need to be used with circumspection. They represent the struggle of theatre practitioners for both legitimacy and unorthodoxy at the same time. 'Fringe' is claimed to have derived from the Edinburgh fringe and still implies marginality. Ironically, much of the work on 'the fringe' is work created to attract the attention of those at the centre, and is often less innovative even than mainstream work – a kind of audition round the back in the hope of being let in at the front. 'Alternative' is more useful in that it does imply unorthodox practice, despite the acquired connotation of being daring in a kind of superficial, scandal-for-its-own-sake way. Significantly, the practitioners who have contributed to this volume tend to avoid such labels altogether, preferring to refer more generally to 'theatre or drama work' or 'community theatre', unless there's a specific application like 'prison theatre' or 'street theatre'.

The word 'facilitator' is close to others which describe similar roles; Boal's 'Joker', the 'Conductor' within Playback Theatre and the 'Questioner' within Instant Theatre. The word itself is relatively new. It's a term which has emerged not as part of some planned cultural programme but awkwardly as an attempt to describe the function which the drama practitioner performs in relation to a group. She or he facilitates, that is, 'makes easy' the task of seizing the theatre language. Sometimes, too, they have to 'make difficult' – hence Boal's coining of 'difficultation'. 'Workshop leader' attempts a similar task of definition although it perhaps fails to incorporate any idea of the enabling, empowering role. Both 'teacher' and 'director' are used sometimes in community contexts, and they help to lend a legitimacy to what is taking place. But there's a key difference between the conventional idea of the teacher and that of the facilitator. The former is more concerned with passing on skills while the latter tends to orientate the work around the perceived agenda of the participating group. 'Director' is more conventionally one who organises actors towards production.

'Participant' is the term used to cover all those who attend drama workshops. Alternatives used are 'community actor' (i.e. non-professional actor) or 'player'. 'Student' is used occasionally but feels less appropriate because of its association with more formal learning processes.

HOUSE OF GAMES

MAKING THEATRE
FROM EVERYDAY LIFE

'Welcome to the House of Fun.
Welcome to the lion's den.'

Madness

PART ONE

FOUNDATIONS

'Socialism will be of value simply because
it will lead to Individualism.'

Oscar Wilde

'I would not create a School of Theatre.
I would create a School of Audience.'

Jonathan Kay

Peter (*a father interviewing a prospective son-in-law*):
'As a father, I have certain responsibilities towards my
daughter, and I have to find out certain things about you.
For example, where you went to school. Not that it
matters, but it is important.'

Peter Cook and Dudley Moore

FOUNDATIONS

THE POTENTIAL
OF COMMUNITY DRAMA

As an art form, drama has considerable advantages over music or the visual arts by criteria of accessibility. There is an immediacy to its practice. There are no scales to be learned or arpeggios to be practised, we can begin creating material straight away. Drama's language is simply the language of social experience – what it 'feels like' to be alive – borrowed and fashioned for other purposes. So it's easily accessible to those who lack professional arts training. We can claim, reasonably enough, that *everyone* has a basic proficiency in its grammar. Everyone 'improvises' from the moment they get out of bed. We all feel pain, experience joy, and learn to 'act a part'.

The medium is also – despite appearances to the contrary generated by professional practice – non-discriminatory. There is no physical or mental condition that debars entry to participation. Those in wheelchairs, those with mental illness, the very young, those who are hospitalised or suffering from depression, none are excluded from participating at a grass-roots level. The medium is sufficiently malleable to adapt to different circumstances and sufficiently multi-faceted to contain appropriate strategies which will harness the strengths and capabilities of different comers. And it can do this without losing sight of its core idea: the interpretation of experience through deliberate, playful enactment.

The art form has a special aptness for groups who are excluded or choose to exclude themselves from mainstream culture. This is due to its plasticity and multi-functionality. In essence theatre is but a set of masks which can be designed and selected from, at will. It's difficult for civic authorities to control this process. They can suppress its visible manifestations but they can never dominate or eliminate it. Even mild suppression is problematic; the censorship of plays in Great Britain by the Lord Chamberlain became increasingly fraught and absurd until censorship was abandoned in 1968. Drama and theatre are by nature subversive media. They thrive on difficult, subversive voices. Technology may come in useful but it's not essential, the medium can be explored quite well with the energy of commitment alone.

Drama is also appropriate as a specifically *community* activity because it nurtures values which are concordant with community ideals. These I would describe as broadly humanist; respecting co-operation, sociability and equality of opportunity while engendering mutual respect. The drama process relies upon the active respect of these values while the mechanics of drama encourage their promotion. So the relationship is mutually beneficial. The more we engage with the art form, the more we appreciate and value collaboration. The more we collaborate, the more possibilities open to us as theatre-makers – which is why, at the beginning of any group drama process, there needs to be emphasis placed on these key values of mutual respect, free expression and collective discipline.

Usually these values are tacitly accepted by those coming into drama. Participants instinctively understand that a willingness to enter into the spirit of the exercise is an obvious precondition to entry. They understand also that drama is, despite appearances, a natural leveller. If someone claims to 'know it all', their comeuppance may not be far away. For the medium depends on expression of human frailty for its mechanics. The primary currency of our interaction is the quality of feeling, which is exposing to some degree. But feelings have to be offered voluntarily, in a spirit of generosity. It's very hard for any director to instruct feeling. (The only emotions I can be sure to generate are so-called negative emotions; fear, insecurity, distrust – the emotions inspired by coercive behaviour.) So we recognise the need to collectively generate sufficient mutual respect to enable this emotional generosity. It's the facilitator's task to establish an appro-priate regime. The group has to trust me as the facilitator, I them, they each other.

If the appropriate conditions are created, then it becomes a matter of faith that the synthesis of values and art form traditions will create a successful marriage. Success can never be guaranteed but if parti-cipants attend voluntarily, they automatically have a vested interest in learning this relationship and profiting from it. I would propose the potential of community drama lies principally in four areas: recreation, solidarity, study of conflict and celebration. We'll take a brief look at each in turn but I would stress that these *different* functions are often mixed together in the *same* project.

A. RECREATION

Firstly, drama facilitates playfulness which revitalises our inner energies and extends our self-perceptions. It is axiomatic that drama begins with play. However, it is only relatively recently that 'play' as an idea has achieved the respect it currently deserves within scholarship. Indeed, so much has now been written about it that Richard Schechner proposes: '*Maybe scholars should declare a moratorium on defining play!*'[3] However, let's be awkward and propose, in a tradition of practice rather than scholarship, that play is 'directed activity, engendering live-liness, interaction, imaginative excitability and the reduction or removal of conventional spatial and temporal boundaries, in an exercise which is releasing and rewarding, often merely for its own sake.'

And for many groups, 'to play' is sufficient. Recreational drama facilitates individual and group expression and involves the pleasurable breaking of taboos around touch and language. The exercise is a welcome escape from the constraints of orthodox behaviour. The experience is invigorating; it allows for inner selves, inner personalities denied elsewhere, to emerge. As Sybil Thorndike said: '*When you're an actor you cease to be male and female, you're a person, and you're a person with all the other persons inside you.*'[4] Here is their place of emergence. Or as an elderly lady who used to attend a regular drama workshop told me, '*And on Thursdays, I'm silly. That's my day for being silly and for playing about.*' Which was quite enough for me. It would have been inappropriate to demand of her that she combine with us to make a play, research social conflict or do Forum Theatre. For her, she sought an outlet for her frivolity and her sense of humour, which elsewhere felt stifled. It was precisely the rebellion against sense, against order, which she chose. And the English often feel a great need to be released from their good sense. We're perhaps too sensible for our own good. As Simon Callow points out: '*one of the great contributions of the English to world culture, is nonsense. A great deal of English humour is based on nonsense . . . It goes right across English culture from Lawrence Sterne to . . . Monty Python.*'[5]

Drama for re/creation arguably contains all the medium's future challenges in microcosm. The work of Jonathan Kay, Phelim McDermott, Guy Dartnell and many others could be said to take place within this territory. While nonsense may be what's on the surface, there is real value in working backwards, against sense. As McDermott observes, *'What I try to assert is that we're doing something very important by mucking about.'* And many would recognise the supreme logic in Lois Weaver's intent to: *'set up an environment where the illogic is primary, where nonsense is the basis. Because I think theatre should be unpredictable. I believe life is more chaotic than we're led to believe . . . In this workshop we may be a Margaret Thatcher-like tap dancing Canadian who sings Barry Manilow songs. Why not?'*

Such work is frivolous but not unserious. It proceeds from what Guy Dartnell refers to as an 'intelligent foolishness.' Nor is there any assumption that 'play' cannot take you into difficult areas or even into what Schechner calls 'dark play' – which *'subverts order, dissolves frames, breaks its own rules, so that the playing itself is in danger of being destroyed.'*[6] What play *can* do, is generate a shared vulnerability which allows us to get closer to our secret, irrational selves. For the truth is, we may not always know ourselves. We may discover in the characterisation of the tap-dancing Canadian, something in us which is more truly ourselves than our preferred self-image.

Drama is regenerative when participants are able to incorporate into their daily lives these secret discoveries. 'Different' feelings and ideas are provoked – can these be acknowledged and incorporated into everyday behaviour? Such feelings have emerged from our own memories and desires. Perhaps these have become boxed away by daily responsibilities. Through incorporating them, individuals may grow from the experience. We may become less frightened and more knowing of ourselves, accepting – as children can do through the assimilation of folktale wisdom – that we have inner strengths to deal with external challenges.

B. SOLIDARITY

Often people come into community drama not just for recreation but to positively leave behind their isolation. They want to bond with others and share experiences. Drama offers the means to do it. The means are appropriate because the abiding characteristic of theatre work is its collaborative nature. Within group membership there are duties and responsibilities – we have to nurture and appreciate others, take care of others, share their inventions – and they must do the same for us. Effective performance work relies on this gregariousness. Not that it doesn't go wrong – we can't deny just how fractious, embittered and painful things *can* become if personalities clash and the working process breaks down. But we can minimise the chances of it happening by working methodologically, i.e. by following recognised teaching patterns.

The process of bonding with others happens in this way: if I feel marginalised within society, my position is relatively weak because I've accepted that what defines me by sexuality, ethnicity or disability acts as a brake on the social participation I can achieve, which others enjoy as a matter of course. And it's still true that heterosexual couples can behave publicly in ways not acceptable for gay people. Black people are consistently more subject to stop and search procedures, and to guilty verdicts in the courts, than white people. Those with disabilities are still regarded as inadequate and careless parents.

By combining with others in a group, I can find support to resist those negative social projections which reduce my freedom to function as a citizen. As Lois Weaver observes: *'In a gay and lesbian environment, a lot of our concerns are with . . . being whole people because we live in a society where we're being told we're sick.'* The temptation to see myself as 'sick' can start to be overcome through a process of articulating interior anxieties. For example, I may achieve this through characterisations. I can delegate to my outer (fictional) character the responsibility of speaking all those (actual) inner thoughts which I can't bring myself to articulate in daily life, and which I've introjected from others' projections. In this way, we give each other permission to draw into the open, parts of ourselves which are not viewed as acceptable by society. And in the context of the group workshop, these parts of ourselves *will* be accepted, even celebrated. So we recognise the similarities between us. We share our insecurities and so begin to find common cause. The net effect is educational; what I previously saw as a 'normality' from which I was excluded, I now start to view as a matrix of social taboos and projections that are discriminatory. Recognised as such, the projections become less powerful.

So what we're doing is taking our own situation, as a minority group for example, directly or indirectly as the subject of our playing, and examining causative patterns of behaviour around it. In this way the relationship between public prejudice and private lack of self-esteem becomes comprehensible, no longer concealed by hegemonic ideology. Drama in this model is about shifting perceptions to foster mutual learning. It's about bringing secrets to the surface of shared consciousness, secrets which are sometimes due to the repressions of social conditioning.

A further step may involve extending our communication skills. By using roleplay, we can learn to deal with social situations which are customarily problematic. From this point, it is a short step towards exploring strategies of active control over our own lives. We might move towards Forum Theatre for example, in which we 'rehearse living', or agitational theatre where we challenge public assumptions. It may even be that we start with the desire to create performance, and use our shared anger as a springboard into direct, demonstrative, political work. David Slater, who works with retired people in Rother-hithe, East London, observes that *some group members are recognised now as the theatre-makers of the area*' despite the fact they may be up to 90 years old and long since retired. But these individuals, through their relationship with theatre, have taken the opportunity to place on the local agenda, key issues about retirement and public resources for the elderly. They've refused to become invisible.

C. THE STUDY OF CONFLICT

The drama process also allows us to research behavioural conflict. As Nic Fine and Fiona Macbeth's training handbook observes on its first page, the Chinese character for crisis encompasses both the concepts of 'opportunity' and that of 'danger'. With this model, drama is used as the means for participants to *explore situations of conflict and potential violence . . . practise skills for dealing with them, and rehearse possible strategies and techniques for future use*'. Fine and Macbeth go on to argue: *'The key principle embodied in this . . . is one of individual respect, the trust that every life is valuable. We need to be able to respect ourselves; we need to respect others.*'[7]

This model finds most common application with groups whose behaviour is destructive to themselves or others. These might include offenders, youth at risk, or groups with special behavioural concerns. Why is drama a tool here? Because, as John Bergman says *'The first thing which theatre does is hold up a mask but in a way which is not censorious.'* Drama can freeze time, travel in space and speculate about the future. So we're able to put recurring conflict situations under the microscope. Theatre has what Augusto Boal calls a diacthonic nature, that is, it's able to happen on two levels simultaneously. Let's call these the true and the false. Arguably real life happens in a way that is consistently true – or, if you like, consistently false. What takes place on stage is false in that it is constructed. There isn't a 'real' fight taking place (we hope). Yet it's real in that the emotions and sensations generated by the actors are truthful. By moving between these two planes of reality, we can speculate about outcomes, try out alternative actions and see what happens. This duality of operation enables us to handle flammable material and avoid getting burnt – providing safety structures are in place. Participants can 'see themselves' in a way not possible in any other medium. Boal observes: *'I see myself yesterday . . . The "I-today" can see the "I-yesterday", the converse obviously not being possible . . . In this ascesis, the protagonist becomes subject of himself and subject of the situation. Within the theatrical fiction, of course. But let us not forget that in the theatre everything is true, even lies. At least, that is our hypothesis.'*[8]

I remember a workshop with offenders where a participant was placed in an imagined social situation – a tube station platform – and various characters were sent to interact with him. Each one was to bring a provocation. The actor's task was to avoid any destructive conflict building up between him and them. He soon got himself into a violent argument with the ticket inspector. We argued with him that his own attitude was largely the cause for this. He didn't believe us. But when another participant 'acted out' what he had done, again with the ticket inspector, the participant was amazed. He simply could not believe that he operated like that, in such a situation. Soon he was on his feet to handle the provocation another way.

In this model, drama functions as an adjunct to other forms of learning. What we're placing under scrutiny are our impulses, triggers to anger, perceptions and projections. Hence the need for clarity on what the facilitator's own values are, which underpin this process. If these are vague or undefined then the premise on which we question others' behaviour may itself be significantly inadequate. And the facilitator is always open to challenge by participants on this issue.

Within the body of work that takes place under this heading, I would identify these particular strategies: techniques of co-operation, analysis of conflict situations and rehearsal of new behaviours. Some exercises necessarily draw directly upon individuals' personal histories, so we're touching on therapeutic concerns. However, this does not necessarily classify the exercise as therapy unless there's an agreed therapeutic contract between facilitator and group. In community drama, the participants may simply be keen to explore self development, they don't wish to make such a contract. Their purpose is to improve their social and communication skills, express themselves and perhaps learn better how to manage emotions.

D. CELEBRATION

There is a celebratory role for drama. This function is again linked to identity; exploring and celebrating what defines us as a group. A workshop to explore, for example, the specific Asian, elderly or lesbian identity of the participants might come under this heading. So we're building on what is felt to be a prior solidarity. We're bringing to the surface what is sacred or common to us. We can nurture qualities of our lives here which elsewhere have to be down-played because they're not celebrated within the dominant ideology. On a larger scale, the community play might be conceived as theatre for celebration; it celebrates the shared local history of participants, as in the Barrow plays developed by Welfare State or the Dorset plays by Colway Theatre Trust.

Drama for celebration is about exteriorising our dreams. It recognises that below the surface we have aspirations and imaginings which never fully find expression within day-to-day living. And through the daily grind, we suppress and dishonour these dreams. Drama, through its transformations, can provide the means to publicise these powerful, imaginative contents. And crucial to this is a sharing process, working together *as a group* in a way which allows a loosening of our individualities sufficient to develop a creative, liberating momentum. As Phelim McDermott observes, *'If you put a lot of people together, there are a lot of dreams that are trying to come into being from that group. And you want to try to cook them up so they present themselves to the whole group so everyone thinks; "Yes, that is what I'm dreaming".'* R.G. Gregory argues in his book The World of Instant Theatre that it is exactly this quality of 'group dreaming' which reveals us most effectively to ourselves.[9] Yet such a 'theatre of dreaming', created through processes that are impulsive, emerging in shapes and forms that are ambiguous, does not necessarily lend itself to easy interpretation or analysis. We cannot reduce its productivity to an easy handful of maxims; we are, as it were, moving into an archetypal world.

Drama for celebration naturally lends itself to performance. From carnival to kitchen sink naturalism, groups have explored a thousand different ways to celebrate cultural identity. When West Indians in this country began in the 60s to recreate the carnival idea, it was not just celebration but cultural assertiveness. Some argue that cultural forms such as carnival provide a kind of safety-valve, an escapism for the oppressed. But this may be too simplistic. Baz Kershaw argues that *'the roots of carnival are to be found in the self-organization of the community for the production of its own participatory pleasures, in opposition to the hegemonic imposition of the pleasures of the mass media and cultural industries.'*[10]

Storytelling can serve a similar purpose. Through the use of selected imagery, character and incident, a storytelling tradition allows a group to express subversive ideas without the exercise becoming pedantic or overtly pedagogical. When the group makes up its own stories, they begin to celebrate what is culturally distinctive and unique about their world. In Word and Action's Instant Theatre practice, the theatre professionals invite the group to make up a story, in the moment, collectively. The rules of the exercise force the group to project its view of the world into the story format. An avoidance of censorship by the facilitators results in a tale which stitches together mundane and fabulous elements into the same tapestry. The narrative begins to take on a mythic or folkloric resonance, moving between apparent symbolism on one hand and obvious vox-pop humour on the other. When the story is acted out, it works as theatre on a number of levels: as social commentary, as exploration of the archetypal world and as celebration of shared experience. Instant Theatre is one of the very best examples of theatre practice which celebrates society without avoiding the necessity for simultaneous social critique.

SOME HYPOTHESES

Before moving to techniques, it may be useful to identify some of the assumptions which underpin drama facilitation practice. These hypotheses necessarily reflect a certain cultural perspective, so not everyone will share them. But I imagine most practitioners will agree that without some similar latticework of presuppositions, it would be difficult to set up safely the kind of power structure which the medium requires. The hypotheses attempt to answer questions like: What benefit is it to me, to participate? Why should I accept your authority in this room? Why should drama make any difference at all to my life?

I

Sometimes participants come into community drama imagining the only thing that matters is whether or not they have 'talent'. They under-rate themselves or perhaps over-rate themselves on this basis. While this notion of talent clearly has merit – certain individuals *do* display abilities beyond our expectations, it can become problematic when associated with a series of further popular assumptions which disempower those struggling to access their own creativity. The ideas sometimes form a value-set associated with the professionalisation of the arts which crystallised during the Renaissance and have set hard some four hundred years since. In the West, we sometimes accept these supposed truths too easily: some people are artists, others are not, some have talent, others have not, some are stars, others are not, and so on. Now by some criteria these distinctions may be useful, but in the arena of community drama, they may disenfranchise newcomers and weaken their self-confidence.

Community drama proceeds from a different principle; that to all intents and purposes, everyone is an artist. It matters not whether you have prior creative experience, whether or not your father or mother was creative, whether or not you 'feel' yourself to have creative ideas. Everyone can be creative. It's an important assumption because without it we run the risk of establishing a creative hierarchy within the room. 'Alright, let's have all the talented ones down this end – as for the rest . . . ' Often it happens that newcomers assert their creative inadequacy by arguing they 'don't have what it takes'. But what are these qualities they supposedly lack? Sometimes it's said that 'genius' or 'charisma' are the hallmarks of the artist. And they certainly don't have any of that. If we quiz further, we might get reference to an ability to manage shape, colour, light, language or melody in a way which others can't. Well, none would deny that Tolstoy, Shakespeare, Van Gogh, John Lennon (make your own list) access and articulate extraordinary, passionate and eloquent statements about human nature. However, these statements may be less the consequence of unique human attributes than the determined application of attributes which are commonly held. In other words, it's the quality of a vocation which is important, and the determination to access what gifts you possess and can identify. Alongside, we have to remember that different societies are willing to recognise and pay for creative products to different degrees at different times. Can we really only validate those creative artists who are 'recognised'? The long list of artists recognised after their death would suggest not.

Surely the talents which 'successful' artists have drawn from to create their works are in fact possessed by everyone – memory, imagination, emotion, impulse, movement, rhythm, language, a sense of colour? Perhaps the doubting participant simply hasn't accessed her own creativity before now. She has accepted by default a self-image of creative inadequacy. Perhaps for years this individual was told she was talentless. Or perhaps the time spent in offices or factories has atrophied creative libido so much that the struggle to release it feels more painful than the assertion it's absent. As a result, the claim 'I have no talent' or 'I have no imagination' represents yet another wrong solution to a problem. A different strategy can be tried within a drama workshop. Here we can start to identify the repression and so begin to validate the creative impulsiveness. If participants can *think* of themselves in this way, as *already* creative, their self-confidence grows and they become immediately more capable. Without this leap of faith – and how to encourage that leap is part of the business of this book – we remain imitators. We remain trying to imitate that television programme, that film, that story. And yet our strength as creative individuals – whether professional or non-professional artists – lies in the uniqueness of our perceptions, always changing and never inter-changeable with others. R.G. Gregory argues that the task of the theatre is to get *'ordinary people to see that imagination, in particular, is not the weapon of the professionals alone – imagination and the ability to use it, is the gift of everyone. And if we don't exercise that gift in some way, then we hand over our responsibility to other people who always misuse that gift because it's not theirs.'*

I remember an exercise with one participant who was determined not to recognise that he had any creative impulses. He was in a dialogue exercise and it was so clear to everyone present that he was blocking his own spontaneity. He was creatively closed down. Yes, he admitted to being frightened. But he insisted his fear was based on common sense. What does it 'feel like', I asked, this need for security? He said it was like he 'was a naked boy, hiding behind a wall. The group are on the other side of the wall, waiting to have a good laugh.' What I was doing was urging him to leap out and show himself. I was impressed; the image was worthy of an artist.

The emphasis here is consciously on artist rather than actor. Lois Weaver observes that she's *'not training actors but creating the independent artist. People who come into that situation often think about what it means to be an actor. But what we're thinking about is what it takes to be a creative person.'* Perhaps that person will become a dancer, a visual artist, a photographer or a writer – the drama is there simply to open the door. Following this is an equally important presupposition. Whatever individuals bring – as life experiences – is valuable. It doesn't matter whether you've spent your whole life in a quiet English street or have spent years saving elephants in Africa. There is no special qualification required to participate in drama work. You do not need to have lived a particularly vivid, difficult or disaster-strewn life to contribute; to have lived thus far is sufficient.

Part of my induction into community theatre practice led to this understanding, that notions of the extraordinary were inflated and self-defeating, the pursuit of extraordinariness perverse and self-denying. It's not that we don't want to enjoy the extraordinary but we don't want to feel extraordinary experiences are the only material for drama. Many of the shows I saw in the 70s and 80s, by Word & Action (Dorset), by 7:84, by the Open Theatre (three contrasting examples), persuaded me of this. They showed there was value in working simply, with dramatic material which had its roots in the everyday experiences of people's lives. R.G. Gregory's theatre practice in particular demonstrated to me the value of working with nothing but the essential elements of theatre: impulse, language, action. He argues that 'anything that is not ordinary is dead. The whole avant-garde movement's impulse has been to go so far away from the ordinary that it's spectacular, farther and farther away from what was seen as the bedrock of ordinary life. And it struck me . . . that with all that going on, what we need to do is to start where we are, where people are.'

It's this principle of starting 'where people are' which must be one of the key foundations of community drama. It means reclaiming ordinary, day-to-day experiences as the meat and drink of what happens on stage. Not that this is any more than an assumption about starting points. It doesn't mean limiting our ambition to be spectacular. It doesn't mean limiting our genres or use of language. We may well transform the everyday into the spectacular but we don't initially search for the spectacular within ourselves. We can still start with a cup of tea and end up with circus if we choose. For after all, while on the surface everything may be banal and inconsequential, summary detection quickly shows that underneath are passions and dreams which, whether they are fulfilled in life or not, represent the staples of dramatic conflict. Jane Austen and Elizabeth Barrett-Browning may have apparently led dull lives but what is brought to their writing proves that imaginative transformation of inner feeling leads to work of great consequence.

It's also very possible that participants may associate creativity with only limited activities; daydreaming, decorating a mantleshelf, telling anecdotes, gossiping. They have little sense of the big ideas that run through dramatic literature. So here the work becomes about deepening that sense they do have. It involves taking what is offered, the anecdote or daydream and transforming it into something greater, without losing the truthfulness of the original impulse. So the issue is less about 'Where's an extraordinary idea/story/image?', than 'What process can we use to transmute our seemingly modest material into stuff which is challenging to work on and could create performance?' Turning to Lois Weaver again, she says: 'I try to create an environment where people feel the mundane details of their life are interesting. And have significance. And can be exploded.'

II

How we fashion this process is a question of craft, one about the relationship between form and content. It's about knowing the drama forms to work with, and understanding their appropriateness for each particular group. It's also about determining which comes first: form or content . For twenty years or so this was the subject of much debate amongst English theatre practitioners in the Association of Community Theatres. There were two camps: some practitioners argued that to make theatre of any kind you needed to decide 'what you were going to say.' There was no point slipping and sliding amongst theatrical images if you didn't know what would anchor them. The best way to anchor them was knowing your analysis of the social phenomena which was your chosen issue. It would be practice amongst groups holding this view to precede rehearsals with many discussions and much research. The work was politics-led. Once a position had been arrived at, for example identifying the causes of unemployment or who science really benefited, only then would practical work begin. The play or workshop would aim to reveal 'the truth' of the prior analysis. Much of this work was highly effective and companies such as Recreation Ground, Red Ladder, Cockpit TIE and Greenwich Young People's Theatre toured plays following this pattern.

There was a much smaller contingent which argued differently. Their position was that theatre was not a medium for the delivery of a set of ideas or a means to expose the contradictions of a capitalist economy – rather it was a set of tools or 'forms' which enabled groups of people to speak about inner concerns. According to this viewpoint, politics did not come first. Decisions about form should precede decisions about content. You could not discuss content first because content would always be modified by the nature of the theatre or drama form you adopted. So if a show espoused a libertarian political viewpoint but the dramaturgical form of the show was authoritarian, the purpose became self-denying. The overall message given would be to favour authoritarian values. This was how the argument ran. Theatre's role should therefore be to develop forms which allowed the audience to interact with the company and share responsibility for the creation of the material. Word & Action (Dorset) argued this position and by implication others such as Professor Dogg's Troupe (Interaction) assumed it.

At time of writing, the landscape of debate has shifted and opposing flags do not fly in conflict as before. Radical political orthodoxy came under criticism for being over-prescriptive and for its insistence on an unassailable objectivity. At the same time, the terms of the debate were shifted by new developments. Augusto Boal's insistence that subjective experiences were valid as starting points for political theatre-making encouraged those who argued against the politics-first position. It seemed there was some coming together, especially around the recognised necessity for efficacious relationships between professionals and communities. It was also recognised that there was a shared value-set within drama and theatre practice that permitted the adoption of a range of content issues. In a way, the growing emphasis on values subsumed some of the form v. content argument. This development was considerably assisted by practitioners concentrating on women's and disability issues for whom a linear, politics-first argument was always inadequate.

Community drama workshops in my view are more effective by criteria of self-empowerment if they place the participating group in the role of content-makers. This means the facilitator becomes responsible for looking after forms and facilitating structures as a priority. Now immediately there are several caveats to this. An absolute division of roles is impossible. Many facilitative decisions are about content. The nature of group engagement always influences selection of exercises. Besides, the drama forms must be appropriate for the purpose. The car has to be built for the surfaces it travels on. There's no point learning cabaret skills if the group wants to explore difficulties around intimacy in male-female relationships.

But nevertheless, this broad distinction represents a useful starting point. So what is a theatre form? For our purposes, it might be a game or an exercise. It has the capacity to transform content. It has rules or conventions to ensure that a specific dynamic is generated which is concordant with the values of the exercise. Certain kinds of expression are encouraged and certain are forbidden. For example, in Game A, you're not allowed to speak, only to move. Or you can only say one word at a time. The rules ensure the form can be effective. It's not vastly different in football. Once the rules are ditched, skill and flair and attractive play will pretty quickly disappear too. So this is how content is generated – as activity, words or movement – by the maintenance of form. This 'content' may later, if we wish, be separated out and called the 'material' which might be used in a group-devised play.

If the facilitator takes for him or herself the business of creating content, there may be problems. After all, what is there left for the group but to simply interpret another's ideas? For example, if a facilitator says to the actors: 'In this scene, you are going to accept a £2500 gift in exchange for agreeing to drive the getaway car for a bank robbery', this is to give the conclusion of the scene in advance. There's little room for the group to be inventive. Professional actors should be able to work backwards from this given conclusion and invent their own journey, but community actors may find this hard. They may feel they're being put to a test. The fun for them is to take the scene in their own direction.

Rather than give the outcome, it might be wiser to set up the conflict and see what emerges, giving guidance as necessary. For example you might say that character A is desperate for money while friend B has a car and friend C has just returned from a successful bank robbery. They meet – and what happens? Yes, elements of the content have been chosen but the group is still being given an opportunity to stamp their identity on the scene. The conclusion might be, A and B get C drunk then A steals all C's money!

So the facilitator looks after forms and structures enabling the group to generate content. This arrangement reduces any tendency the facilitator has to use the group as a vehicle on which to project their own creative ideas. Of course the facilitator may come in with 'hard' content to use as a stimulus, like a photograph or a story – but this does not have to involve prescribing outcomes unless the actors are asked to remain completely faithful to that stimulus. There are of course situations which are not clear cut, where this division is blurred, for example when working with folkloric or mythological material. Here, deviation from the storyline probably involves loss of the archetypal qualities of the characters. If so, the benefit to the actors of playing those roles – Red Riding Hood, the Wolf, the Woodcutter – may also be lost. So the facilitator probably needs to keep the players to a given track. But this exercise is quite specifically about aiding participants to find and nurture certain qualities which the characters embody.

The workshop leader therefore needs to select the most appropriate games and exercises to bring out the best of the group, which means looking carefully at the geographical, social and cultural context of the workshop. There can be no assumption that an all-purpose methodology will be appropriate. Exercises which have worked for Augusto Boal in Brazilian villages or Keith Johnstone at the Royal Court Theatre will not necessarily produce the same results in an English youth centre on the edge of a run-down Midlands estate. It's not that the work of these practitioners cannot be drawn on – they can and should be – but they have to be examined in the light of what you know of the strengths, qualities and dispositions of each new group of attenders.

There are many who've been eaten for breakfast, lunch and supper because they never made reconnaissance. It's not only comedians who die on stage. I once went into a youth club where the club leaders had decided drama would be a good idea because of the destructive rivalry between the girls and the boys. Only no one told me. My approach at that time was not to plan things too carefully but to follow the group's momentum. When the two sexes began to separate out, I thought, let's see where this leads. It led not to acceptance and bridge-building but to hatred and chair-throwing. The particular context required its own agenda but I hadn't sufficiently researched it. There's a real obligation to think site-specific. The drama process is potentially so exposing that a breakdown in trust or a key problem in any part of the work can fatally compromise the whole endeavour. Disgruntled or upset participants who walk out have no obligation to return: it's not a maths class. There's a clear need for methodologies to adapt to circumstances. There *are* a few exceptions to this rule especially in the area of recreational drama and performance models, but not many.

Working with respect for context means working with what the group gives you. Even Augusto Boal whose respect for the rigours of methodology is well-known and even a source of contention, tells this story:

> '*Sartrouville was the occasion of my first meeting with such people (those suffering from mental illness) . . . Annick kicked off the session:*
> "*What do you want to do?*"
> "*Nothing.*"
> *All were agreed on this point. Annick as well.*
> "*Fine. We'll do nothing. With that in mind, we'll divide up into two groups who will each do nothing. Augusto will go off with one group and I'll stay with the other . . .*"

I went off with my group . . .

"*So*" *I said* "*We're going to try doing nothing. What does anyone suggest by way of starting point?*"

"*Nothing*" *said Andres.*

"*Yes, OK, that's already been settled. But how are we going to show this 'nothing?' We have to show that we are doing nothing so that has to be clear. For example, if we stay like this, they'll say we're waiting for something: which is already doing something. We must show them we're not waiting for anything, that we're doing nothing. How?*"

Andres thought quickly.

"*Ah yes, right – this is what we do: I lie down on the ground and pretend to be sleeping – and that's it –* "

Andres was still doing all the talking.

"*OK you lie down on the ground and pretend to be sleeping. So we've already got something to show them. How do you sleep?*"

(Augusto then got Andres talking about his dreams.)

To one side, Georges was watching us. I became aware that I was not talking to Andres alone. Some small progress had already been made. We could change interlocutors so as not to put too much pressure on Andres, not to tire him out.

"*What about you, George, what do you dream about?*"

"*The cinema.*"

"*You dream of being an actor?*"

"*No . . . Director.*"

"*Great . . . Perhaps we could act that out to show the others.*"

"*Yes. We could.*" [11]

Even allowing for Boal's mythologising of his own event, the story shows clearly how methodology is subordinated to the reality of what's possible in the circumstances. Of course it takes courage to follow this path. It's easier to walk into the room and impose a pattern irrespective of context. There's a story of a facilitator who did just this with another group having learning difficulties. Katina Noble told me this story because it was she who volunteered to assist the process. The facilitator walked in and presented each of the group members with a copy of a play he'd written based on the nativity. Some of the group even had serious difficulties with reading!

This is not an argument to suggest that a difficult group should have low ambitions set for them. Rather that various factors need to be squared at the planning stage, in particular *context*, *methodology* (forms and exercises) and *objectives*. If a challenging and exciting programme can be built from these, this will best facilitate the creative expression of the company. There's a balance to be found between being challenging (setting goals which will stretch the group), and being safe (playing to existing strengths). There must be a clear understanding as to which of the functions given earlier – recreation, solidarity, etc. – are perceived as underpinning the project, or which combination of functions. We cannot always determine games and exercises until the twin issues of context and objectives have been aligned.

III

The careful selection of drama forms is essential because after all, theatre is a subversive medium. Theatre which is conceived and organised to reaffirm political or cultural orthodoxy sits ill-at-ease with itself. Madame Mao's great dance-dramas applauding cultural reforms may have made bright, bold spectacles at the time, but history disposes of them quickly enough. Playwrights who aim only to applaud the status quo, find their work lacking essential dialectics. There is a reliance within theatre on disruptive voices. In community drama work the same is true. Augusto Boal's insistence on the oppressed being the true authors of their work is a natural corollary of his perception of drama as a crowbar to unseat the comfortable building blocks of hegemonic power. The energy of discontent fuels a drama process. But this is no rewriting of the first book of theatre. The best work in either sphere proceeds from a recognition that the medium is appropriate for, and suited to, subversive purposes – be those the deliberate provocations of a playwright or the conscious empowering of the creatively dispossessed at first base.

Should we seek evidence, history provides it in the documented closure of theatres by regimes aiming to establish a strictly centralised ideological power: Maoist China, Cromwellian England, Pinochet's Chile, Hitler's Germany. Theatres tend to be perceived by such regimes as potential cauldrons of discontent which at any time might crack open and spill revolution on to the street. Even in relatively liberal regimes, it is warily suspected, their very uncontrolled and unsupervised presence, openly trading in uncensored opinions as they do, might injuriously affect the sensibilities of the vulnerable. There is some justification in this, for if one examines the contribution made by the small theatres to the Velvet Revolution in Czechoslovakia, there is much here for dictatorship to fear.

Even in contemporary, liberal regimes, there is a perception that drama and theatre practice cannot be allowed to grow uncontrolled and unmonitored by political powers. While greater attention is given to so-called 'politically biased' film and television, it has also been apparent that in the case of subsidised theatre practice – while its benefits are recognised – there is a stringent check on guarantees of longevity lest such practice leads to an independent cultural momentum which begins to move against the prevailing political powers. It appears to matter little whether that momentum be expressed as social criticism, political satire or as arguments for revolutionary change – the fact remains that a subsidised theatre is rarely allowed to plan beyond a year or two ahead. If we look back to the 60s and 70s, it's interesting to note how the community theatre and the theatre-in-education movements in England were first nurtured and encouraged, then, in the late 80s and 90s, were cut down by a series of widespread cuts and initiative-thwarting activities. And what civic repertory theatre had not boasted of its little touring theatre company flying out of the side doors?

The drawing in of resources followed the 'last in, first out' philosophy, undermining previous intimations that community theatre and theatre-in-education were to be the essential ingredients of a new, democratic, civic idea. The scope for maintaining life after cutbacks was always possible, but generally involved a closer relationship with the funding authorities. And these same authorities would often require, in return for granting financial stability, an influence in artistic affairs. As a result, some companies struck out on their own, while others were brought closer to a 'centres of excellence' way of thinking, with the criteria of excellence uncomfortably drawn up by those who were never theatre-makers themselves.

For drama as for theatre. Theatre, the production of plays, makes public our difficult voices while drama coaxes these privately. People go to the theatre to see the rules of society broken. People go to theatre workshops to break them themselves. Any workshop which does not channel these subversive desires, risks being subverted in turn. And it very likely will be, by discontented participants. For in either medium, the same is true; energy springs from the expression of conflict, the articulation of paradox and difficulty. It moves outward towards the exploration of emotional extremes. Such expressions do not find easy incorporation within the status quo; were they to do so, people would be less drawn to the arts to give expression to these energies. This doesn't mean being in a love triangle or a revolutionary cell to justify membership; rather, the medium tends to attract those for whom unresolved feelings and suppressed thoughts and ideas are an everyday part of life.

Drama relies on the breaking of social rules within a fictional framework; hence it is attractive to those whose natural instincts lead them in that direction. Previously in our cultural history, ritual played a role in codifying times on the calendar and places on the map when we could break out, let loose and behave badly without the social framework being too seriously threatened. Today, in a society without unifying rituals, football, royal weddings and funerals do their best to fill the gap. But population growth and technological enfranchisement of society prevent these events reaching beyond small pockets of people acting independently. As consumerism fails to provide the stabilising of national identity as advertisers persuade us it might, those on the edge of mainstream culture – which different commentators argue form any proportion between a tiny minority and everybody – instinctively seek other means to break the cultural knots that bind.

So the challenge for drama facilitators is: given that we are working with these difficult, subversive energies, how can we harness them to positive effect without their becoming destructive and turning in against their possessors?

SIX POLARITIES

One way to ensure drama work is effective is to understand the laws that govern it. I propose the territory of community drama is defined by six key, polar relationships. It's the responsibility of the facilitator to manage the exploration of these while maintaining the safety of the group. Each relationship contains a spectrum defined by two opposite yet complementary poles. For example, there's a relationship between the performer and the audience. Each role is dependent on the other yet they are opposites, the performer performs but is nothing without the audience. Likewise the audience cannot function without the performer. Other key relationships include those between surface and depth, the fixed and the free, and the centre and the edge.

The facilitator is constantly moving between the different polarity sets according to the demands of the situation. Choosing which axis to explore at any one moment, and how to explore it, is a matter of skill and judgement. If for example, we never look at the issue of surface and depth, or if we constantly perform and never discuss how the audience is reacting, the work remains unfulfilled. If on the other hand, we forever analyse everything, or if we only ever talk about the audience's view, that too would be counter-productive. We need to experience and consider all the different polarities and to move between the poles in each, not allowing ourselves to become immobilised.

1. THE FIXED AND THE FREE

There must be a balance in drama workshop practice between fixed elements and free elements. At the beginning of a project, there is an apparent freedom. Nothing has been set. We can do what we like. We can run around, take our clothes off, argue, adopt characters, whatever. But this freedom has no meaning. We cannot assess whether this running around is successful or relevant because we haven't defined terms. We haven't set ourselves goals or challenges so we can't assess whether we're making progress. It's probably quite good fun but after the initial excitement has worn off we may start to feel bored. Some in the group may feel upset or taken advantage of. So we need to introduce some fixed elements to regulate the activities.

Creative adults need structures to funnel their creativity. The structural elements we can introduce, like a theme ('betrayal') or a restriction ('no speech') or an objective ('to win favour'), anchors participants' energy. Now we can begin to find a sense of role. We can enjoy our freedoms more because we know where the boundaries are. We feel safer – therefore, paradoxically, we can start to take more risks. And in contrast to what happened before, when our invention flags in an exercise we don't just collapse exhausted, we're fired up again by remembering the structural components of the exercise which might be tasks or prohibitions.

We can see this co-dependency between fixed elements and free elements echoed elsewhere. We can see it reflected in the relationship between the body, the dimensions of which are fixed, and the imagination, the dimensions of which are infinite. Some practitioners refer to similar relationships between order and chaos or chaos and structure. R.C. Gregory talks about this relationship using an astrological analogy: *'Saturn is the planet of order, of form. If you don't follow the form, you don't get anywhere. You have to satisfy Saturn before you can get into transcendentalism . . . Neptune is boundless imagination. Neptune is the sea, the collective feeling that has no bounds. And is very dangerous unless it meshes with Saturn.'* It is a characteristic of the relationship between freedom and structure that an increase of rules does not necessarily give you less freedom. This seems perverse but it is so – the more restrictions placed on how a task is performed can lead to the creation of something like a funnel, the participant's energy getting channelled down a narrower and increasingly restrictive tube which engenders a 'freeing up' of energy. Let's take a workaday example. Let's imagine a participant is introducing a story about being mugged in a park. Initially the facilitator offers complete freedom to the group to interpret the story how they like. The chances are the group will simply 'act out' the story. But the experience may not animate the group – they may simply choose a rather prosaic form of staging and dramatisation. Let's imagine instead we're going to introduce a series of fixed elements, an increasingly narrow and rigid set of instructions for each subsequent interpretation.

First, we say, 'no speech'.

Next time, we say, 'no more than three characters'.

Next time, we say, 'one person – not the person whose story it is – tells the story with speech directly to the audience.

Next time, that person has to tell the story to the audience using sounds or movements only.

Next time, the group has to make a single image of the attack.

Next time, that person has to walk into the space as if they were revisiting the site of the mugging for the first time.

If the group stuck with this exercise – although it's pretty unlikely we'd go through all these permutations – it would probably experience with each new challenge a 'freeing' of its creativity. Doors would be closing on some options, forcing others open. This is not completely dissimilar to what happens when people are confronted by restrictions on their political freedom – it challenges their creativity. In Tibet, as a protest against Chinese occupation, Tibetans put up pictures of the Dalai Lama everywhere. So the Chinese banned the pictures. How did the Tibetans respond? They hung up empty frames! Then empty frames were banned! Doubtless the Tibetans will have a further response.

The imposition of rules has meant the group can stop worrying about certain tasks. If words are banned – now I can have fun with movement. If planning is disallowed, now I can be spontaneous. So after completing a series of exercises like those above, the single actor may do no more than walk into the space and out again, but I suspect that watching it, we would note the tension, concentration and truthfulness of the actions. And we'd notice how the actor came alive in that space.

So imposing fixed elements helps to create a sense of freedom. The fixed elements may vary, but their presence creates a structure to the work which helps participants feel 'free to fail'. In a drama GAME, the rules may provide the fixed elements – 'You cannot touch' or 'You must touch' or 'If Grandma sees you move, you have to start again'. In an EXERCISE, the tasks may provide that – 'You must mirror everything which your partner does' or 'You must accept all offers which are made'. In an IMPROVISATION, the motivations may provide that – 'When your character comes in, she is solely concerned with getting money to support her habit' – or 'Everyone in this scene is jealous of everyone else'. If such structural elements are abandoned in any of these contexts, there's less freedom. For example, in playing Keith Johnstone's dialogue game, YES, AND, if I break the rules or move too far outside them, the exercise may crash. If I stop saying the phrase 'YES, AND' each time I speak; which is the game's rule, I fail to engage impulsively with the dialogue and the exercise loses energy.

Should fixed elements be abandoned, safety may be jeopardised. There are a number of freedoms which the medium offers us and which we need to protect, for example, the freedom to speak out, to use words of love or hate, the freedom to touch and to be touched. We need to give permission for display of vulnerability or the breaking of taboos around language, for example. But if these permissions are to be given, exploitation of opportunity also needs to be protected against. People's rights have to be defended. As Tom Paine observed, liberty is not the same as licence. People can't be allowed to use the freedoms of the workshop to take advantage of each other or insult each other. This kind of behaviour would be damaging not just to the aggressor's victim but to the work as a whole. Participants won't introduce sensitive material if they feel they'll be laughed at or taken advantage of. For example, material about an abusive father or a broken affair won't be introduced if it's anticipated that people will laugh or criticise. It's the facilitator's task to ensure that fixed rules or conventions are in place, and are making people feel safe. There needs to be a hard shell maintained to protect a soft centre. This may mean that at the beginning of any project a set of 'ground rules' are established. These will set down what is permissible behaviour and what isn't.

Staff within institutions often look puzzled when a drama facilitator insists that certain aspects of a residency are non-negotiable. For example, that latecomers cannot be allowed in after a certain time or the workshop room absolutely *must not* be used as a corridor. Or the girls and the boys *must* agree to integrate during the workshop process. Or there absolutely *must* be disabled access. They express surprise because they may not perceive straight away how important these absolutes are, to the success of the work. It's probably correct to insist on them however, because to give up on these, is to create unworkable conditions which threaten group safety. Without those fixed elements, creative freedom or emotional safety may be compromised.

Participants can move towards creative freedom and experience its power, but only if structures are secure. Carl Jung knew both James Joyce and his daughter. The latter spent much of her life in distress, consumed by a love for Samuel Beckett which was not reciprocated. Jung commented that both she and her father were 'travelling to the depths – only one was diving and the other, falling.' Maintaining structures enables the group to dive, and safely return. Understanding the dialectical balance between fixed elements and free elements remains a consistent responsibility.

2. SURFACE AND DEPTH

Deadly theatre, to borrow Peter Brook's phrase, exists largely on the surface. It may wear its heart on its sleeve but it still lacks depth. To an audience this is disappointing because we want our own depths mirrored in the play. We want to see a comparable relationship between surface and depth to that which we understand exists in our own lives. We want that acknowledged, even though the characters may be strange and their dilemmas unfamiliar. We may not have been where that hero has, but we know we want him to suffer when he smiles.

Drama workshop practice should be similarly ambitious. It must acknowledge this relationship and arrange journeys between the two poles. This will give participants the chance of a more complete engagement with the form. It will enable them to express something about their inner lives – feelings, memories, hopes for the future – as well as their worldliness; jokes, trivia, flamboyance, opinions. In some ways it's easier to talk about the relationship between surface and depth, using analogies. We know the iceberg has 10 percent of its bulk out of the water, while 90 percent is hidden. We only see the 10 per cent and imagine that's all there is. Of course what makes it an iceberg of that shape is the bulk beneath the sea line. If in workshop practice we *only* look at what's on the surface or *only* what's beneath it, we reduce the scope of our potential material. As with the iceberg, there are always hidden dimensions.

A further analogy is with the actor's body itself. Expressively speaking, bodily and facial gestures are on the surface while memories, feelings and desires are internal and in turn provoke external gestures.

What an actor's training is about is understanding this relationship so the surface becomes consciously a moving pattern of signifiers to the inner life. An important tool in this training is the mask. What the mask does is fix the face so attention is drawn to the body which can then become a more graphically communicating instrument. A key plane on the surface has been immobilised to accentuate the depths. The actor can then explore internal feelings more nakedly, through the whole body.

But how is this relationship between surface and depth manifested for a group? It often happens that a group membership is quite varied – temperamentally, opinion-wise and in terms of class or race. But *beneath the surface* there will always be a commonality of experience – especially if they're of similar age, have a similar class background or share a profession or vocation. This common pool of shared experience is what we have to bring into awareness, in part through the drama language. If achieved, it will not only bind the group together, but will throw into focus images and themes which are collectively important to the group, and which could be turned into plays. But because this below-surface territory is in part hidden from immediate consciousness, we have to start to work with what we don't know about ourselves, as much as with what we do know.

Our bodies however, remember. In particular, they remember much that the mind has forgotten or doesn't want to access. It is this recognition of the body as a gaoler of strong, hidden feelings which is part of the argument for working physically. By so doing, we start to silence the cerebral reflexes and release emotion. Emotions come out to play, triggered by sensations which are themselves more easily engineered. (I'm always reminded of the body's independent memory when about to board an escalator which is out of order. However hard I tell myself the escalator won't move, my leg nevertheless shudders in anticipation of movement. This event doesn't trigger emotional feeling particularly, but even today the sound of flames crackling brings back the panic of when my bedroom was set on fire.)

We need therefore to be able to release material without self-censoring. Structures which allow for playfulness certainly help but alongside must be a recognition that content generated whilst 'mucking about' in this way can be attributed with significance. We also need to be prepared to go into difficult areas, perhaps against our resistance, to find a richer vein of experience than logical, reasonable behaviour will reveal. There are parallels with shamanism here, and with forms of therapy. Phelim McDermott draws from the work of Arnold Mindel who argues that illness is often the body's way of alerting the person to changes that need to be made in life. Mindel's experience of working with people in coma involve him 'going with them' in order to 'bring back' stories and myths which have a resonance for the patients' lives. In the same way, McDermott hopes to find – within areas which are felt by the performers to be emotionally 'difficult' – *'the seeds which will help us to tell the story (which needs to be told.)'* There are, in effect, *'diamonds within the shit'*, but we have to be prepared to go into those difficult areas and grab hold just when our instinct says we should move away.

If the group does, in its improvising, start to touch on any of those key human paradoxes which we all recognise but rarely take time to articulate, the retrieval of them can be a rewarding experience. The emotional energy released by the effort involved contributes to our self–understanding, even if this happens at an affective rather than at a cognitive level. We feel better for grappling with the devil, even though it's hard to say precisely *why*. If the language of the exercise remains a mythological one, by contrast with psychodrama, for example, where we name our devils, then we're speaking of our concerns only meta-phorically. So the material that we create in the process can be said to have a duality consisting of the dramatic/metaphoric and the examined/psychological. We have a choice whether we subject the created material to analysis or leave it to function as a kind of group dreaming.

If we choose the latter approach, then we make up stories and leave analysis of them largely to one side. After all, there may be reasonable group resistance to analysis. However, a point to remember is, even apparently light-hearted, spontaneous creativity is often charged with profound thematic content *whether we choose to analyse it or not*. R.G. Gregory argues that Instant Theatre for example, *'is bound to concern itself with the central issues for that group whether or not the group knows that it is doing so...since it picks up all the fluff that is flying around in the minds of people, it must also pick up the deeper concerns.'*

Work of this kind draws from what is unconscious, lending the imagery a certain opacity. There are no easy interpretations to be made of it. Tales from folklore are similar in that what often appears full of non-sequiturs can also be said to be most revealing of what is intrinsic to our human nature. They also resist comprehensive interpretation although we may wish to contextualise their histories sociologically. Perhaps we should maybe rest happy with this. As McDermott points out *'If we talk too much (about the work), we reduce it.'* It may be that such material 'works' for us metaphorically *just as long as we don't* unpack all its possible meanings.

If we do take the other route and analyse the work, certain observations can often be made. It's striking how a group whose members share a history can leave a coherence and clarity of impression on its dramatic material. A teenage group will tend to concern itself with the transition from childhood to adulthood, almost whatever you throw at them. Older people are more likely to be concerned with reflecting on the past, balancing out achievements and mistakes. Important to note is, whatever the group, what is on the surface of their stories and what those stories mean, is not always an obvious relationship. If teenagers introduce themes of sexual adventurism into their improvisations, this may not necessarily imply anxiety over or enthusiasm for sex. The primary concern may be with authority, and they're using the language of sex to mount a challenge to the authority's view on a range of topics, which include sex. They know that sex is very likely a weak point. The content cannot be viewed separately from the process.

Another way to talk about what is 'below the surface' for any group is by reference to secrets. Jonathan Kay argues that *'at the end of a week, I'd like people to see in everyone – if they're prepared to flip into it – an amazing sameness in their commonality of secrets. Personal secrets aren't that unique. . . . If they were told they would lose their power because someone else's secrets are* equally *harrowing, if not more harrowing than any you're holding on to. The theatre itself is a secret. We wouldn't go there if it was about things we knew about. It's about a dream, a place which is not accessible.'*

How we go there is taken up in the second part of the book. Suffice to say here, it's important to mark the roles physicality and spontaneity must play in the task of pursuing revelation. If we want to access concerns below the surface we can't sit around on chairs talking, we need to disable our conscious intelligence and think less. For in guessing and fumbling we may start to give ourselves away. The secrets start to speak through us – and then we may begin to recognise each other as fellow travellers. As Arnold Mindel writes: *'Body work cuts through a lot of junk in consciousness and gets right down to brass tacks quickly. The advantage to this is that the Self appears and a real relationship between persons often improves rapidly.'*[12]

3. THE CENTRE AND THE EDGE

Imagine the group sits down in a circle. This means everyone has equal access to the stage area. In a literal way the 'audience' defines the stage. Now if you look to the centre, there's nothing there, only space. Those who have created it are on the edge. But we're led to believe that 'the edge' is somehow lesser than the centre. If I'm on the edge of society, I'm a lesser person. Yet the centre wouldn't exist without the edge. In fact, the edge is where the life is. If there's to be life in the centre, it needs to come from the edge. We see this in the theatre: mainstream producers enticing fringe actors and playwrights into the centre with lucrative contracts to resuscitate an ever-tiring repertoire. But they don't do it to remove the edge. Those at the centre, the movers and shakers, *need* the outcasts and the low caste and the not-yet-cast to make them feel better about their own achievements.

Every group has its centre and edge. Understanding the relationship between them is part of the facilitator's brief. Mediating the interplay helps to maintain the health of the group as a whole. After all, in a way the group is a microcosm of society. There's assent, dissent, loyalty and doubt. Keeping in mind the values of non-exclusion, it's important that no one feels they are 'not part of the group.' It's important that no one feels consistently 'on the edge.' Everyone should feel, in some way, part of the centre. A group that is split or fractious, may carry their rivalries into the work. So the work begins to be about the group's troubles with itself – there's no free play of inspiration.

You can always ask the group how they feel. 'Imagine this room is the world of the group. Where would you place yourself? At the centre or the edge, where?' If you do this exercise with teenagers, everyone will cluster at the edges – everyone wants to be seen as a rebel, an outsider, someone who has withheld commitment. They know the benefits of being on the edge, you're closer to the door for one thing. But then you can talk about where people have placed themselves. There may be comments like 'Jane should be in the centre, she's always the first to arrive.' And questions can be asked. 'Pete, why are you near the door when you earlier said how much you enjoyed the workshop and wanted to do a show?' Quickly we're sharing doubts and problems about the work.

In a way these doubts and problems are what exist on the edge. By bringing them into the centre, their destructive potential is reduced. If there's commitment, it's because there's been a leap of faith over the doubts. I've noticed on several occasions when devising a show, there is a crucial moment about two thirds of the way through. Suddenly the whole team, after a period of being reserved and holding back, suddenly become terrifically animated – especially criticising the whole project. 'None of it's working.' 'We've lost all those good ideas we started with' 'I haven't a clue who my character is.' Everyone sparks off everyone else, like fireworks set too close together. It can be terrifying, and off you go home, convinced the project is in terminal throes. In fact the group may be opting in rather than out. It may be bringing doubts and fears to the centre as a necessary prelude to the final stage which requires more commitment than any previous stage. The group may be 'taking possession' of the play through redefining it. The piece may drastically change, but if the facilitator keeps their head it may be transformed into a more powerful vehicle. Alternatively, the project may collapse. But at least you've got a result. Better that than produce a play which everyone hates and no one believes in.

The same can happen within a workshop programme. Individuals – as individuals – may get to that point of being ready to jump off the edge. They feel like they've had enough. But having got to this point, if they can, by expressing their feelings, jump back in, it could prove profitable. As Jonathan Kay pointed out with reference to a particular participant who wanted out: *'What's so difficult for that person to see is they've just come to a very good thing. But because they don't see it, they just go, "I'm off. Sorry, Jonathan, it's been nice talking to you, but honestly I feel so pissed off." And I say, "Now hang on a minute because you just got to the best part." And they go, "Why's that? How do you mean?" I say: "You're just becoming an individual. You're not going to be in this herd. That's what the fool is. The fool is something that is not prepared to move with the herd. But is able to do something more than just criticise the herd. It's too dogmatic to just say "I'm off." The fool comes back. The fool goes "I feel animated now, I feel alive".'*

Kay's vision of the fool is that of an individual who is emotionally committed to the process of play within theatre. His argument is that an individual cannot progress without abandoning the critical ego.

This assertion complements our common-sense awareness that we need at the centre of the group all those dissenting, complaining, difficult voices which otherwise remain at the edge. When they come centre-stage, drama is occupying its properly subversive role. I remember an occasion working at the National Theatre when it was at the Old Vic. I worked as a stage hand on a production of Webster's *The White Devil*. We had large, white blocks of scenery to move on and off. After the play had been running for a few weeks, I noticed that at the edge of the stage actors waiting to come on weren't patiently waiting, thinking about their previous circumstances, they were making faces at the actors onstage. It took a while for the impact of this to register: they were trying to corpse them. And they weren't entirely unsuccessful. These were NATIONAL THEATRE THESPIANS! Reflecting later, I couldn't but think of it as an example of dead theatre whose edges were still flickeringly alive. The actors had lost commitment to the production and were subverting it from the edges. Surely this is what happens when core energies disengage; dissent eats into the centre and the centre no longer holds.

It's the same with the physical body of the performer. If the performer is animated only at their edges; their hands move, their feet, their face, but their pelvis is not energised, then they remain uninvolved. They are probably what's called 'indicating' or 'demonstrating'. Instinctively, participants in workshops fall into this peripheral way of acting without examples to work from; they assume that surface engagement is all that's required. The tendency becomes particularly evident when you do rhythm work, which calls for a full-bodied engagement. Peter Badejo, a Nigerian teacher and actor who uses a live percussionist in his workshop, points out: *'The African sense of performance is all-rounded . . . but here, actors find that difficult. They find it hard to do a simple 4-4 beat without falling off the rhythm.'* He argues: *'It's not just industrialisation. If you look at the influence of Christianity in this culture, there's total separation of mind and body. And it stems from there, even though it was centuries ago.'* Rhythm offers one means to help the group *learn* how to energise the physical body at the centre, solving the mind/body split. In this way, energies which exist at the edge can be transferred *into* the centre, and the body animated. When this happens, the edge just looks after itself.

To return to dissent, and complaining. What's required is to find ways of integrating naturally subversive energy into the stage work, so it drives creativity instead of disrupting it. Phelim McDermott points out that such energy can often be found in gossip. *'That is what alchemy is about, in my simplistic view. This prima materia, you put it in a crucible and you cook it up. It's taking that thing which comes from the edge and cooking it up. It's the group gossiping about the director and saying "What's he doing? He's rubbish. This isn't what I paid my money for." And that's a signal you can choose to ignore or you can amplify it. You grab hold of it and cook it up and what's in that gossip, what's in that edge is the solution for what you're dealing with at the moment.'*

This observation is especially relevant for groups who find the process of drama unfamiliar or difficult: school refusers, those with special needs, probation groups. They may appreciate the appropriation of their private joking around into the process. It reduces the status of the work; drama is no longer something for other people that we must try and aspire to, it can be about us. In time, the group can put more of themselves into it. Roger Hill devised a series of exercises especially to incorporate the contributions of those who felt themselves alienated from drama, and who preferred saying no to yes. *'Sweden has had an awful lot of Keith Johnstone. And after I'd been there a while, people said to me, "This is so interesting, what you do has got all the energy of Keith Johnstone, but it's so opposite. Keith Johnstone is all 'Yes, let's!' 'Go for . . . !' 'Do it!' and this is all, 'No, please let me off' . . . " And I said, "What this is, is DRAMA NEIN DANKE. And it's built out of the energy of people who don't want to do drama."'* Hill's techniques illustrate the value of using structures rather than persuasion to deal with disaffection. Because where there is disaffection there is rarely reluctance to accept a reasonable challenge, if in taking it, you're not left looking stupid.

Teenagers are especially terrified of ceasing to look cool. Saying no is extremely cool. They may even have come to drama for new opportunities to say no to things they've never been able to say no to before. But at least we can give them a chance to say yes inside themselves. Drama Nein Danke builds the drama from activities more easily entered into – saying no, trading blame, gossiping. Material is created out of people's wish to avoid an individual responsibility for anything, and using that gradually to create a group responsibility for something. Examples of exercises are given later.

But of course coming into the centre always involves some element of emotional risk. It's about saying 'Yes, I will make myself vulnerable'.

Out on the edge is safer, that's where the observer is, who enjoys being detached. In the centre there are fewer places to hide – there you're observed. There, you're more reliant on your own spontaneity. You can give yourself away. Of course you can always hug the back wall and get some measure of protection that way. This is one reason why a round staging is to be preferred for much improvised work – there's no back wall, there's nowhere to hide, once you're in, you're in. The degree of vulnerability is increased, and yet it's less pressured because the gaze of the audience is spread out, not concentrated. In fact, perversely, the actor feels more protected there, despite being vulnerable, because she is never 'confronted' by the audience, the audience surrounds her.

Such is a journey of the heart. It is about an emotional leap, not knowing the outcome, trusting that you won't fall, or if you do, the falling will be fun. Jonathan Kay argues: *'In workshops I am asking people to go to a metaphorical heart. A metaphorical centre. Which is usually dictated over by a dictator, who doesn't enable the fool to arrive. But the fool is the thing which the king or queen will eventually hear about – he's knocking about in the pubs or whatever – and eventually he'll be invited into the court. And the fool will make the court alive. Because up to that point it's all full of dryness.'*

A NOTE ON PERIPHERAL VISION
Let's return for a moment to the group sitting in a circle. If you step into that circle – effectively a theatre-in-the-round – and stand there, you can't see more than about half the group. If you focus strongly on just one face in the audience, other faces lose their distinction. You can switch your gaze around but it remains very 'directed.' But if you use a soft focus and allow awareness of other faces on the edge to come into you, you're beginning to use your peripheral vision. Over-controlled, technical actors won't use this, because it means they might be surprised: acted *upon*. The use of peripheral vision is linked to vulnerability and feeling.

Responding to signals from the edge is part of holistic awareness. In a way, peripheral vision is emblematic of awareness itself. It represents an ability to avoid narrow-mindedness or a tunnel-vision view of life; instead it assists responsiveness and an inner flexibility.

4. THE INDIVIDUAL AND THE COLLECTIVE

When a participant moves centre stage, she is also declaring her group membership. She's saying, 'Yes, I'm a member of the group and this is what it means to be that.' Because it's the stage area which is the symbolic territory of the group. To belong, you must be ready to occupy the centre. That's where the group *is* the group. (People who come in wanting to be stage hands or designers quickly realise they can never be *in the group* in the same way, so they have a choice – start to perform, or remain on the periphery.)

Membership is about commitment, risk and trust. We don't have to make a big deal of this, it's not like signing for the army, but there is a quality of commitment involved, otherwise the energy generated within the room will be insufficient to raise temperatures above the norm. And we do want to change the temperature. Often newcomers to community drama are willing to accept this premise, but see it as a membership subscription. In other words, there's a session or two thinking about other people but after that, they imagine it's forever 'their turn'. They see membership, once acquired, as consisting of rights only without obligations. Strangely, that's how drama is perceived; as a vehicle for individuals to display their 'talents'. Such newcomers find it shocking to be asked to spend so much time thinking about others in the group and supporting them. Instead of their individuality being promoted, it seems they're consistently being asked to sacrifice it. And what's more, this sacrifice is being asked without evidence of apparent reward!

But there are rewards. They lie in the complicity which is achieved in teamwork. And the paradox is, if teamwork is put first participants discover a new, stronger individuality for themselves. Their 'rights' emerge from fulfilment of their obligations. But it does take time for this process to work. And it's hard to recognise that the key to progress lies in immersion of self into the group nexus. It means looking at what aids others' creativity before looking at what aids your own. *But* if your partner is taking the same view (always hard to believe!) then of course you're flying because each is looking out for the other. Ironically, at the very beginning, participants *are* sometimes completely selfless – in the first session or two, they grasp instinctively what's required and selfishness remains hidden. It's a kind of honeymoon period in which they don't make mistakes because they don't know what the rules are.

It's during the second period that selfishness and egotism can enter in. At that point what's required is to work backwards to that first, instinctive enthusiasm albeit this time with increased awareness.

This process of discovering how you can take a lead only after submitting to the leadership of the group can be observed not only in a player's growth into group membership but also *within certain exercises*. Such exercises explore microcosmically the balance between allowing yourself to be led, and leading. Phelim McDermott and Guy Dartnell use an exercise called THE GAME where this can be observed. It's built on a technique of copying. Quite simply, a group of players copy each other, one person leading at the beginning, then another leading and so on until the leadership function gradually falls away. Eventually all are copying each other, with no one leading. As Guy Dartnell observes, *'What you try and get to, is a point where everyone is willing to let go doing what they want to do. Because part of them goes "I know where this should lead, we should all do* this." *And another one is going "No, no we should all do* that." *What it involves is just releasing and letting it go where it must go. Now some people understand this intellectually but don't do it in practice or think they're doing it but they're not. If you do get to the point where everyone has let go and the whole group unites, you get to the point where people can lead again. And they can lead in a much more total way.'* So it comes down to a willingness to play, to be flexible. And in being led, letting any anxiety about your vulnerability being exploited, fall away.

What we hope is to arrive at is an embodiment of complementarity. There's no assumption we should create a company of clones. We don't want everyone to be / act / behave similarly. A collective is not about everyone being the same, but about tolerating difference. It's about the celebration of difference. Shafiq is very loud, Mary is quiet, Hanif is comic, Sandra is instinctive. Different qualities of character can be respected. These different qualities will be shown in how individuals lead. It's for the facilitator to find strategies which facilitate a sharing of constructive leadership. In one scene a quality of aggression is necessary and we can call on Shafiq to bring that, to power the scene forward. In another, Mary's quietness may provide the necessary still centre.

There can be movement back and forth between prioritising the group and prioritising individuals within it. The group will always be a conglomerate of unique personalities, some having backgrounds in a well-balanced life and others who are used to struggling along on a day-to-day basis. Some will require more personal attention, others will be happy just to be 'in the group'. It's the facilitator's task to work with them *as they are*, using the context of collectivity to help the individual. Sometimes this means consciously encouraging group members to learn the qualities of others. If you admire what another person does, can you take that quality for yourself? Can you borrow that attribute? Guy Dartnell here observes the differences in what men and women bring: *'Male energy is about – you come up with the idea, there's a space and you put an idea in the space – so there's always a leaning on the male side to be doing something, to be creative. The female side of that is to be the space, to wait and to allow the idea or the creation to come in. So there's women on the side saying "Don't push me to do something, I'm waiting for it to come." And the man is going "But I've got to do something." In a sense part of the workshop process is to make people learn to inhabit the opposite energy from themselves – men to inhabit more the female energy, and women the male.'*

And it's true to say, the greater the degree of difference, the more need for mutual understanding. We may be talking about the differences between men and women or about class, race, background, personality – all may divide people. But if we're learning to integrate, this learning requires us to move outside our personal criteria and understand those of others. The groupwork needs to make space for a culture of tolerance. Such learning often takes place happily, invisibly. Other times it has to be made more obvious: 'If you block Jenny every time she puts forward an idea, of course she'll get fed up and feel like blocking you! Why are you doing that when you didn't block Michael?'

With a sufficient mutual acceptance, we can begin to make statements – through theatre – which embody the spirit of the group. Such statements hope to articulate shared dreams, paradoxes, archetypal struggles. This is what the work is leading towards, where group members can reap the benefits of earlier self-sacrifice. Individual performance cannot achieve this. It is only with the fusion of individualities that such synergy is possible. R.G. Gregory, drawing on the ideas of Joseph Campbell and Dane Rudhyar, argues that this is where the true potential of theatre-making begins. And this potential is inseparable from the idea of subsuming individual egos into the collective process. He looks at the struggle between the individual ethic and the collective ethic in a wider context: *'What Campbell points out is that up to about the thirteenth century, which is really the beginning of the*

Renaissance, every major statement had been a collective statement. All major statements came up through collective religions. What happened in the beginning of the Renaissance is that these statements began to come up through individual people. And that's when we began to name our artists... Now Dane Rudhyar picks up on this, saying there aren't these individual voices any more capable of expressing the human condition. What Rudhyar argues is that this is what the Aquarian age is about, the destruction of the ego as we now know it. The ego is coming under such enormous pressure that it can't sustain itself. And we have to look to a system where the ego – in the same way that thought has to move into and be absorbed by feeling, sensation and intuition – can be balanced by the other elements, to allow some other way that we don't quite understand yet, to speak for us.'

A defining characteristic of community drama is that a group without formal training can often make statements which have a resonance beyond the group's limited situation. It may even happen that performance work taps into universal issues, while the content itself remains largely parochial. The enjoyment for a group making this journey is that material starts to appear 'from nowhere' – no one can say this was 'my idea' or 'her idea' - it comes from no one, or all of us. Given this momentum, all find themselves travelling in one direction. The show, if there is one, starts to build up from concerns which many can recognise, perhaps across generations or countries. The work starts to bear out Pete Brooks' observation that *'art is about the expression of what we might call truths - a word I would disagree with - shapes or ideas which have resonance for ourselves because we have experience of them. But they also have resonance for others because they recognise the community that makes us human.'*

5. THE PERFORMER AND THE AUDIENCE

The performer and the audience represent mutually complementary, co-existing functions. Together they make theatre. The world is not divided into performers and audiences but into people who are both, exercising these abilities at different times. The task in a training situation is to separate out the qualities that are associated with the different functions. This involves identifying not only what it means to be an actor but what it means to be a spectator. Actors coming into community drama find it difficult to make that separation; they can't get out of their audience mind-set when they're acting. So they become self-conscious and self-critical. When this happens, they are not *'leaving the audience part of themselves in the seat'* as Guy Dartnell puts it. *'But you have to leave that there because it's no use to you when you're performing. It actually gets in the way and judges what you do.'* Even professional actors are familiar with this syndrome. The brain is buzzing away going 'this is dreadful, it's all wrong, can I start again PLEASE?' while the body is just hanging off the brain like a dead thing.

Much of this self-consciousness is about fear of the audience. Or rather, fear of *what we have projected* into the audience. Jonathan Kay: *'The reason you can't perform is not because of you at all, it's because of what you place in other people . . . The reason you get nervous before going on stage is because you hope they won't eat you up. So you throw it out to the audience – "I hope they don't eat me up" – then they eat you up and you say "I told you so." But it's not them that's eaten you up, it's the thing you projected into the audience.'* Jung writes: *'Projection is an unconscious, automatic process whereby a content that is unconscious to the subject transfers itself to an object, so that it seems to belong to that object.'*[13] In this case it goes something like 'They hate me.' Well, they probably don't. 'They're judging me, they think I'm useless.' It's possible, but unlikely. 'They're all better than me.' In fact they're probably just trying to decode what's happening on-stage, assuming you the performer knows everything. This projecting on to the group happens in part because of misunderstandings, so a possible first step is to recognise such fears for what they are. Jung again: *'The projection ceases the moment it becomes conscious, that is to say when it is seen as belonging to the subject.'*[14] So it's for the facilitator to try and make clear how this is happening; how the group doesn't really have an intention to eat up the performer. This is not Emperor Nero out there, we only think so. In fact, in our group-membership part of ourselves, we know the health of the group depends on individuals shamanically venturing into difficult territory. The audience wants the performer to succeed. For if a performer does break through into more dangerous, emotional playing, it's easier for others to climb through the gap.

But even if we accept this thesis, relaxation and spontaneity in performance is still hard. Ultimately there can be little substitute for getting up – often – and trying stuff. Practice teaches the body to function in spite of fear. Physical exercises discourage a reliance on thinking. As we think less, we become more open to emotional impulse. The body gets used to behaving emotionally, while being watched. And when we reach this point of welcoming feeling, we can start to use the audience's reactions as a resource. Having learnt not to fear the spectators, now they can be allies.

They can be allies because they perceive potential in the performer which the performer never can. Of course it's not true the audience has no expectations. We know from being spectators ourselves how we perceive unfulfilled potential in a play. In the pub after the show we say 'It was great, but it never got going' or 'I wasn't moved' or 'The acting didn't develop.' In a workshop context, such awareness is useful. It doesn't have to be expressed as negative criticism, it can be offered as 'what the audience want to see more of'. And this can be passed on to the performer in feedback. The performer can learn about how to fill out the potential of the *next* play or improvisation. This is not the same as wanting to eat the performer, or about giving permission to the audience to say 'You were rubbish'. It's about learning from the audience's observations. The audience may observe that Jane performs in a very introverted way, while Jason seems too involved in telling jokes. So perhaps the audience can be encouraged to advise them, telling Jane to 'open up more', or Jason to 'stop telling jokes, just be in the situation more'. This is not to destroy what Jason does well, it's about adding to his repertoire. And the performer may accept these comments more readily from peers.

The point is to develop a critical language which allows participants to help each other. Here are some questions which avoid judgementalism: 'Did you recognise what was performed?' 'Did you identify with what was performed?' 'What would you like the performer to do more of?' 'What parts of the stage would you like to see used more?' 'Can you say one thing which was exciting and one thing that was confusing, in what you saw?' In such feedback, it's often good to silence the performer to avoid an unhelpful dialogue in which the performer tries to 'justify' their acting and the spectator to 'justify' their observations. If observations are presented, the performer has the choice to accept them. A conscientious performer will at least listen, knowing that it's the actor's job to reflect the audience back to themselves.

But when they get up again to perform, there is some reflectiveness which must be left behind. They must allow a certain foolishness to prevail. This foolishness allows the performer to draw from any aspect of the psyche. When I first arrive, I can probably only access a small part of myself – the equivalent of a little finger. As time goes on I hope to access more and more of myself; any memory, any feeling – the equivalent of the whole body. Jonathan Kay uses this idea of 'foolishness' as a key concept to understanding what performing is. Foolishness here does not imply stupidity – this fool is intelligent. But the point about the fool is: the fool does not mind what happens. The fool within, Kay argues, does not mind what part he plays; Emperor or beggar, it makes no difference. It's only the dictator within us who minds, the dictator who wants to control and plan everything. The dictator is terrified of things getting out of control, so always wants to know the future. If the dictator element becomes too strong, that's when we seize up and become insecure. Improvisation, drama, play are processes in which the dictator naturally feels uncomfortable. They are the natural territories of foolishness; they involve 'giving things away'. So the facilitator's task, in Kay's view, is to help participants find and cultivate this quality of foolishness so it is not overpowered. *'The fool is walking around and there will be something about the fool that the dictator cannot avoid. Which is that the fool loves them. And that is something that the dictator does not understand. So will want to banish it. For the fool is unrepresented in any hierarchy yet it is represented in every heart. Which is why the fool can talk with everyone. Because the fool talks to the fool in each person. Whereas the dictator talks to the dictator in each person.'*

Exploring foolishness allows vulnerability to be expressed. The dictator cannot see the value of that so will resist it. 'Why should I be emotional, what's the point?' While the fool engages with emotion for no reason at all but that it's playful and an act of generosity for an audience. And the audience appreciates it. If the performers cannot make this leap into foolishness, the audience feels dissatisfied. They've given the players licence and the licence hasn't been taken. The performers do have a brief. As Kay argues, the performer *'has to move through demonstration, into feeling. If no one is prepared to enter into their feelings, they're not prepared to enter into the play.'*

The challenge of allowing your performance to be feeling–driven is as difficult for the old hand as for the newcomer. While the newcomer may struggle to avoid being overcome by emotion, or to identify it at all, the old hand may be stuck in tricks to avoid it altogether. Besides, the old hand knows how to represent feeling in a way which disguises its absence. *'There is a danger in improvising in that ostensibly it looks like a skill. And there are specific skills that can make you a good improviser, an impressive improviser. But actually it's deceptive. It's not what makes good performers. The skills are there to lead you into an area of vulnerability.'* Phelim McDermott. Actors who rely on tricks often give themselves away with their eyes. They don't keep their eyes open. They're placing their body's actions and reactions under a strong, personal control. And this control extends to their eyes. They are always 'looking somewhere' with a clear focus, not allowing themselves to 'catch sight' of anything, for example 'out of the corner of their eyes.' Their peripheral vision has been closed down.

A NOTE ABOUT STAGING

In some respects, the question of the audience / performer relationship cannot be separated from the question of staging. As the stage shape changes, so does this relationship. At different times in history different stages were preferred, evolving to suit the prevailing ideology. Our stage architecture is still largely dominated by Renaissance ideas of giving the single actor maximum contact with and control over the audience. Hence a proscenium stage which is built around a vanishing point perspective. Paintings of the Italian Renaissance can be seen as having power emanating from a single point in the high middle distance. This use of perspective complements the idea of the single individual as the vessel through whom inspirational authority is channelled. The idea was appropriate for a culture which promoted individualism, professionalism and the idea of individual genius as a source of wisdom.

When we move from a proscenium to a theatre-in-the-round, the relationship between actor and audience changes. The round is ideal for community theatre because it emphasises the 'relating' aspects of drama, less the 'singular' aspects. It does not favour the individual, heroic actor because it offers him little opportunity to dominate or dazzle the audience. It favours instead the ensemble through a status reduction of the actors generally. The audience are not placed in such a way as to emphasise the actor's charisma, instead they are given higher status because they have the actor 'trapped'. In the round, actors must work together if they want to dominate the space. There is no single spot on the stage which if inhabited, allows the actor complete power over the audience. So the single actor has to keep moving or invite others in. In fact there's often a sense of unfulfilled potential with a single actor in the round, as if we're waiting for a second. (When talking about the round, this does not have to mean the literal round which can disorientate actors, it can mean a rectangle with audience on two longer sides and two shorter sides. Looking out from the stage, the audience is still there whichever direction you look.)

6. THE SIMPLE AND THE COMPLEX

The natural progression in community drama is from the simple to the complex. We start with a simple idea and explore it until we arrive at a more complex expression. The basic, most simple building block, is the game. A drama or theatre game, the terms are interchangeable in this context, is really an assembly of commands, prohibitions and rewards. Altering any of a game's components will alter the dynamic of the game. Why games at this early stage? Firstly, they assume no prior theatre knowledge. Secondly, they animate people easily. Children don't usually need the format of a game; adults have lost their instinctive playfulness and tend to put physical spontaneity under mental command. So they require formal permission to release this.

How do games work? How do they engender creativity which is beyond simple, childish play? Here are two different answers from Viola Spolin and Clive Barker: *'The game is a natural group form providing the involvement and personal freedom necessary for experiencing . . . Skills are developed at the very moment a person is having all the fun and excitement playing a game has to offer – this is the exact time he is ready and open to receive them.'*[15] And Barker's view: *'My own work with games arose out of a need to find a method of actor training that did not make the actor self-conscious, as technical exercises seemed to do. I discovered that in many children's games the "rules" constitute a resistance against which the players struggle to raise their skill to a higher level . . . This way of working appeals to an area of memory which is pleasurable and anxiety free.'*[16]

Moving from games to more complex improvisational structures is conventionally the next step. First, we establish a territory which is familiar – games – second, we build more and more difficult challenges into this territory. Clive Barker summarises his own move from the simple to the complex: *'I have accepted Callois' thesis that theatre is simulation play, and developed a method of improvisation which begins with children's games and proceeds through rule-changes to structures which approximate to the scripted scene. In this I recognise that some areas of what we might observe as free play in children are, in fact, highly structured events involving incident, narrative and characterisation.'*[17] Ed Berman, the founder of Interaction and Professor Dogg's Troupe, developed a similar premise to construct a Creative Games Theory. This allowed users to perceive games as based on the addition of rules to propositions: X plus one plus one. This formula, he hoped, allowed everyone to see that you could adapt and change drama games to suit the group. Ali Campbell, who trained with Berman, explains the theory: *'Berman observed lots of children's games with Miriam Stoppard, particularly the under-fives, and went "Ah, if we can extrapolate this, this and this . . . then we can invent a game that has this agenda, this line up and moves people from A to B." This is where the Creative Games Theory came from . . . The theory went "Y plus one plus one plus one." I always remember the women teaching this – "If Y is a game like TAG, I tag you and then we rush about till everybody's gone." And then "plus one" is "It's hospital time – now you have to hold yourself when you're touched – and the next "plus one" would be to blindfold someone . . . " (In this way) you can change the line-up, the agenda or the task. You can change whether it's co-operative or competitive. And you would be not just unlocking their problem-solving abilities, you would be moving them towards a goal; a play, a song, a raised garden in the city . . . and you would start with TAG.'*

With the atmosphere altered by the spontaneity of games, the facilitator can capitalise on the resulting shifts of perception. Participants have been pushed literally and metaphorically 'off balance' so they're less guarded. Chances are, they're now more open to accept unusual challenges. How fast you move from games to exercises or on to improvisation, depends on context and opportunity. If time is short, there is within the Berman Games Theory the idea of 'the game that takes'. This is the game which *'chimes with the agenda of the group.'* Once identified, it helps further planning. Campbell was working in HM Prison Ford with inmates still to be sentenced. They were very nervous, very frightened. Campbell discovered that the games they liked were about sussing out who was in charge; BANDLEADER and MATTHEW, MARK, LUKE AND JOHN. The following day, Campbell proposed GRANDMOTHER'S FOOTSTEPS which was successful enough to run for about half an hour (a *very* long time in that situation). *'Then I went – "This isn't Granny, this is the judge. And every time Granny turns round, you (Granny) point at someone and say 'guilty!'"' And then we froze images of people being sent down – and then asked them what music we could create for that, and someone suggested Chariots of Fire.'* In this way, the group moved towards creating a thirty minute opera piece, ready for performance.

Let it not be assumed only existing games are valid. The formula of task + penalty + reward (e.g. Players have to touch Granny, Granny has to see them moving, if a player is seen moving, they have to go back, if a player succeeds they become Granny) is relatively easy to apply from scratch. New games can always be made up, and should be. It may be that your 'new' game is a variation on an 'old', but the act of tailoring it for a group gives it a unique purposefulness. Berman argued that 'the game' was a fluid not a fixed entity. You change the rules to suit the circumstances. If for example an existing game is inappropriate for a group with special needs, rule-changes can be employed to make it appropriate.

How is a new game made? The way I use is to hold in the mind's eye an image of where the group is now, and a second of where you would like them to be. Juxtaposing the two, suggests ways to travel. They're lethargic, you want them to be energetic; what if someone is chasing someone else? They don't empathise with each other, they're constantly giving each other a hard time as actors. Maybe we have to make them 'responsible' in some way for their partner's fate, so if their partner suffers, they do too. What if they're thinking too much? Then maybe we add a structural device which makes planning and thinking very difficult to accomplish during the exercise, a word-at-a-time technique or a time penalty.

Working with students, I needed an exercise which helped them to learn about focus. I devised THE TV GAME in which players acted out a documentary television programme. The game placed great stress on the necessity to pass focus. Some played presenters, others reporters in the field, others interviewees. It was quite successful. Some time later I saw an almost identical game on 'Whose Line Is It Anyway?' Had I unconsciously copied it? 'Whose Line . . . ' had only recently come to TV. Did someone copy it from me? Unlikely. Did different people, with similar knowledge of other games, come up with a similar format? Very probably.

Later in the work it may be necessary to move in a reverse direction – from complexity to simplicity. With participants in the role of generating content, they may give birth to a multitude of ideas and images. Participants can get lost swimming about in a sea of ideas. So a discussion which allows ideas to be written up and put into categories helps to keep the group on top of things. In some situations a Polaroid camera may be useful, and images can be put up around the walls.

A NOTE ON RULES AND LAWS

There is an important distinction to be made between rules and laws. Laws are what the medium depends on – the medium's equivalent of the law of gravity or what is required to make water: H2O. If we ignore these, if we try to defy gravity or make water from bricks – it may end badly. Whereas rules are changeable – they are man-made, so can be altered. Rules are the 'plus one' in Berman's games theory: 'Now if you're touched, you have to start hopping.' We invent and alter the rules to take advantage of the laws. We want the laws to work for us, and rules enable that.

The laws encompass the quintessentials of drama. We are all familiar with the fundamental tenet that to create theatre, we need an audience. As Mark Long pointed out in his 1995 lecture at the ICA, *'If I go out of my house, walk down the road and buy a packet of cigarettes, that's living. But if – before I do this – I persuade someone to stand on the street corner and watch me come out, walk down the road and buy a packet of cigarettes, then that's theatre.'*[18] In other contexts we might discuss the levels of awareness involved in this event but for community drama, this dictum will suffice. It's another law that two characters with opposing motivations will inspire conflict. If one of the characters in a play is poorly motivated, we know the rival will win. As Boal observed, if a boxer comes into a ring for a match on crutches while the other is jumping around waving their fists, you know spectators won't get their money's worth. Equality of motivational intensity is necessary to sustain a scene, and we can achieve this by altering the rules or giving actors certain instructions.

There are more complex laws too; those governing space, distance, emotion and the flow of creativity. In terms of the latter, if one actor consistently blocks (ignores or rebuts the imaginative inventions of another player) pretty soon the creativity of the first will dry up. The non-blocking player will get exhausted. If this blocking persists, we can introduce rules: NO BLOCKING. Or NO BLOCKING WITH JUDGES where the audience throws off the 'blocking' player and gives another a chance.

There are laws regarding status, distance and personal space. In some aspects, these laws function in the same way in society but on the stage they carry particular significance and can be studied. For example, if one player stands and another walks slowly towards them, the standing player will – at some point – feel the walker is invading their personal space. Doing this exercise will discover this 'edge' of their personal space. People's 'sixth sense' even allows this to exist behind ones' back. If a player knows about this, they can use that knowledge in their characterisations. Does my character invade or respect other characters' space? In society, we know that people in their professional roles have different status expectations; kings and princes demand a lot of personal space, they have minions to clear it away in front of them. It's an honour to be allowed into that space. When I met the Queen I realised that her signal for me to leave the space was simply to stop talking to me. My permission to be in her space had been withdrawn. Policemen for their part are no respecters of private space – they believe they can walk anywhere; their power depends on that right. In prison and in the army, low ranking soldiers have their space reduced to almost nothing – the belief being, that's how to 'bring that tyke into line'.

In his book *Impro*, Keith Johnstone talks in more detail about how physicality is influenced by distance between people. Note that he refers to space in this context as an aura or personal energy belonging to each person – an energy which passes through the air: *'If I stand two students face to face and about a foot apart they're likely to feel a strong desire to change their body position. If they don't move they'll begin to feel love or hate as their "space" streams into each other. To prevent these feelings they'll modify their positions until their space flows out relatively unhindered, or they'll move back so that the force isn't so powerful. High status players will allow their space to flow into other people. Low status players will avoid letting their space flow into other people.'*[19]

Just as in science these 'laws' are always up for modification and discussion – but again as in science the big theses change very little. There is also discussion to be had about how different areas of the stage have different functions, in terms of performance. Jonathan Kay argues that on a proscenium stage, each section of the stage offers different scope. Frontstage naturally invites commentary, speculation, storytelling, while the central area is the area of emotional play. The rear of the stage is the place for expression of archetypal qualities. It gives us access to the gods. Such perceptions are useful because they help us to develop a sense of the medium's full potential. They may also help to understand why, for example, a performer avoids one area on the stage and always prefers another.

In terms of applying rules to what the performers are doing, the facilitator has a number of options. She can establish rules at the outset, ('Now we're going to play TAG, NO BLOCKING or BOXING) or progressively add rules as she goes along. ('Ok, Everyone just start moving around the space. Good. Now imagine the floor is red hot . . . ') The same is true for improvisations. The technique of rules as you go along is particularly useful in improvisations when actors meet problems. For example, the actors are blocking each other or not using the space properly or their work lacks energy. Let's imagine two actors are playing a scene. I've asked them to explore what happens when a gift has been lost or destroyed.

'Hi, Robert.'

'Hi.'

'I came round to see how Henry was getting on. Henry – you remember? The hamster we gave you for Christmas.'

'He's fine.'

We know the actor must be lying. So we have to impose a rule –
 (I could just propose or encourage, but let's make it a rule.)
 So I might say:

'You're not allowed to lie. Tell the truth.'

'Yes, I wanted to talk to you about that. Um . . . would you like a cup of tea?'

Now he's hedging, putting off the inevitable. He's not disobeying the rule, but avoiding its implementation. We haven't got time to waste so we'll give a direct instruction.

'Tell the truth of what happened to Henry.'

'Yes, I'm afraid Henry's dead.'

'Oh no, what happened?'

'I'm afraid he crawled into the liquidiser when I wasn't look- ing . . . '

Now the scene can move ahead. Sometimes an actor says 'Well, the character *would* lie in this situation' – and it may well be true although we have no way of testing that. But the point is, because it's drama we need to impose *different rules from life* to create the vivid, provocative, revealing entertainment which we want. As Guy Dartnell put to me, *'Life is walking while theatre is running.'* Why come to a workshop to simply carry on walking? We want to show what's below the surface of life, hence the imposition of rules which force us, as Rousseau insisted, to be freer than we would be without them. In the example given, we want to explore the guilt that Robert feels because of the loss of the gift. We want to enjoy his desperation at being found out. The rules push him towards that exploration.

But sometimes it's necessary to break rules. This rule-breaking is justified when we remain within the spirit of the game. I remember an exercise called FOOL FACTORS which involved a player having to achieve a certain number of tasks in a given time. It's a social skills exercise. He had to drink a glass of water, move furniture round, change his clothes ready to go out, talk to his mother on the phone and deal with a visitor. He got so far behind the clock that when the visitor arrived, he took his jacket off him, made *him* talk to his mother on the phone – then sat and poured the water over himself. Ok, he broke the rules but his ingenuity was clearly within the spirit of the exercise. There are exercises which specifically nurture lateral thinking. The NEWSPAPER GAME works by very strict rules. Here, it's necessary not to break rules but to scrutinise them carefully to identify *the freedoms which are hidden within the rules.* The puzzle of the game can be solved once these freedoms are found. Augusto Boal once offered a diagrammatic equivalent of this process of 'thinking round' rules. He was trying to make the point that as an intervening spectactor in Forum Theatre, it was foolish to assume that because one set of rules applied others also applied *which in other circumstances would be associated with these.* He asked us to take a piece of paper and draw nine dots, like this:

The task was to connect all the dots with four straight lines, without allowing the pencil to leave the page. When the problem is solved, it's useful to look back and examine what assumptions were made in initial, unsuccessful attempts.

PART TWO

FACILITATION

'You teach what you need to learn.'

Michael Chase

'And our big tough leader, away he wails
He thinks he is the kingpin but he's outraced
by that weedy little stranger with the grin on his face.'

Robin Williamson

'Chaos has to be very well organised.'

Joan Littlewood

FACILITATION

SOME PREDECESSORS

The drama facilitator, working amongst communities, arguably performs a contemporary, radical and innovative function. It's different from a theatre director or drama teacher, yet it borrows aspects of these roles. Modern practice leans on old disciplines. Where then are the role models? The following offer reference points:

THE SHAMAN

The shaman's primary function is to serve as a conduit to the spirits. He or she does this on behalf of the tribe, acting as a bridge to the spiritual realm. The shaman however operates differently to those who become subject to spirit possession, for the shaman always aims to remain in control of the visiting/inhabiting energies. This enables him or her to licence and supervise a controlled disorder. To achieve the means to perform this role, the shaman goes out from the tribe into another place then returns to infuse the tribe with energies which have been contacted elsewhere. This process of interacting with the tribe is begun by the shaman's provocative behaviour. The shaman hopes to release energies within the participants which are powerful, sometimes disturbing, often invigorating. Encouraging this process are the uses of rhythm, movement, mask and symbolic objects.

THE THEATRE DIRECTOR

The director conventionally organises the actors in such a way as to make the play coherent and effective for an audience. It's understood that George II, Duke of Saxe-Meiningen was a founder of the theatre director idea. He is credited with providing Germany with a core of basic principles upon which the modern theatre is built. He established the importance of the regisseur, integrating the actor and the *mise-en-scène*, perfecting ensemble playing and making decisions around the style and historical character of the production. But all this appears to have been achieved through the imposition of strict, autocratic rule. The director made the key decisions and the actors fulfilled them albeit within an ensemble idea. Finally, even Stanislavsky found the overall effect reduced the actors to the status of 'a stage property on the same level with stage furniture.'

The twentieth-century theatre director has moved towards a less autocratic, more inspirational idea. Far less common today is the image of the tyrannical director/actor/manager who employs actors as satellites to their own personality. Instead, directors such as Brook, Mnouchkine and Lepage tend to be ensemble-builders, allowing the theatre language to be pulled by the varying talents within the company while harnessing these within an overall conception. Actors are allowed greater control over how they interpret their roles. And in devised work this aspect of production is taken a stage further. The director Mike Leigh invites actors to create their characters from scratch and structures improvisations to facilitate a play-building process. So the final play is built on what actors have brought that is unique to them, albeit under his controlling direction. With another group of actors, the play itself would be different.

THE DRAMA TEACHER

It was in the nineteen fifties and sixties that the schools drama movement opened the way for teachers in the UK to use drama as an important adjunct to the regular curriculum. The drama teacher saw games-based play as instrumental to child development. Through play, the children's social skills, mutual tolerance and sensory abilities would be improved. The teacher's role was to release the children into more freeing and imaginative modes of interaction.

Later, Dorothy Heathcote and Gavin Bolton altered the focus of the work through deliberately linking it to educational and thematic content. The drama session became a means to engage with historical, political and cultural issues. The drama teacher introduced educational themes and harnessed the drama to understanding these. The teacher might go into role, taking on the part of a character to stimulate and direct the course of the improvisation. This role work shifted the whole idea of what a teacher was, and what a teacher could do. While earlier the teacher would direct sessions and run games, now she moved from the periphery of the group into the middle. She led from the centre, inviting pupils to follow on an imaginative journey, the pedagogical parameters of which were carefully pre-structured.

In a theatre rather than a schools context, teachers like Keith Johnstone and Viola Spolin were less interested in the knowledge arrived at than in the journey to get there. While Spolin in the US adapted a Stanislavskian conceptual vocabulary to stimulate actors to function as creators of their own material, Johnstone's techniques were designed to release content from part of the psyche which lay beyond rational control. His 'rediscovery of the visionary world' was intended to rebut the more negative consequences of orthodox teaching. A teacher's role, in his eyes, was about using games and exercises to liberate actors from their usual thought and physical patterns, so to become more effective, inspirational artists.

THE POLITICAL ACTOR

This is the actor who sees their professional calling as an opportunity to project their political view of the world. Acting is perceived as a political act, theatre as a political tool. In the UK, Joan Littlewood's Theatre Workshop extensively toured to community venues in working-class communities between 1950 and 1965. Influenced by Chinese and Russian models of politically proactive troupes, there was a conscious determination to link with working-class traditions and assist a process of cultural change. They were followed by companies such as CAST, 7:84, Monstrous Regiment and many others in the 60s and 70s whose actors perceived their work as one dimension within a life of cultural activism. What would characterise the actor's role, was a considerable influence over choice of play, style and audience. The actor would be expected to join in discussions about the content of the play in all its political aspects. In terms of training, the drama school might be valued less than an apprenticeship on the shipyards or in the mines. For when the company moved amongst the audience, either within a show or within its cultural work, this personal experience would win friends and strengthen complicity.

In the US, libertarian/anarchist companies such as the Living Theatre modelled company membership on an idea of combining anarcho-liberal idealism and acting. Membership was a life statement, a vocational subscription to a set of ideals, not just an enthusiasm for theatre. As Julian Beck wrote: '*The purpose of taking the theatre into the street is to smash repression. To disconnect art, artists and public (people)*

from the repressive arts of civilisation . . . Liberation is the word.[20]
Performance structures similarly elided into improvisation to facilitate
the expression of the ideals. Direct challenges would be made to the
audiences, to stand up, join, engage, perhaps even leave the theatre and
move into the street – if they weren't already there – for direct action.
Other companies were less politically strident, yet still assumed
commitment to a cultural role for theatre which moved beyond the
traditional. The Open Theatre, Theatre Libre, the Bread and Puppet
Theatre all called for a personal commitment from actors to a shared
ideal. The actor was to be a living embodiment of a set of alternative
beliefs, acting, provoking and enthusing.

THE ACTOR/TEACHER

The theatre in education movement which grew up in the 70s in the
UK, expanding at one point to 30 companies at its height, developed a
new hybrid, the actor-teacher. Otherwise known as the TIE actor, this
role aims to combine the best of both worlds. From teaching it drew
the practice of leading pupils through a series of intellectual
challenges, asking questions and eliciting debate. From theatre it drew
the idea of the performer 'in role', posing these challenges from inside
a fictional construct. The pupils, either as witnesses or participants,
therefore experienced knowledge as inseparable from the subjectivities
of living human beings. Even if the subject matter was historical,
issues were brought to life through recreation happening 'in the
present tense'.

This allowed for the actor/teacher to switch between objective and
subjective modes of engagement. The actor-teacher might play a
character one moment responding to pressures outside their control,
then step out of character to ask pupils questions about that character's
decisions. Working as a team, actor/teachers can set up quite
sophisticated interplays with the pupils which allow a shifting in and
out of theatre time, in and out of fictional worlds, within moments. At
the core of the actor/teacher idea was a notion about facilitation; direct
contact with the client group, building relationships, using drama as
means to question preconceived assumptions. The great strength of
role work, pace Heathcote and Bolton, was how it brought to life the
affective and psychological dimensions of political and historical
issues. Learning was not only absorbing but acting on information –
testing it, 'living' the events which were the subject of the learning.

THE CULTURAL ACTIVIST

The cultural activist who goes into a community and organises, stimulating educational programmes, has been seen as a force in both social development and political manipulation. The history of Chinese social development bears witness to both during different moments in the Chinese Revolution. When the community in question is asked to accept an ideology promoted 'on their behalf' without their compliance, we tend to recognise the influence as manipulative rather than educational. Paulo Freire, through his writings, offers a model of non-manipulative community activism appropriate for a population with extensive non-literacy. His writings place pedagogy clearly within a political analysis and emphasise the need for those on the margins of society to seize the challenge of literacy as a means to advance their rights within society. Literacy itself is seen as a tool which will assist social progress and social equality.

If the UK were to claim its own educational innovator, it might be Ed Berman whose Interaction Company aimed to provide the local community with the means to make its own theatre, on its own terms, to its own agenda. The theatre company Professor Dogg's Troupe was based on the idea that actors were also facilitators, able to teach as well as act, able to combine with local people in the making of workshops and shows. The theatre work was avowedly populist; it was a tool for communities to seize hold of and use to advance their interests. The company was widely influential during the sixties and seventies, generating a multiplicity of theatrical off-shoots, as well as actor-facilitators who went on to form their own companies.

THE JOKER

The role of joker is part of the mechanics of the Theatre of the Oppressed. It is close to being a facilitator, provoking and animating the group. It refers to the joker in a pack of cards where that card can take on the face of any other. The facilitator too has that chameleon-like functionality to respond to any situation with a different response. However, the Theatre of the Oppressed is perceived by Augusto Boal as a unified system, hence the joker function is intimately related to the purpose of this system which, at its simplest, is to rehearse behaviour for radical personal, cultural and political change.

The joker's function therefore derives from a responsibility to present groups – or audiences – with theatricalised opportunities for change. There is an assumption that the aesthetic sphere functions as kind of double for the social. Within Image Theatre work, this means directing exercises and managing a process which moves towards articulacy. Within Forum Theatre the joker's role moves further, working as the bridge between actors and the audience; summarising, encapsulating, stage managing. The joker is neutral, he or she does not 'argue a case' despite what is often the openly political nature of the exercise. Instead, the joker summarises options and provokes participants towards making choices. The joker is also able to speak about the consequences of choices, feeding back the implications of what has occurred after ideas have been tried out.

THE THERAPIST

Firstly, the pyschodramatist. He or she deals directly with the particular life experiences which are informing the client's behaviour. Psychodrama is an action method of group psychotherapy created and developed initially by J.L. Moreno whose descendants today acknowledge his founding influence. Psychodrama deals centrally with those personal issues of group members on which they wish to work. These issues form the subject of the group work. Drama techniques such as role play, role reversal, mirroring etc. will provide the means to investigate and illuminate those issues in a group context. So the function of the psychodramatist is primarily to organise and stimulate the group, run the enactments and lead the learning process in such a way that is therapeutically beneficial to the group members.

The dramatherapist by contrast, while sharing therapeutic aims, works analogically and through different forms: folk tales, metaphor, playtext, puppetry, myth and ritual. There is a wider remit of theatrical traditions employed. Again, the dramatherapist is working in a mutually understood therapeutic environment; it's understood the therapeutic goals are primary and not incidental to the ongoing activity. The work may remain within a private workshop situation or move out towards performances, perhaps using scripted material which might be generated from the group or drawn from literary sources.

RESPONSIBILITIES AND TASKS
OF THE FACILITATOR

A. SAFETY

Often safety issues are thought about by default after the accident has occurred. I've never known a participant ask to see an insurance policy but if a leg gets broken, they might. It's the facilitator's responsibility to ensure that a policy is in place which indemnifies against personal injury or damage to the building.

Here are three examples of incidents where safety had been neglected. The first took place when amateur theatre members were combining with a special needs group. There was only one workshop leader. The group had been divided into pairs with each pair having a member from the two sides. Then the group began to do some physical exercises, lifting and pushing. While the leader's back was turned, one of the special needs group members sat on his partner's back while he was lying on the floor, face down. The individual was quite heavy and a serious back injury was caused. It involved hospitalisation for several weeks and the problem continued beyond hospital.

The second example took place in my own workshop for probation clients. There was a young man in the workshop who had come out of prison that week after several years. But I didn't know that. I hadn't taken the time to find out about his situation. He appeared very confident and I found myself upping the challenges. Before long he was doing an improvisation with his 'girlfriend' and during it, jokingly threatened to strangle her. Appreciating the laughter, he commenced a demonstration. I was worried for a moment, but let the exercise run. For a few vital seconds too long. When I did stop it, alerted by her behaviour, she was shocked and upset. Luckily, there was no injury. The man had not intended to hurt her but simply didn't know his own strength. He was not yet sufficiently in control of his physical impulses. As he commented to me later, it was several years since he'd been in a room with women on a level of equals.

Clive Barker offered me the third anecdote. *'I have had only two accidents in all the time I've worked, discounting people biting their tongue or stubbing their toes. The terrifying thing is both accidents have been identical . . . (both individuals concerned) snapped Achilles tendons, while hopping. According to the surgeons, who were very laid back, it could happen to anyone at any time . . . but I was responsible and I've spent a lot of time going back over it and looking at the specific circumstances. As near as I can see on both occasions I was working with smaller groups than I have been accustomed to recently and, with the excuse that I was working with fit people in full training, I cut down the heavy tag games I usually start with.'* [21]

Within these stories come a roster of issues. In the first, there is the question of the team – is one facilitator enough? Leaders need to know enough about participants' situations to reasonably assess how they're likely to respond to different stimuli. There's also the issue of the training of volunteers and what responsibilities should be given them. Lastly, the careful matching of exercises to the group. Activities which involve lifting, carrying, jumping, running all involve elements of physical risk, the value of which must be considered against the capabilities of the group.

With the second story, insufficient preparation had taken place with that particular individual. I hadn't questioned him or his Probation Officer sufficiently. He was still an unknown quantity. Charming and self-effacing on the surface, he simply wasn't familiar with issues regarding drama in a mixed-sex environment nor could he understand the sensitivity which that entails. He was given responsibilities as a player which he wasn't yet able to manage.

The third story suggests that if activity is too strenuous too early, it puts participants at risk. There needs be slow development of activity to allow for bodies to adjust to the changing demands made on them. If bodies are stressed too quickly, something may snap. Sometimes – not in this case – facilitators import exercises from aerobics, sport, dance or karate which only occasionally have a place in the workshop room. The exercises don't transfer because an athlete's fitness requirements are not the same as an actor's. A degree of muscular strength is usually necessary, and a general fitness certainly is, but there's no point aiming for the stars when we only want to travel to Wolverhampton.

Then there is the issue of emotional safety although an absolute distinction between the two is artificial. Emotional insecurities or emotional excess can easily precipitate physical injury. It's not so different in sport. The English cricket team that went to Australia in the winter of 1994 suffered a series of debilitating injuries. One couldn't but suspect these were caused or at least aggravated, by stress. The team had just won a match after a long run of defeats. There was an almost desperate determination to maintain the momentum. Every time a fielder forgot technique in a headlong dash for the ball, there was injury. Australia, calm and much less anxiety-prone, suffered few setbacks and won the series.

Participants don't just want to know the floor is sound, they want to 'feel safe'. They need to feel comfortable with the project. Otherwise, why risk oneself? For a participant there's nothing worse than showing vulnerability and having it disrespected. So there's an onus on the facilitator to create the right atmosphere. How to do this? The first available strategy is the employment of ground rules. These might cover issues such as personal behaviour, lateness, use of drugs and alcohol, language, smoking. Some facilitators even use written contracts which are signed by everyone in the group. The contract can't ensure that rules aren't broken but it represents a code of practice which has been accepted *in principle*. So if it is broken, reference back helps the offender recognise the significance of transgression. Ground rules also help to publicise that the facilitator is determined to create a safe, ordered and hassle-free environment. This is a fuller list of what might be covered in a contract:

Arriving Promptly. An agreement is made around what is an acceptable and an unacceptable time to arrive. I've found constant lateness to be one of the most draining aspects of community drama. Valuable time is lost, and those who come late, arrive in a defensive/aggressive frame of mind. Perhaps the group has already started, in which case the latecomer will feel 'out of it' for the rest of the session. This is where the workshop leader's patience is most likely to be tested.

Smoking. For example, smoking is disallowed while the session is in progress. It's OK in the breaks or in designated areas at given times. There is occasionally a case for smoking a cigarette during a scene, but this can easily be taken advantage of!

Drugs and Alcohol. Participants are not allowed to bring either into the session. Nobody is allowed to attend the sessions under the influence of drugs or alcohol. If they are under the influence, then they may be barred from that session. Usually it's very evident that someone is under the influence. There's little benefit in their participating, because they won't be able to channel their feelings or ideas with sufficient focus or co-ordination.

Mutual Respect. It's important that participants acknowledge and respect every other participant's right to express themselves. This extends to disallowing remarks or behaviour which are abusive, or which 'put others down' by referring to their race or gender or sexuality. Often it's the unintentional remarks which cause upset. When this occurs, it may be necessary to engage a process of extending that individual's awareness of the impact of their remarks, either through an immediate comment or during feedback.

Confidence. Stories and experiences which are shared, are confidential to the session and should not be repeated elsewhere. A hard one to police. I've probably broken it in the book.

After establishing ground rules, much will depend on the facilitator's personal style; how they trust the group, and how they deal with the interpretation of rules. 'Feeling safe' is about creating the right atmosphere; informal yet disciplined, relaxed yet spontaneous. Katina Noble, previously with Spare Tyre, puts emphasis on people enjoying themselves as a way towards feeling safe: *'I have to make the group feel safe, by having fun and being aware at all times of combinations of people working together . . . so we want games which are confidence-building, like WHOSE STORY IS TRUE? . . . I'm always aware of not putting people on the spot too soon.'* The avoidance of high focus situations is particularly necessary with those who are not natural performers. If they're ask to walk naked through fire on the first day, they won't necessarily see the point. Maybe the purpose is to confront them with the full implications of their own fear. But as Chrissie Poulter observes: *'The terror can be worse if they are expected to perform or demonstrate abilities which they feel they don't have. As a result they feel foolish and oppressed by the situation.'* [22] The most high focus situation of all is one where the individual acts alone in front of the whole group. Almost as difficult, is acting with just one or two others, in front of the group. It's a feeling of maximum insecurity, minimum safety. It stimulates all the fears; they rush up to the head and one's mind is taken over by panic: 'how on earth can I stop myself feeling this way?'

Of course you can never make people feel safe all the time. The stage is a dangerous place else it's not worth visiting. There will always be moments when participants are invited to take a leap into the unknown – and may need pushing. How and when the pushing is justified, will depend on context. But the element of challenge should never be removed. As Keith Johnstone observes, talking of drama students (so they can be pushed harder): *'I used to think that I should try to prevent the student from ever experiencing failure – I thought I could do this by always selecting the right material, and by grading it in tiny steps. These days I think it's more important to teach ways of dealing with the pain of failure. I tell the students, "blame the teacher, laugh, never demonstrate a determination to try harder".'*[23]

Some facilitators like to demonstrate a game. The virtue of this is it shows you're willing to go where the group must follow. It says, 'I can be foolish – and I don't mind.' It's not only breaking the ice, it's taking your clothes off and chucking yourself in. The value lies in demonstrating the mechanics of the exercise if people can't 'see it.' The disadvantage lies in appearing to 'set standards' if you happen to be particularly adept. If I do it, I aim to try and show the mechanics but not in a way that inhibits others.

Whether you demonstrate or not, doesn't have to become a rule. Such a convention may prove counter-productive. It leads to 'Come on, show us – you did before.' It's true some facilitators prefer to be 'inside' exercises, others prefer to be 'out'. But most will agree that in/out depends on the situation of the group at any time. Some groups need provocation from inside, others are naturally courageous but could benefit from guidance at the edge. Again, if the facilitator works with a partner, there are more options. One can be inside leading, the other can be out, observing. Whatever the pattern, we're trying to inspire confidence that the medium is worth tackling so we'll do whatever is necessary to achieve that.

The appropriateness of different safety strategies will vary. Retired people may feel happier with half an hour of tea and socialising before any drama at all. Groups of individuals with learning difficulties, may feel less inhibited if their day-to-day supervisors find themselves busy elsewhere. Younger people will have different resistances again. Clair Chapwell and Harriet Powell observe the particular defences that teenagers have. Harriet: *'There is a cool barrier we have to break through. They're desperate to be cool. They want to be good at everything. So we have to tread carefully not to make people feel stupid.'* Clair: *'You need to get through the cool, because it's an insecurity barrier. They may not all become actors or musicians, but they'll learn about something, they'll get excited about something and they'll see words they've improvised acted on stage. So we're saying . . . "Maybe it's OK to be excited about things."'*

Ali Campbell, who works with a range of community groups, uses positive acceptance of all suggestions in the early stages. *'I will say yes to everything for at least the first half hour or hour, before anyone goes – "No, let's do that bit again and let's miss out the waving of the sticks this time." It's true that there are things we're not going to do. But I'm going to embody yes-ness.'* This helps people to realise that every contribution is apposite. Sometimes a facilitator will take the route of so-called trust games. A particular problem with these games, though admirable in intent, is they're more often 'dare' games. 'If I dare to do it, I must trust you.' But if I *don't* dare to hurl myself from a height into anxious arms, we're left with an uncomfortable feeling of failure. We're left feeling an *absence* of trust and perhaps there are no further strategies to deal with that, so little is achieved. Another difficulty with some of these games is they pay insufficient attention to the differing physical makeup of men and women. What is OK for physical contact between men, it is assumed, is fine for women. But often women feel less comfortable with them, the areas of permissible touch not being the same. Some of the gentler trust games may encourage people to loosen up physically but to simply run 'trust' games does not necessarily engender trust. And if individuals start feeling awkward, and frightened by the explicit challenge element, group confidence may suffer.

B. MANAGING RELATIONSHIPS, METHODOLOGY AND TIME

Prior to a workshop project beginning, there may be management issues to be addressed. Negotiations between staff and facilitators probably need to take place over formats and objectives. (Dealt with in Part Three.) This is often the case where the group members need personal support, or are institutionalised. One aspect concerns relationships – it's the facilitator's task to monitor these throughout the project. This might involve relating not just to the group, but to staff, volunteers or carers.

RELATIONSHIPS

The most effective workshops in institutions take place with the active support of staff. There needs to be a coincidence of objectives; this assists the development of relationships and positive feedback. In short, several minds are better than one; if they're all focused together, the participating group is well supported. This may mean discussing all aspects of the project in advance. Will staff be present? On one hand, with staff absent, the group can experience more sharply a difference of atmosphere. They may appreciate the freedoms. But with staff present, they may be able to key in information about the group, or constructively help with the process. Of course each situation varies widely; in prison there are security issues, in a hospital, health issues. And if staff are present, should they participate, or watch? Saul Hewish on working in prisons: *'I used to say to staff "Get involved" – after all, it's a way of validating the work, having them see the benefits. But now I leave it up to them. Or they may choose not to do certain exercises. For example, women staff may feel uncomfortable doing physical exercises with . . . offenders, and I understand that.'*

With carers and groups having special needs, some similar issues apply. Often there are strong reasons for the presence of carers. For example, they may be able to assist the participants be creative. They may have information about what animates or worries the participant. Janet requires medication every so often. John can become distressed if family situations are discussed in any detail. Yonic always responds well to music, and rhythm work. These titbits of information can be invaluable. However, there can be problems if staff, trying to be helpful, intervene counter-productively, for example, 'on behalf of' their client. They haven't understood the facilitator's methodology which involves the participant being allowed to struggle for a solution. Geraldine Ling works with Them Wifies in Newcastle, and her comment underlines the need for co-operation: *'I prefer for staff to be involved but they've got to be sensitive to the needs of the session . . . Mostly it's best to say to the worker "Please, just don't do things on behalf of the others." Because they'll say "I'll do that. Look, John, this is how to do it." But if there's someone who needs help to move, then help them . . . As for volunteers, it is good to have people who are enthusiastic about the work, but you can't be looking after them as well. It's better to have people who've had training beforehand. It's the dropping in and out you need to have control over, because it can be destructive.'*

While identifying pitfalls, the impression should not given that if staff are collaborative, their presence is not beneficial. They can be helpful in interpreting instructions to the individual participant whom they know personally. They know best how to phrase the challenge so it will be more readily accepted. Which brings us to volunteers. In 'Safety' we identified the problems which can occur if volunteers are not properly trained. However, if they have a clear function in the room, their presence is invaluable. For example, they may bring complementary skills to a partner, so the two can work together as a team. Amici, led by Wolfgang Stange, is a workshop and performing company, which has combined blind members with Downs Syndrome members and active volunteers. *'In terms of the able-bodied members of the group, the volunteers are supporting the blind members. I have to have someone who is audible and clear, to give instruction when I'm somewhere else. If one Downs Syndrome person takes over leading the exercise, for example, then someone has to explain (to the blind person) what's happening, because they can't see a thing. But then when the blind person takes over, she doesn't need any support there . . . And very often the blind person doesn't work with an able-bodied person, but with a Downs Syndrome person.'*

METHODOLOGY

A methodology is defined in Chambers Dictionary as 'a system of methods and rules applicable to research or work in a given science or art; evaluation of subjects taught and principles and techniques of teaching them.' In other words, the governing structures which incorporate most of the issues raised in this book. In practice, this involves the facilitator maintaining an overview of what is to be achieved, and controlling the strategies selected. Without an appropriate methodology, there is always the danger of the workshop being hijacked. The group may appropriate it for their own devices which may not be particularly educational. In the late seventies I understood little of any methodological approach to working and had only one or two rather inappropriate maxims as my guide. One of these, which I believed in passionately at the time, was 'whatever the kids want, they must be right.' With a group of unemployed teenagers attending a drop-in centre, this proved a little inappropriate. It was a group of 5 or 6 school refusers. The first session went well so in the second I suggested improvisation. And I asked them what they'd like to do. 'A robbery in a post office' they said. So that's what we did. It went well. The robbers got away. Next week, 'What do you want to do?' 'Robbery in a post office.' 'But we did that last week.' OK. So how can we do it different today?' 'This time we'll use guns.' 'OK – fine!' So we did it again, with guns. It went well. The robbers got away. This time they left the postmaster dead. Next week, same question. Same answer. 'But we've done the robbery for two weeks now. Can't you think of something else? 'This time we'll use machine guns.' 'Er . . . OK, fine.' It went well. This time there were more dead. The following week I came in and there was no one there. The youth leader emerged from his office and took me aside. 'I'm afraid there's been a problem.' 'Oh, really?' 'Yes. It appears some members of the group have been arrested.' I tried to look bright. 'Oh! How so?' 'It appears they tried to rob a post office . . . '

Your methodology comes under inspection at moments like this. Perhaps there was fine tuning to be done. I'd had the sessions hijacked. The group had been allowed to determine form, content and process while I, in my liberal naiveté, permitted it all. Effective methodology seems to depend upon a conjunction of objectives and strategies, underpinned with a core understanding of first principles. Without such infrastructure, your house is blown down faster than First Pig's.

TIME

Managing time raises the issue of objectives and how these need be aligned to the situation of the group. Disappointment and confusion can arise when objectives are set beyond the abilities of the group. You run out of time trying to achieve them. Similar disappointment happens when dramatic styles are adopted which the group are unfamiliar with, and cannot quickly learn. Perhaps the facilitator has imported a theatrical style from another context, and it simply doesn't work with this group. So there's always that sense of struggling against the odds. We can't always succeed on every occasion, but we can monitor the relationship between the group's ability and the challenge offered, and if necessary make changes.

Which challenges can the group address in the time? When Clair Chapwell and Harriet Powell moved from working with teenagers to working with retired people, the need to change expectations became apparent. Clair: *'Harriet had worked with older people before, and I hadn't. So first I said "Let's get them moving around the room." And she* said *"Are you kidding? That they get moving* into *the room will be their achievement for the day."* And I thought *"Surely not."* But yes. In fact we had two one and a half hour sessions a day, which was about right. We'd have a theme every day, for example holidays and we'd use objects to pass round.' Harriet: 'We used the same process as we normally use (to build a play) but it took three months instead of two.' Clair: 'I was clueless and I said "Let's talk about their lives, let's start with – " and of course they hang on to those early memories. They're precious. And there was one man who said "You have stirred me up so much, I'm not coming back. And he didn't come back."* Harriet: *'That particular man, he wouldn't let anybody else talk, you couldn't stop him. It all came out, from the dead horses in the first world war . . . but as soon as we wanted to focus on one particular thing, he wouldn't have any of it.' Clair: 'But at the end he came up and said it (the performance) was beautiful.'*

What Clair also found was the necessity to switch from her normal role. With a group of kids from an estate, she played high status: *'I'm in charge!'*. But in the old people's home, that would have gone down like a visit from the Benefits Agency. So she was *'like a grand-daughter, always putting my arms around them.'* An element of trust, friendship and relaxation was essential. As with all groups, if key members are won over, others follow.

There are also issues about the number of sessions, the length of each and how the project will conclude. Often a facilitator is working within given constraints either of finance or time. Individual sessions may last a fixed period; one hour, two, perhaps three at most. There is always a need to have one eye on the clock, not only to honour agreed coffee breaks, but to anticipate the end of the session, and to allow for a winding down – and possibly feedback at the end. Roger Hill argues that a session can be divided into three sections; the warm-up and preparatory work, the main part of the work, and the winding-down. Facilitators rightly place much emphasis on the latter part which includes feedback. It's not that everything *must* be talked about, but ideas, feelings and opinions which have been withheld may usefully be offered then. There is also perhaps further planning to discuss. Roger Hill: *'Even before we leave this room, let's share what we've done. We should share the energy so it seems to be completed. And if you don't have a sense of completion, if you're a loose ends type, your group performs in a particular way. I'm not a loose ends type. If we're going to leave all these notes on the wall, that's something we've agreed. It's a sense of closure, which is a formal thing. Each one of those closures works towards a final closure which is with the audience.'*

There are many different ways to evaluate during feedback. Have participants enjoyed the session? What have they learned? What would they like to do more of, next time? Nic Fine uses two particular techniques during a closure which may be appropriate. Firstly, he may ask the group members to give 'appreciations' of contributions made by others. Secondly, with some groups he may insist, to avoid the feedback becoming acrimonious, for each contributor to summarise the previous contributor before a new comment is added.

Very little is possible if the group has already run out of time. The temptation to run 'just one more exercise' is often strong. If it fails to finish, or if there's a man waving keys at the door as it closes, we may feel that earlier good work has been compromised. Certainly any feedback session has been lost. Roger Hill: *'The strangest place you should reach is two thirds of the way through the session. Thereafter – recuperation, reflection and recovery. There was a story that we used to be told in school assemblies. There was a man who was told he could have as much land as he could walk around between sunrise and sunset. This guy is really greedy, he sets off and goes round and round. Two thirds of the way round he realises he's going to be cutting it fine to get back to the point he's started from by sundown. So he starts to run, he starts to hurry, but he's a bit old, a bit tired. He's just going to do it, he's almost there – yes, he's got there, he's claimed this massive amount of land. Then he dies of a heart attack.'*

C. BUILDING THE GROUP

I am always impressed by anyone who can make a group gel. Pete Brooks held Impact Theatre Co-op together throughout the eighties when other companies fell apart or constantly changed their line-ups. He told me; *'I'm very dictatorial but I'm very loyal to my performers. Impact was a co-operative but I've always been a strong figure. My skill is in creating teams, people who like each other. It's the most fundamental skill and the most indefinable. I'm quite conscious of my attempts to keep people happy in the sense of who I'm giving attention to and who I'm not. I try to distribute my attention. I do a lot of flirting, self-deprecation, the usual stuff.'* What does this usual stuff consist of? It involves giving attention not equally but fairly, reading the group, observing how individuals are, seeing if they become troubled by an exercise or a comment. It's about choosing the right exercises, making sure they match the mood. It also involves what Phelim McDermott calls 'building the myth of the group', which means nurturing a sense of identity, a sense of who we are, us few.

GIVING ATTENTION

Running a group is an act of emotional generosity. It can't be done without warmth, affection and good feeling. As Roger Hill observes: *'You have to love the idea of group. In the sort of work I do, you've got to believe that coherence and inter-relationship is the natural and preferred way in which human beings co-exist.'* Of course, any group is made up of individuals who are respectively introvert, extrovert, intellectual, instinctive and so on, they're different personalities. These personality differences will inform how contributions are made. So 'coherence' in the sense which Hill refers to it, means drawing from and respecting these differences. Giving attention means understanding these differences – and 'seeing' what different individuals need. One of the hardest balancing acts is between being *challenging* and being *supportive*. Training actors for the professional theatre, if my own training is any guide, is a lot about the former and little about the latter. But in community drama, it should tip the other way. Especially with those who feel themselves vulnerable and shaky day to day, supportiveness is essential. Sometimes a challenge may be misunderstood. Often I've upset someone unwittingly by drawing attention to a failing. I'd thought it a gentle observation, then the next day someone tells me how upset Jack was, my commenting on his reluctance to take off his hat.

Working with offenders, the challenge element may be more justified. This is because we may be pushing to encourage disclosures. Saul Hewish: *'Being supportive and challenging is a real tough skill. I don't always get it right. But if you're co-working, good and bad cop routines are not unknown. Then your partner can see what's needed . . . '* Working with other groups, the balance may need to be different. With a group of individuals having learning difficulties, there's a balance to be struck between permissiveness and strictness. We want Maureen to meet a particular challenge. But we're tempted to accept whatever she offers, fearful that's all we'll get. If we don't push, nothing may come of it. But if we push too hard and she withdraws, that may create enmity.

There is always a sub-text to group relationships. Part of this is to do with the fact that theatre is an erotic medium. 'Giving attention' by the leader to the group and vice versa, always involves an element of flirtation. Pete Brooks observes: *'There are complex psychological games that you play that you're not aware of . . . maybe there is an erotic relationship between you and your cast. And if that pretend flirtation isn't there because you're preoccupied with something else, like a break-up in your relationship, maybe they sense it. They all want you to be in love with them whether they fancy you or not . . . And it's got nothing to do with gender sexuality.'*

READING THE GROUP

is a natural corollary of this. 'Reading' means constantly watching, registering and noting signals. It means observing all those behavioural signs being given off by participants – both the intended, directed signals: questions, statements and movements – and also unconscious gestures and body language. A workshop is a constantly buzzing human–electric field of such signals. Monitoring these is an important skill and a precondition for decision-making on the spot. Since we're looking to fill the stage with energy, that means learning how the group's energy functions, and therefore how it can transfer to the stage.

Of course I will read some individuals well and others less well. This has to do with my own blind spots. Some individuals I see and hear more clearly. Some individuals, perhaps because of class or culture, I find more difficult to read – not because of any lack in them, but because of a lack in me. It's often the smaller signals that are the most important; the danger signals: those that tell you that if Jane gets any more attentions from Vince, she's going to burst into tears or hit him. In which case it doesn't matter how brilliant is Danny's improvisation. The signal that tells you that Bob has been quiet from the start and cannot engage. Maybe he should be asked how he feels, or be given more attention. Maybe something's happened in his private life which is affecting his behaviour.

In the early stages of a project, you can run games which specifically help you to 'see' how individuals are responding. Their responses may indicate how they'll react to harder challenges. Saul Hewish uses GRANDMOTHER'S FOOTSTEPS in this way. How do the individuals in the group tackle the problem inherent in the game? Who hides behind someone else? Who rushes at Grandmother? Who gives

up quickly and goes for their packet of cigarettes? Who starts shouting
that Grandmother is breaking the rules? Jonathan Kay tells me that
with groups who are more experienced, he'll throw them in at the deep
end with a high-focus exercise at the first session. It enables him to
'read' their approach to performing under pressure; this enables a fast
track to discussion of the basics.

Cultivating harmony is also related to the CHOICE OF EXERCISES. It's
easy to set people against each other. It's a great way to get 'instant
conflict' so things 'appear to be happening'. Wow, people are shouting,
it's theatre already. Challenge and competition games are useful, but if
they become the common form of expression, rivalries can spill over.
The group starts to see itself as one which thrives on conflict. It's also
true that certain co-operative games can get hijacked and become
competitive. I've never been able to play FREEZE TAG in a mixed
group without the men taking it over for a display of their talents. The
freezing which goes on . . . is of the women being frozen out.

If in doubt, I use exercises which rely on warmth and generosity.
I've borrowed and adapted Keith Johnstone's PRESENTS and I use
DANCE DIALOGUE or SELLOTAPE GAMES. There are also quite
well-known games such as WIZARDS which while being competitive,
rely on teamwork first and foremost. An easy sociability is encouraged
by changing the format of the exercise quickly in early sessions, so
participants interact with everyone; they get used to changing partners
and stop relying on 'being with friends'.

THE MYTHOLOGISATION OF THE GROUP

These are important ways to bond a group which start offstage, in the
coffee bar, on the telephone. What defines a group is both inclusiveness
and exclusiveness. Some are in, some are out. What kind of identity
does this give us? Phelim McDermott: *'The way that I work and try and
help people with their creativity, whatever the environment is – a six week
rehearsal period, a four week workshop – is to create the myth of that group.
And the improvisation and the games for me are ways of making a sort of
world which is their world, our world, which supports and makes the rules of
the games clear. Now sometimes those games might be very specific. On first
day this might be a trust game. You get up and lead people around with their
eyes shut. But also there are lots of games which come from the edges of the
group, which start in jokes in the coffee break, jokes about the group, which
may be important ways of helping that group be creative.'* Perhaps a

shared anecdote or a curious turn of phrase from an improvisation triggers the group imagination. There's a joke which seems to pull everyone into its slipstream. David Slater, working with retired people, tells the story of how a pensioner announced her company from the stage as 'The Old Crocks'. A younger group called themselves 'The Copycats' from a copying exercise which worked particularly well. If these strands of energy emerge from *within* the group rather than from the leadership they may be more powerful in building a group identity.

D. DEVELOPING THE ARTICULACY OF THE GROUP

Drama facilitation is about introducing a language which is already familiar, but unused. The teaching element lies in encouraging participants to become conscious of the potential of this language. The teaching enables them to train their dramaturgical eyes on to any aspect of their situation and appropriate what they see. In making this appropriation, the material becomes something else. It becomes dramatic vocabulary, something separate from life. This distinctiveness is important. At drama school I was shocked to see how someone could get muddled about the difference. I was going out with another student. During a lesson we had to play boyfriend and girlfriend. The scene was, she was to find me in bed with another girl, and get angry. Furniture was to be thrown. We played the scene. She got very angry. Furniture was thrown. But in the coffee bar she turned on me. 'How could you do that? I'm very upset. I never thought you could behave like that.' Were these not confusions about what was real, and what dramatic? (An actor friend has similarly commented to me that whenever he plays villains in a show, he always meets with persistent distrust from his colleagues.)

The facilitator needs to nurture a sense of this division. It's a matter of safety: if the lines are blurred, stage revelations may become judged 'as if' the events were real. Then those who revealed something become vulnerable to mockery. It's one reason why I encourage the use of character names, even for brief exercises. As soon as a participant is addressed by their own name, they start to feel this is real life again. They feel 'this is me here, so I must only do what I would do offstage – I need to defend my identity.' Now there may be moments when this is appropriate – when working on personal stories for example – but otherwise a fictionalisation is more appropriate.

Fictionalising stage action demarcates it as a world apart. We can never lose complete touch with our own reality since everything is proceeding directly or indirectly from memory, but we can optimise our imaginative possibilities by acknowledging that here, rules are different. Augusto Boal draws a triangle to illustrate the relationship between lived experience, and theatre. We make a journey from our lived experience towards theatre. Then we play with that theatre material; and so make a journey with it. We arrive at a new point, allowing us to return to the start point. Through the playing we hopefully reach understandings which help inform us about our start point. However, while we're *within* dramatic play, we operate in a non-linear mode; by association and impulse. Inside this theatre world we can amplify, exaggerate and stylise according to whim. Participants may be unfamiliar with just how plastic the language is. So there's always a demonstrative element involved in facilitation. However, the facilitator should generally avoid taking responsibility for content. In Mike Leigh's film, *Nuts In May*, the referee of the boys' football game keeps getting involved, just can't resist getting control of the ball and becoming a player. And who's to dispute then he's scored a goal? Roger Hill: *'You are occupying one seat in a circle of seats. You have no greater status than anybody else but you have a function which is different. First of all, you are there to ensure that everyone in that circle has a chance to, is encouraged to, articulate something . . . Then you have to ask as many questions as possible to establish what sort of shape that material can take. Then you have to challenge them, in a potentially autocratic way, of that shape and of that material. 'We need someone to play the nurse. Mary, I think you should have a go.''*

Often facilitation fails when strictness unhelpfully replaces openness, or too much openness is allowed when strictness is essential. At the beginning, when participants are tongue-tied, a certain sensitivity is in order. We want to be open and encouraging. But this doesn't mean people can just opt out. We have to establish that drama is about contributing stuff, even on Day One. The challenge element has to be there from the outset otherwise people opt to be audiences all the time. In difficult situations, there is always the tactic of incorporation – doing what good improvisers do – accepting offers even though they haven't been made. Ali Campbell: *'I could be talking about any group here, but I was working with some very confident kids doing GCSE drama. But there were two absolutely terrified girls. When it came to their turn to sing their name, they practically flipped . . . I give people the power to pass but I don't give people the power to say "pass" straight away . . . I make sure that everyone is relaxed, and I say "That's OK, come on" and I just wait. Neutral status. I just wait. And they'll go "Tch! Oh . . . " And if I'm asking for a name and a movement, I'll go "That'll do." '* Usually the participant is so relieved to see the focus pass, they have little sense of the ploy adopted. And besides, they learn that what you contribute doesn't have to be thought out, or profound.

From this starting point, the level of articulacy can be raised to where you can be more discriminating about material. The group can collaborate on choosing material from a selection of what individuals have contributed. It becomes acceptable for the group to recognise that a certain idea, story or image does speak more effectively. A different route might use an exercise like THE BRIDGE which aims to link all ideas offered into a pyramid of scene-making.

Articulacy also means recognising and validating dialects. It means acknowledging that the vitality of drama work is fed by spoken language in all its variety. Group members are likely to feel more comfortable if they know they can use those speech patterns, rhythms or patois which are their own. I remember a workshop where we played the TV GAME which was commandeered by the Afro-Caribbeans present for a satire on American street gang culture. The group generated more energy and vibrancy than almost anything I'd seen before or since, using that exercise. A similar argument can be made for the argot and display of sub-cultures. Punk, Rastafarian, Teddy Boy, Gothic, New Romantic, all hold a fascination for any age group which is experimenting with identity. Improvisations can give full reign to that experimentation. The suppressed colours of language, gestures and behaviour can quickly revitalise dull material.

Group articulacy does depend on even-handedness from the facilitator. Favouritism drains the group spirit. Instinctively you know sometimes that somebody's idea won't work. But to crush that idea too quickly may be undermining. It may be necessary for the weaker idea to be tried along with the rest, so its weakness becomes evident through playing. And what may happen is that the supposedly weak idea turns out stronger than all the rest! You just didn't see it. Even playing out a genuinely thin idea may spark useful observations. As John Bergman observes: *'Psychology and drama are not sciences. They are evolutionary art forms where we reach for something that opens a door – that then gives us something else. And we don't always get it right. But we don't have the same need to work logically. We're in there to achieve an affective result, and some self-awareness.'*

The development of articulacy does not happen in straight lines but by a zig-zagging of associations, leaps, guesses and experiments. There is no royal road to articulacy. It is the lateral leaps which often take us closer to where we want to go. Suddenly when the workshop appears to be disappearing down disappointment, something happens which takes everyone by surprise. Some facilitators try to exploit this lateral, non-linear logic in their game plan. Lois Weaver: *'I try to keep people from worrying whether it (their character) makes sense or not. "Oh, my character never would do that." I try to push people beyond what their character would or wouldn't do because I feel that's where we constrain ourselves in terms of our own identity . . . I try to set up an environment where the illogic is primary, where non-sense is the basis.'* Weaver's process may involve writing by free association then selecting out an idea and building it up. Facts from personal history may be deliberately fictionalised to get on a different track. A character may be quizzed about things which are absent in their (fictional) lives and then *this* be used as a start point.

Ali Campbell uses the ambiguity of imagework as a means to take off sideways. He uses a game called THE TRANSPORT MUSEUM which is about the group building different shapes. It starts off building letters of the alphabet – *'So you get six people making the letter B. Then I say "Supposing you just walked into the room and you didn't know we'd all been making the letter B. What else might this be?" And last week someone said "Oh, it's people doing a ritual to make the crops grow." And another said "It's people in an art gallery looking at pornographic paintings of the Queen." Well, we were away.'* So the group has shifted sideways, played into a new area, and there may be richer pickings there. There are good exceptions to this rule, but in terms of developing articulacy, the material which comes from unplanned, spontaneous leaps at the edge may be what's required for centre stage.

Allied to this, is the notion of the facilitator as someone who 'divines' the group. The art of divination in this context is about seeing patterns below the surface. Such themes might be present in the group but unarticulated or unconscious. It's the facilitator's task to read below the surface and discover what these are. If appropriate, an analysis can be offered back. This was an aspect of Boal's practice which most impressed me. It was not just the techniques – though they were magical – it was how he wrote down descriptions of all the images we'd made, then returned the next morning with analysis of the key themes. It was as if he looked primarily, and centrally, at sub-text. So we were introduced to the essential paradoxes embodied in our work which we weren't aware of while making that work. Through his and others' example, I learned detective skills. I worked once with a group of 11-13 year olds in a youth theatre context. They were constantly doing improvisations in which animals featured, and usually died. There were also improvisations involving people of their age being let down by teachers or parents. Probably neither of these motifs seem surprising. However, I began to realise that the animal scenarios were at one level about a sense of loss of their own instinctive, childish natures. After all, they were all on the cusp of adulthood. While the other theme was about wanting to test their powers as young adults. I decided that the play should be set on a desert island where the young people had opportunely landed. Conveniently no adults had survived the shipwreck. I hoped to create a world where the twin themes of loss of innocence and assumption of adult responsibilities could be explored. Interestingly, the group then 'killed off' the immature characters who couldn't adapt to the situation on the island. (Their actors conspired in this.) This allowed a key debate to take place on the island, which was about the rules which should be in place for this 'new society'.

In any devised work, different individuals will have different relationships to the key themes. Some feel closer to them, others less so. The facilitator tries to read the book of the individual as well as the book of the group. And very often identifying the key themes for individuals is a key to their individual articulacy. It is not infrequent that someone comes into community drama, finds a characterisation for themselves through impro, builds it to a point, then leaves the group. For example, Andy begins playing the role of the father all the time. He appears to have a real energy for this, and everyone is delighted by his playing. His characterisations are funny, bawdy and not a little critical. One might say he is achieving a kind of Brechtian distance on his characters which allows him to inhabit the Dad, but also comment on him. Then suddenly Andy leaves the group. Everyone is disappointed. But perhaps what he came into drama to do – consciously or unconsciously – is now completed.

To refer back to Roger Hill's earlier comments about articulacy and his asking 'Mary' to play 'the nurse', he goes on: *'and I'm asking her to do this, because of what I know of Mary and because of what I know of the nurse.'*

This may be a simple, but it may also be a complex relationship. Mary may be asked to play the nurse because Mary is new to the group and the role will be fun and easy to play. Hopefully Mary will grow through it. Or perhaps Mary has been months or years in the group, is constantly playing rebel characters and giving her the nurse role is about casting against type. In which case it's about asking Mary to extend her expressive range through working with a caring archetype. This deliberate casting is particularly useful for groups with less developed social skills. Through such character play, an individual can surface some of their hidden, inner potential. It's possible that Mary will have a resistance to playing the nurse – which is why some measure of persuasion may be necessary. After all, 'caring' roles may be viewed as uncool. But if she does do something striking with it, others may follow her. By contrast, in a group of individuals having learning difficulties, participants may be keen from the start. For when participants are constantly in the role of being 'cared for' the chance to flip into the opposite, is a bonus. The same occurs when a person with disability becomes a mother or father – care staff are astonished that the participant demonstrates such effective parenting skills!

E. TROUBLESHOOTING

Here are some typical issues which come up with groups whose behaviour is challenging:

Lateness
Argumentativeness
Apathy
Fear
Offensive Behaviour
Splits within the Group
Egocentricity.

Broadly speaking, these issues can be divided into those which can be dealt with within stage work and those which have to be dealt with separately, offstage. Some issues may need to be addressed in both areas. Ultimately it's difficult and probably inappropriate to lay down the law about *how* any dispute should be tackled; so much depends on the individuals, the group and the circumstances. And let's make no assumption that the facilitator cannot contribute to things getting out of hand. A facilitator running a group who cannot admit their own mistakes or is incapable of changing their mind, can only present an unhelpful image of inflexibility.

Disputes which occur on-stage are more easily dealt with because they probably relate to the work in hand. There may be misunderstandings about the exercise. There may be frictions building up because of an exercise not working. Participants may become frustrated and start to blame each other. In this case, the facilitator's task lies in restarting or restructuring the exercise. It's important then to identify how the exercise might be accomplished more easily. Perhaps a different exercise altogether is called for.

As far as offstage behaviour, a contract about ground rules may be an appropriate first strategy. When it comes to managing ground rules, the *circumstances* surrounding a breach offer a yardstick for deciding what action to take. Those who wish to impose hard and fast rules may discover more is lost than gained by being ruthless. For example, the issue of sexist remarks. We're assuming the remark is made off-stage (if it's on-stage, we have to consider its appropriateness in terms of character behaviour). Most facilitators agree that there is little to be gained by immediately jumping on the offender. A knee-jerk response only reproduces classroom authority patterns. The offender can easily retreat into belligerence. It may be wiser to tackle it in a different way. It could be addressed in the feedback session, or during a moment when working on a scene when the stage action connects in some way with the issue. If such remarks are commonplace, there may be good reason for structuring the work around related themes.

However, given the above latitude, major transgressions do have to be jumped on or the safety of the other members will be jeopardised. Nic Fine has worked extensively, running conflict management sessions in a range of institutions. Here he talks of a particular workshop where *'one guy got aggressive at the beginning and got more and more aggressive as time went on. This guy didn't keep to any of the guidelines that had been set out. And by the third day things were beginning to get violent. He really flipped out . . . whenever family was mentioned.*

It was obvious the guy was in a lot of distress. Things shouldn't have been allowed to get to that stage.'

It's very difficult for participants to sustain commitment if ground rules are consistently broken. Far better to work with a smaller group who will accept and work within the guidelines, than a larger group which won't. Especially in a youth club I give clear options at the beginning. 'In three minutes the door will be closed. You can leave now – now you know a little of what we're going to do – or you can stay. If you stay, you can leave later but you can't return. Similarly if you leave now, you cannot return. There is no returning once you've gone!'

There are clear examples where if an individual displays behaviour wildly in breach of the contract, there's no alternative but to send them out. There's little point in a participant joining in who's clearly under the influence of drugs or alcohol. Blatant possession of banned substances is usually grounds for expulsion. But the majority of cases happen in the twilight zone where responses are negotiable. For example, problems may arise out of the behaviour of not one, but several individuals. Antagonisms develop between them. Who is to blame is unclear. Then a decision must be made about the seriousness of the dispute. Can the current work absorb it, by bringing the disputants into the centre, into the improvising? Or do we need to sit down and sort it out? It may be a hard decision. If a meeting is called unnecessarily, the group begins to feed off the facilitator's anxiety. But if the work is carried on and issues are not dealt with, frictions can cause explosions later. Let's look at a situation where a major argument did brew up, and the work was stopped. In this case it's between young men and women in a group devising project. There was to be music in the show. Harriet Powell and Clair Chapwell tell the story.

Harriet: *'The women were very angry about some of their experiences – and we wrote a song, "Women's Blues", a powerful song about what had happened to them. They felt angry, and this song emerged. I think I wrote it, and each verse drew on a different woman's experience. And the men got so threatened by it. It was as if they said "This isn't us, we don't behave like this. We're not having a song like this in the show. We want a men's song to redress the balance." And there had already been quite a lot of stuff about men. They just couldn't see it. So, they had their own song.'*

Clair: *'But also they wanted to change a verse (of the women's song). And I remember Adele saying to Brian "And is it better now?" And he just* said *"Fuck it"* and stomped out. And the women were outraged. Just completely ... We were so angry at this stage I thought *"I'm just going to re-write the whole show for women. I don't care if I ever see those shits again".* '

Harriet: 'The women at that point were bending over backwards to make everything alright. As women will always do ... '

Clair: 'What was interesting was there were different shades – in the men – but they all got swept up.'

Harriet: 'What happened then was a meeting was arranged for the following afternoon. The whole group assembled in a circle.'

Clair: 'We had a choreographer working with us who was also a therapist. And he said – *"You can have four minutes each"*. And he said things like *"OK, I want to talk to an angry woman."* And interestingly the giggly, sort of good-times girl said *"OK, I'm an angry woman."* She told about being raped, about her son, and her complete fury. And then one of the men talked about his mother and what he felt about her, and how he didn't want to go back to Jamaica, so it was just – '

Harriet: 'The men were crying, we were crying, it was the most emotional thing. But we all learned a hell of a lot. And it moved it all along ... That completely knitted everybody together like nothing I've ever seen.'

EXERCISING THE ROLE

Arguably there are two aspects of the facilitative role; the formal and the informal. The formal would cover division of responsibilities in a team situation. The informal would concern what kind of status is played, what kind of relationship is cultivated. But even this is not the whole story. When talking to facilitators I asked two further questions; what qualities did they think were required and what are the recurring mistakes?

FORMAL ROLES

There are strong arguments for team working, especially with large or difficult groups. Here, a minimum of two facilitators is usually essential, each adopting complementary roles either by *sharing leadership*, by leading in different *skills*, by taking different *functions* or by representing different *communities*. They may of course combine some of these functions.

The two leaders can operate simply by sharing the leadership between them. One sits out as an observer while the other runs the session. The second facilitator is ready to come in and take over. This strategy is particularly useful if there is a possibility of the relationship between facilitator and group becoming argumentative. Nic Fine observes: *'Two heads are better than one. One of us may go down a path that is not particularly productive and one of us will always try to keep ourselves unhooked, or at least a little more objective. Someone will press one of my buttons. Release one of my prejudices. It's helpful having a colleague who can spot that.'* And as John Bergman observes of working with inmates in prison: *'The most important function a co-facilitator can play is in helping your partner out if he gets into shit.'* Besides, with one person always observing, there can be a payoff when it comes to feed-back where notes are exchanged, and the session evaluated.

The group members' previous experience may have only been of *individual* teachers. Nic Fine observes: *'One value of working with a partner is modelling something for participants. They can see two people working together successfully. And co-operating together. The theory is, you're giving them a model . . . Also it's important for both the men and women in the room to have a man and woman facilitator. For their feeling of safety.'*

Secondly, the facilitators can bring complementary *skills*. Clair Chapwell and Harriet Powell have a background in drama and music respectively. Each takes a main responsibility for each area. One will tend to run the first half hour then pass over to the other. Ali Campbell, working with Glyndebourne Opera, works with a choreographer, a musician and a storyteller in quite a large team. They are all present, but pass the baton between them. They have recently devised a role of the Green Man/Woman who is the leading co-ordinator of the team on any one day.

Such team working is helpful in extending the participating group's vocabulary. They experience different forms of expression. This may happen mechanically, by one facilitator handing over to another after a preordained time, or it may be more impulsive. For example, there may come a point in the work where it feels appropriate to hand over because *that particular territory we're touching on* will be better explored through movement or narrative or singing and with a different leadership. The participating group gets a sense of the theatre language as able to stretch in different directions, to meet different challenges.

Thirdly, we may divide according to *function*. For example, one facilitator might be *inside the group*. To all intents and purposes they are a group member, accepting all the disciplines and challenges of membership. However, in a Wooden Horse operation they help the group develop from the inside. They can pose questions to the other group members in ways which the external facilitator cannot. Or they can ask questions of the facilitator 'on behalf of the group'. Crucially, they can be called on by the external workshop leader to demonstrate or lead a particular exercise. They can break the ice, make the first jump, and demonstrate to others that it's safe to follow. I've found this role partnership useful when working with ex-offenders. The co-facilitator might balk at running a group perhaps, but is happy in this half-way role. He or she acts as a bridge between me and the group, as a conduit of information and as a radar to any developing difficulties.

It's also possible for one of the two facilitators to work *in role*. After training with Dorothy Heathcote, Geraldine Ling has adapted role

techniques for special needs groups. By going into role she can provide
a challenge which will precipitate a dialogue not otherwise possible.
*'The use of full role was chosen in the case of a group who were having real
difficulty sitting around and having a meal together. Continual rows. . . .
So we created a role who was even more awkward, more dreadful, a woman
who had been sent away from her own people. She came with a letter,
demanding all sorts of things. The group began explaining to this woman
about why she should not be so horrible to people, helping her so that
eventually she could go back to her own people.'* For her part, the
facilitator is constantly modifying her performance to bring out the
positive, problem-solving capabilities of the group. By embodying
these anti-social tendencies, she compelled the group to address this
misery-making behaviour. And as a result, they did become somewhat
more skilled in recognising these negative patterns when they
recurred.

Fourthly, the two facilitators may reflect different *communities*. In
this event, the team has been assembled to reflect the balance within
the participating group. If the group has men and women in it, there
are advantages in having both a man and woman facilitator. There are
more possibilities here to meet across the divide and more scope for
unearthing private experience. The same argument applies with the
racial mix. Participants feel their experiences will be more easily
identified and respected. They also witness a model of co-operation
between black and white.

Finally, individuals who work together as teams over a long period
find areas of *complementarity* which are not formal as such but devolve
from the personalities of the facilitators. Powell and Chapwell have
found that they tend to complement each other: Harriet: *'We're very
different. I'm much quieter, much lower status. But somehow the
relationship seems to work. If we were both Clair, we'd probably drive
people out of the room, we'd self-destruct.'*

Clair: *'I think sometimes you get upset with me being so high status and
sometimes I also get upset with me being high status. Don't you think? . . . '*

Harriet: *'Early projects, I very much wanted to be liked. I was one of
them. Always smiling, always enable, enable, smile, smile. Clair didn't smile
much and I was smiling for both of us. Progressively I've got more
distanced. I feel I'm getting progressively less smiley. I'm not sure I know
what that's about. I'm not in isolation, we play roles that have to do with
each other.'*

INFORMAL ROLES

Learning facilitation skills, there is a strong temptation to take on the mantle of a facilitator you've observed. You copy his language, the stance, the status. But ultimately each individual has to find their own style. What is right for one is not necessarily right for another. There needs to be a groundedness in first principles but beyond that, there is considerable room for personal interpretation.

Inevitably the group will tend to project certain characteristics on to the facilitator. For example, they seek approval so they see that person as an approval-dispenser. They see that person as a judge so they expect adjudication on success or failure. They may even see that person as parent figure who will console or nurture them. So in the choice of informal role there must be some degree of distance which implicitly rejects any unhelpful projections, while at the same time offering the necessary support and guidance. In this context, it seems fitting to let facilitators speak of their own approaches:

PETER BADEJO: *'The best teachers are leaders. You have to have confidence in yourself. And in what you have to teach. And at the same time, recognise you are dealing with the most difficult form of machine in the world, which is human beings. I'm not afraid to criticise, and you shouldn't be afraid, as long as one is not insulting. In fact I've been accused many times of being too plain. When I tell people to jump, I may say "why are you landing like an elephant?" I don't mean it as an insult, I speak a plain language.'*

PETE BROOKS: *'You have to be genuinely interested in the group you're working with. You can't be egocentric. But you can pretend to be. For instance, I will say to a group "There are no stars in this company except me. This is my show." And everyone feels really relaxed, and they laugh at me. It relieves the tension. You pretend, and they know you don't mean that . . . and at the end, and I'll always say it: "It was a great show because you were all fucking brilliant."'*

JOHN BERGMAN: *'I play any role necessary under the sun, to get what I want . . . Sometimes I play fool with them, sometimes Grand Inquisitor, sometimes child, sometimes I put a mask on and become a baby, sometimes I become a nightmare. It depends on the place. In Vermont, I meet with the therapist and I see who's been doing what. I may do a one-on-one with someone beforehand, I may do a one-on-one with all of them.'*

HARRIET POWELL AND CLAIR CHAPWELL. Clair: *'With the old people, I was like a grand-daughter. I found myself putting my arms around them and cuddling them.'*

Harriet: *'You were still high status, but very jokey. Clair would come into the room and kick her legs in the air – physically you did things that were totally uncool.*

Clair: *'I'd do things like this (leaps wildly) and they'd go "Whooh!" I don't know where it came from, I didn't plan to do it, I just got sillier and sillier. And I had a complete ball. Such a good time.'*

PHELIM MCDERMOTT: *'I like to play low status. I like to play the ignorant person, who doesn't know, who discovers because he doesn't know. That produces a really interesting dynamic in the room . . . The main thing that I try to do is to keep things fluid, or lubricated. And the way to do that is to keep playing. So my overall job as a facilitator is to say "this is how we play." Now that may involve playing at being an autocratic director, and you can actually bring that in without it being destructive, or it might be playing the trickster who destroys everything, who when things get good, blows it open and shows that you can do it another way. I suppose I have an awareness of a spectrum of archetypal characters or personalities that you can be . . . When I directed* Dr. Faustus *one way for me to release and say "don't take this all too seriously" was to drop my trousers and have comedy underwear on. That sounds very contrived but it grew out of play. So that during the technical week, everyone's taking it much too seriously, it's important to be a director, but with your trousers down. Because when you do take it too seriously, that's when the dead theatre comes in.'*

KATINA NOBLE: *'There's a conflict between my desire to be a director, and my desire to be an enabler. I want to be a friend, but I also know I need firmness . . . What's very important is that people have fun, that they enjoy themselves. But I have to balance that need to create a fun atmosphere with some compassion, with a need to get material out.'*

FRANCES RIFKIN: *'It's a very professional role. Because in your personal life you might be always interrupting people and getting cross and losing your temper – here it's different. In that, you are modelling a very flexible role – supportive is not quite the right word – it's critical, too. Which they perceive as professional. They don't see you as just any old individual.'*

ALI CAMPBELL: *'A choreographer I was working with said "That's what you do, you do the human being thing, don't you?" She said, 'You took half an hour for everyone to get their chairs and to get to a point where everyone could say their name and do a movement. And for some of those adults that was a huge thing.'*

LOIS WEAVER: *'A woman got really angry with me and said "You're a powermonger." I said, "You're right." And I think there's a way to be sexy with that power. I like to sexualise our experience – to make it fun, to make it feel that it's not just hard work, it's like going to a party, it's a good time.'*

NIC FINE: *'For the first few hours of the first day I really try and be myself. I've got a role as a facilitator – it's like a performance – it's more of an energy state. If it's a small group, I might give a quiet, gentle introduction. If the group has a high energy level, I might have a dynamic persona – I might stand up, walk around or do a cartoon on the board.'*

NIC FINE ON JOHN BERGMAN: *'He worked in a team with a psychiatrist. John was the extrovert, the clown, the powerhouse. The other guy was quite gentle, very sensitive. They had a game going between them – it was very powerful to see them work. They were complete and utter opposites: John provided the theatre and the other guy – if he thought John was going too far – he'd call "John in the Dogbox!" and John used to jump on a chair and curl up in a foetal position. All the guys would roar with laughter. John created a lot of laughter in the room. And he would do his most powerful work after the laughter.'*

QUALITIES

What are the aptitudes required to lead a group? It calls for a willingness to be vulnerable because it involves nurturing others' vulnerability. It requires humility because you have the power of bestowing value. And it requires a certain self-awareness because you ask others to search for that awareness in themselves.

If the group is to move from point A to point B while never quite knowing where point B is, they need to trust that person in charge. They need to feel the journey is worth the struggle. So a degree of personal transparency on the facilitator's part is appropriate. Your pedagogy must be open to inspection to some degree. You need to know where you're coming from, so you can articulate and defend those principles which underpin your work. Nic Fine states that his *'foundation stones would be that people develop respect for themselves and each other, and develop a belief in democratic processes . . . Thirdly* (he argues for) *a belief in non-violence and a belief in the creative potential of all people.'* While Lois Weaver argues how important it is to have *'a healthy respect for your own aesthetic.'* And that hers *'is based on chaos'.*

You may need to be prepared to sacrifice good relations for the principles which underpin your work. There may be a moment when you're faced with a choice: to reassure a member of the group or hold to your personal aesthetic. The situation becomes a litmus test. If you offer reassurance, you may betray a value which you earlier defended. But if you don't, the individual concerned may walk out. Guy Dartnell recalls a participant accusing him of trying to convert him to homosexuality (!) so he replied: *'I see you have a problem with this but your problem is not a problem for me. If you stay in this class, I will always encourage you to touch other men. Maybe even to kiss them if the inspiration takes you. So if you're asking me not to encourage you to do that, no, I can't.'* Dartnell concludes *'In this kind of situation, if you go back on what you believe in, the whole thing disintegrates.'*

But having a personal commitment to a set of ideas would go for little without a commitment to enthuse others. Given the group often don't know what's at the journey's end, then the spirit in which the journey is made becomes the lodestar. Guy Dartnell again: *'You have to love doing it. I have an immense interest in what I do. Enthusiasm rubs off on people. It makes them interested because they can see that you like doing it. You need a certain amount of courage to put yourself on the line, to be spontaneous with them, to be intimate with them. And to be challenging in the sense that you can't be afraid to be complimentary if you really like something.'*

Curiously, once you acquire a degree of self-knowledge and can argue your own aesthetic, the 'inner flexibility' which is so important to facilitation comes more easily. It is easier to adapt and follow a previously unscheduled direction if you have confidence in the integrity of your own approach. So should you meet an invitation to abandon that integrity – you know you can refuse it. And the drama workshop is never the event you imagine. John Palmer, formerly of Interplay Theatre, observes the truth of this in terms of working with those having learning difficulties. He argues that what is required is *'openness to different ways of working. Not having preconceptions about how you're going to run the session – being open to what the group offers you . . . Not working to a set format. So for example you don't have to work with any particular attributes, because there might be group members who have no legs. In short, there's a very subtle thing about being led by the group, as well as leading.'* The importance of being humble enough to respect the different priorities of the group, must be a further precondition to working flexibly. Frances Rifkin: *'I wouldn't call it humility, but it's a modest understanding of who and what you are in that situation. You are in the bottom left corner of the picture. You need flexibility and an ability to define objectives* and *change them – but keep a sense of what your overall direction might be.'*

David Slater finds it hard for elderly people to take responsibility for a creative process when they've no previous experience of anything similar. So he places emphasis on the need to negotiate and bring *'an ability to recognise that the potential for theatre is in most situations. So it's to do with finding the connections . . . and creating the time and space to make it happen.'* In turn this calls for a quality of listening – not simply to what is said but to what lies beneath the words. This information will help in determining what direction to take. As Nic Fine comments, what's required is *'knowing what to listen for.'* Guy Dartnell asserts that it is listening which *'in the end tells you what you have to teach. Because what you're teaching is improvisational, the teaching format has to be improvised.'* Finally, Phelim McDermott points to what might be almost the most important quality of all – *'a sense of joy at being together as people. Playing together. And saying "This play is the most important thing in the world. And we're doing something very important by mucking around."'*

MISTAKES

Different facilitators appear to gravitate towards different traps.

GERALDINE LING: *'The main mistake that you can make is trying to block a contribution because . . . you're not on the ball sufficiently to take that in. I'm always aware that it'll come crashing around me later. Sometimes people want you to achieve something particular, and that's when that's most likely to happen.'*

NIC FINE: *'Things that can go wrong are often the things that happen before you walk into a room. Like the assumptions you take* into *a room . . . if you assume, for example, that you can work with anybody . . . that you can make a success out of everyone, open everyone's creativity. That's dangerous.'*

LOIS WEAVER: *'(A mistake for me would be) when I kick something into motion, a series of exercises that have been planned, or are habitual for me . . . and I follow that knowing that people have disengaged. I'm following the sequence rather than the moment. That's when I know that I've lost it. But if I can keep in the moment, in the way that the questioning and answering keeps me in the moment, then I know I'm OK.'*

GUY DARTNELL: *'Things go wrong mostly when people have to sit and watch for a long time. Although it's a necessary aspect of what I do. People sort of think that they've stopped doing it. And so they turn off and their energy seeps away . . . Then if I waffle too much . . . people get confused. So I talk some more to make them less confused, and it becomes a mess. The same applies if I let* them *talk too much, the energy goes – and people go up into their heads.'*

ALI CAMPBELL: *'Other days I've gone in wired. (Mistakes happen) if something has knocked me off centre – or an individual has. A hyperactive prisoner last week got me into the attention trap. I got into this bind with him – I find myself saying things but not really doing them myself. Like "Let's all wait . . . one still image will do" when I'm really sending out a signal about how pissed off I am, and that there really isn't enough material. I'm lying.'*

SOME RECURRING QUESTIONS

SHOULDN'T DRAMATIC MATERIAL BE CENSORED?

Censorship is particularly an issue in schools and youth centres. Staff are sometimes worried that young people will use the opportunity of a drama workshop to break taboos maintained at other times, and this will make it difficult later to 'turn off the tap.' The facilitator may even be approached beforehand and asked for some kind of assurance that they will prohibit bad language.

Such concerns may be expressed from either a conservative, disciplinarian viewpoint or a more progressive, pedagogical one. In either case the issue is seen as one of control – the group is expected to maintain the same standards of behaviour as are normally applied and sometimes this is seen as extending to behaviour on-stage. The proposer may not see the distinction between drama work and other activities. So it is argued that, for example, racist and sexist opinions must not be expressed within the drama. Or if they are, they should be challenged directly. Both of these viewpoints proceed from a perception that drama should be subject to similar codes as that which operate off-stage. Practice however suggests that such codes are not transferable. Given that the world of the stage is ephemeral and illusory, if someone is raped on the stage, it is not a real rape. It will certainly be necessary to question the process which governs that action – does it have integrity? Is the theatrical style appropriate? Are we exploring a legitimate concern for this age group? Are the participants willingly consenting to the action? But the action itself cannot be condemned simply on the grounds that it took place – since it took place within the world of performance. It's very common for teenagers to test the workshop leaders with their indulgence in scatological or sexual material. Ultimately any movement on from these challenges can only come with a deepened relationship with the medium.

Discussion before a workshop between staff and the visiting team will help the team to outline their methodology and what it will involve. The two sides can outline their hopes for the project. The staff always have the option to withdraw the contract. Without a clear basis of agreement, the wrong criteria can be brought to bear in evaluating the project. If the sessions tackled taboo themes, the staffs might comment, 'The drama workers were very good, it was just the kids who got carried away'. Or the inverse; 'The kids were great but the drama workers were leading them on.' In either view, the observer may underestimate the group's ability to handle difficult themes. Perhaps the workshop has led the group to take opportunity of extending their agenda for debate. For the staff, seeing any play which has been created by the group may help them to develop their relationship with the client group in the future. Feedback and evaluation sessions will allow for a handing over of issues which the staff can integrate within the life of the centre or take further in other work.

Perhaps it's worth keeping in mind Keith Johnstone's recollection that: *'At school any spontaneous act was likely to get me into trouble. I learned never to act on impulse, and that whatever came into my mind first should be rejected in favour of better ideas . . . I learned that the first idea was unsatisfactory because it was (1) psychotic, (2) obscene, (3) unoriginal. The truth is that the best ideas are often psychotic, obscene and unoriginal. My best-known play, a one-acter called MOBY DICK – is about a servant who keeps his master's one remaining sperm in a goldfish bowl. It escapes, grows to monstrous size, and has to be hunted down on the high seas. This is certainly a rather obscene idea to many people, and if I hadn't thrown away everything that my teachers taught me, I could never have written it. These teachers, who were so sure of the rules, didn't produce anything themselves at all.'*[24]

Word and Action (Dorset) whose work constantly takes them into schools and youth clubs, experience the censorship issue head-on. This is because their story-making theatre involves asking the participating group questions, the answers to which go into the play, without censorship. The team have often observed how staff in authority can misunderstand the fictional, dream quality of the exercise; they perceive the story as a conveyor of literal rather than folkloric or symbolic meaning. So observers become worried by the contents – swearwords, acts of aggression, acts of sexuality. Hence the importance of developing an understanding with the staff that censorship in this context only forces a concealment of thoughts and feeling which ultimately leads to an ineffective session and a debased relationship between facilitators and group. A founding principle of the company is based on an understanding that anything *can* be acted out if the language of the exercise *allows* it to be acted out, while ensuring that the safety of the participants is not compromised. The style of theatre is deliberately non-realistic and non-naturalistic. Inevitably, accepting this principle becomes a test not just for the the staff but for the actors as well. R.G. Gregory recalls how an actor was confronted with the dilemma of acting out difficult material which had already been accepted: *'The group went to Denmark. (Paul) was playing Frankenstein and it was midnight and the moon was shining and we said "What happens next?" and someone said "Frankenstein fucks Lady Frankenstein." Paul was playing Frankenstein . . . so we needed somebody to come out from the audience to play Lady Frankenstein. We waited for someone to come out. Suddenly this beautiful, tall Danish girl stood up and said "I'll play it." And she came out. And this was our first performance almost in Denmark and we had a local photographer from the local teacher's union newspaper there. And he had a camera and was taking all these shots. And it came to this moment and I as the questioner announced "And now Frankenstein fucks Lady Frankenstein!" and Paul hesitated. He didn't know what to do. Then he thought, "Oh bugger this", and he jumped right on the girl. And the photographer was in there, click, click, click. And it really worked. And that fear disappeared. He had to overcome that. Very often in youth clubs, they put the women through difficult situations – and you have to go through with it. But just as when you have someone "naked" on the stage you don't actually take your clothes off – so you don't do the sex act, you represent it.'*

ARE EMOTIONS DANGEROUS?

Those new to drama sometimes over-exaggerate the potential damage incurred in expressing emotion. They say 'I can't do what you're asking – I couldn't be responsible for the consequences.' They imagine they will combust and all the furniture will be broken. Well, yes, there is sometimes legitimate concern that if an individual has recently experienced trauma or is currently emotionally wrought, they should stay home. But these situations aside, one must be careful not to exaggerate, out of fear or ignorance, the implications of giving in to emotion. This voice of anxiety may be simply that; a voice which is part of an inner resistance. For there's another voice too, saying loosen up and let go.

I've never known furniture broken by emotion alone. What may be dangerous is the lack of structures and support surrounding the expression of emotion. Without emotion, there can be no play. The task lies in coming into a relationship with feeling without being overwhelmed by it which, if it happens, is more temporarily disabling than dangerous. A respectful circumspection towards inner emotion may prove a better guide than fearfulness.

Once the individual becomes comfortable as an emotionally expressive person, emotional impulses can be seen as allies rather than enemies. They are welcomed as the beginnings of genuine creativity. But it takes time for participants to free up their emotional selves. In the world outside, many emotions are simply not acceptable: here, every emotion is acceptable. There, the expression of any one emotion for any length of time is seen as anti-social and indulgent. Here, we can continue to explore one emotion for a considerable time. There, we are impelled to 'make things move for us'. Here, we need learn how to be moved, literally and physically.

It sometimes happens nevertheless that an individual does break down because of the emotional impact of a memory surfacing. Again, this is not necessarily a failure on their part or that of the facilitator. It may be simply an opportune release. It is not of itself problematic unless it's seen that way. The release of emotion may even be beneficial, despite the fact it appears to break up the workshop. Even if the participant feels unable to continue, after a pause, they might be able to return. It may be that an individual needs to be consoled, perhaps by a facilitator while a co-facilitator continues with the group; but this is a matter of judgement. Sometimes individuals prefer to be left alone.

Here, Peter Badejo recalls a situation when a young girl broke down at the memory of abuse which surfaced during the session. The approach which Peter took might in other circumstances be inappropriate, but here it was effective in helping the girl reconcile the memory with her present situation: '*I remember a workshop with children in Greenwich, a two-day workshop. I asked them to bring in stories about their environment . . . One of the girls told this story about this rape situation, and I can never forget it, it was so emotional. First of all I just asked her to tell the story herself. When she got to the middle of it, the incident of the rape, she started crying. I hadn't realised that this story had happened to her, I thought it was about someone else. But she started crying, so I said "Let's go on break". And during lunch I spoke to her. I said "That's a very interesting story, that's a very hard story." And she went into how this guy was so nice to her in the beginning . . . but not all sweet things are good for ever. (And we talked about it) and she said finally "Yes, it's a story about me and now I've grown up a bit I know how to deal with it." So I said "Well, that's a positive thing, isn't it? If you tell the story properly, then you can highlight some of the positive aspects." And this is where the community work comes into it. You are not just telling the story for entertainment, you are telling the story so people can benefit from it. And in the end, she did this story, it took about three minutes, just a young girl, from the sweet beginning to the dark side, to the positive end of how she could deal with it. And when she was doing this story, when we worked on it, she wasn't crying any more.'*

WHAT HAPPENS IF WE GET STUCK?

It's one of the facilitator's fears. Suddenly someone refuses to do an exercise; before long anxiety has spread like an insidious gas; no one wants to get up; everyone is refusing your invitations. Perhaps it's the wrong exercise – the worst response is to turn to the most pliable group member and *demand* they get up. Better to laugh at yourself for pitching down a wrong road, and perhaps ask the group what they would like to do. It may require plucking an exercise out of left-field, something which no one is expecting, perhaps a release game. Or it may be a cue for discussion or a break. If the response is to talk your way out, you may get into what Ali Campbell refers to as 'the attention trap'. This is where an individual manages to steal your attention away from the rest of the group, while the consequence is boredom for everyone else.

Here are some reflections on situations which in some way or other have become stuck. Firstly, Saul Hewish talks about working with offenders addressing behavioural patterns. *'I used to feel anxious about the drama stopping. Like I'd failed. But then, in a way, the techniques that I use are about the way that we think. So shifting perceptions is not a failure. And it may be that if that bit's not working, we could pull back and look at something else.'*

Nic Fine also talks about working with offenders, this time at Feltham where a clump of individuals had moved away – physically and emotionally – from the rest of the group. As his colleague led the session, he took the dissenters. *'I just knew from the body language of these two or three guys, there was no way they were going to participate. So I went over to them and they said: "There's no fucking way you're going to get us to do anything." And I said "No, you're right. I can't." That surprised them. I just sat with them and said "Let's talk, just sitting here." '*

It may be that someone in the group is unintentionally holding the group back by staying with the process but at the same time giving out signals of reluctance. In this case the facilitator may need to challenge them about their attitude. They have a problem, but they're not articulating it. They're holding it to themselves which has the effect of making others wary. In a sense, they've withdrawn from the group while still being physically present.

Jonathan Kay: ' *In the workshop if someone falls asleep, I think it's because they're getting bored. I think it must be something to do with me. So I tap to get their attention. And they say something like "Jonathan, I can't take any more – my head's totally full up. Could we do something else?" All the time looking like they're falling asleep. That would probably be time for a change. For if it persists, that person is taking all the energy out of the group, swallowing everyone's negative energy. That's a difficult moment. Because that person "owns" the circle more than anyone else. So I have to have a set-to with them. So it maybe gets to a point where either they're going to leave or they're going to stay. Once they've gone the circle is better. Once they've decided to stay, the circle gets better. I don't mind which. There was one workshop where unless you said "big huge penises, large, huge, sexual juicy stuff", stuff like that, this guy would fall asleep. And if you said this stuff he'd wake up. Every now and then he'd fall asleep and I'd say "big huge dick" and he'd start to laugh. I said to him, "You're too predictable. You say we're wasting our time here but I can wake you up just like that." And he laughed. He came back the next morning and said "I've been awake all night." I said "No wonder you're tired." He said "I think I'm not going to join in. Because I think you're victimising me." I said "I'm not victimising you. I just notice that when I say sexual things you wake up, and when I don't, you fall asleep. I have no animosity against you. Stay, leave, whatever." What this guy did eventually was he said "I'll flip a coin." He said "Heads I stay, tails I go." It was heads. He had to stay. But because he stayed he had an amazing time. If it had been tails I'm not sure he would have gone.'*

FACILITATOR – FRIEND OR AUTHORITY?

Given the intensity of the process, it's inevitable that boundaries around relationships are apt to be indistinct. The facilitator needs this; if boundaries are too fixed there's less scope to surprise or provoke. 'Is that how you behave to your real mother?' 'Have you never flattered to get what you want?' Keeping things loose allows a feeling that in this space, there is always room for surprises. However, it can work the other way. If boundaries disappear altogether the participant may feel confused or taken advantage of. It's only a drama session, after all.

It's the facilitator more than anyone who defines boundaries. One temptation is to make firm friends with everyone. The work continues in the pub or the coffee bar. And a certain bending of orthodox teacher/pupil relationships can only be advantageous. The danger comes in if the boundaries of the relationship become determined by the traditions of friendship or even intimacy. Then it can become difficult for the leader to challenge the participant beyond a certain point. The friendship has become a trap, compromising scope for leadership. If an extra-curricular friendship has built too far it may be difficult to retain objectivity. This situation is ripe for exploitation by a workshop leader who makes the assumption that liberties can be taken where equivalent permissions have not been given by the participant for this context. Perhaps, in a way, the facilitator knows too much. In such cases, what may be lost is the sense of an objective professional role with its accompanying rights and obligations.

On the other hand the facilitator who always stands aloof may never elicit sufficient trust to inspire effective performance. The participant sees them as if from miles away with communication taking place over great distance by means of semaphore. It feels like school only without the marking. One consequence of this is teacher-pleasing. The teacher, appearing so remote, remains an unreadable authority, a source of wisdom more powerful than any other. So the participant may start to bend personal judgements to theirs and measure everything against their approval. The problem is compounded by the workshop leader giving unclear instructions. Participants cannot grasp the challenge, so they perform in a way which constantly asks 'Is this what you want?'

Participants may also project a role on to the workshop leader which the leader hasn't assumed. For example, there's a danger of falling into child-parent routines. Because the facilitator nurtures and interrogates, they appear like a parent. If this happens, it may take some firmness to break the pattern. I recall a particular participant whose sulky victim stance made life difficult for the whole group. Every negotiation was conducted around the unspoken question 'I'm suffering – what are you doing about it?' It's very easy to become sucked into accepting a stance like that as the basis for your relationship. It also allows the individual to pull the group's attention round him or her like a shawl. The group eventually became frustrated at this individual's determination to get attention at all costs and scapegoated her, providing further fuel to her victim stance.

ARE WE 'SELLING OUT' THE GROUP?

There is legitimate argument about whether or not drama disempowers, despite its claims. In particular, it can be asked whether the recent switch in emphasis from drama-for-recreation to drama-as-social-learning, has placed more power in the hands of those who have a vested interest in quietening disaffected groups? Do drama practitioners sell out their participants by making a priority of incorporation over empowerment? The question is pertinent when we look at, for example, the community play, where class conflict is – the argument runs – muddied in the broader interest of bringing very different groups together and making heart-warming statements about community spirit.

Ali Campbell argues that the aim in such projects tends to be less about amalgamating concerns than shifting perceptions, throwing a new light on to aspects of history, architecture, self-identity and community, and leaving subsequent initiatives in the hands of the various participating groups. He argues that the impulse towards social action is by no means diffused by the community play. However, questions remain. The integrity of the project must always be linked to the issue of 'whose agenda'? Where an agenda is introduced which has neither relevance nor meaning to the group, it's clear that the only benefits can be in the area of skill development. Where the interests of a socially disadvantaged group are ignored in the broader interests of pleasing a larger group, we can conclude that the project is not materially moving them forward. 'Whose play is this?' must be a question that's always worth asking.

Where social skills drama work is concerned, here it's reasonable to assert that the work has a particular objective: that of developing the social aptitudes of the group members. For groups whose energies are fractious, disturbed and self-destructive, a learning about self and emotion management may legitimately prefigure any more outwardly directed work. No social ideology is being sold out by bringing such individuals to the point at which they can make cogent choices about their future. Once a participant achieves mastery in this area, it's for them to choose how to direct their anger in ways informed by an awareness of choices available – which might include radical political action.

A degree of circumspection is always valid. Poor or mischievous facilitation can disempower, and the damage rebounds on others. Other professionals suffer indirectly through association, and the group involved loses confidence and direction. Staff in institutions need to be wary of whom they employ. Facilitators need to monitor their processes. And in some cases it is legitimate to question why an authority is wanting dramawork to be part of their institutional practice. Do they have participants' interests at heart or are they looking to divert energies away from other concerns? Are they looking to strengthen their position through associating their power with the theatre's energy? Peter Badejo offered this story from Nigeria as an example of how cultural theft can occur. It serves as a warning and as a validation of the subversive power of the medium. *'We live in a city where there is a ruler. And the ruler employs someone to be his clown, all his life. And in one of the performances (of this community theatre project), this was criticised. And they used their community theatre to really put that down, to say "Look, this ruler is born equal with this guy – why should he be a clown all his life?" Good enough. Three years later the ruler's clown died. And the ruler needed a new clown. And the guy who played the critical part in the production was selected, and he became the new clown.'*

PART THREE

ANIMATIONS

'I built a road which had no purpose. People gathered.
"Where is it from?" "Where does it go?" Then –
"Is it a road?" Speculative builders narrowed their eyes.
Children crossed, stopped in the middle and laughed.
I have built a hut at either end. One A, the other B.
Sometimes I go from A to B.
It gives the road a bit of purpose - not much.'

Ivor Cutler

'That's enough about lessons,' the Gryphon interrupted
in a very decided tone.
'Tell her something about the games now.'

Lewis Carroll, Alice in Wonderland

Butch and Sundance, while escaping their pursuers, stop above a ravine in which, far below, there's a rushing river.

Sundance: I want to fight 'em.

Butch: They'll kill us. Do you want to die?

Sundance: Do you?

Butch: Alright. I'll jump first.

Sundance: No!

Butch: Then you jump first.

Sundance: No!

Butch: What's the matter with you?

Sundance: I can't swim.

Butch (*laughing*): Why, are you crazy? The fall will probably kill you!

They jump.

Butch Cassidy and the Sundance Kid

ANIMATIONS

WORKSHOP PLANNING

Much of the success of any workshop series lies in the planning. This is particularly true when the participating group are unfamiliar to drama or have behavioural or learning difficulties.

THE INVITATION

Some projects begin without a group in place. When Frances Rifkin as a member of Banner Theatre went to Corby during the miners' strike of 1987, there was merely an invitation to build a project from the ground up. When Clair Chapwell and Harriet Powell begin work in East London it is often like this, the responsibility is theirs to create a group from scratch. Recruitment may mean advertising, lobbying, even becoming a member of that community for a while as Rifkin did in Corby over a two year period. Since the facilitator is coming in to the community from the outside, it's important to build a coherent support structure. Not only does this help with managing the programme, it means there are advisors on hand if things go wrong. Rightly enough auditions tend not to be a feature of such projects; other strategies are preferred which don't give preference to those who have previous experience. Besides, these sometimes oppressive rituals can strike the wrong note and suggest a policy of exclusiveness. Some likely contenders may feel their place in the project has no worth if there are no auditions – 'Hey, if anyone can join in, I won't.' But it may be more important to establish a different value-set at the outset, and stick to it.

THE GROUP

What is the situation of the group? Are they a group? Have its members ever acquired a sense of themselves as a group? They may have shared a factory canteen or residential lounge for decades, but that doesn't mean they've formed a group. They may never have thought of themselves in that way. Some members may still be unfamiliar to each other. What's the balance between those who are friends and those who don't know anyone? Existing relationships can provide an early foundation. But if these are already fractious, some renegotiation may be necessary. How have these individuals come together? Have they opted in to the project individually or has the group signed up as a group? Individual commitment makes for a strong starting point, but others may need to be won round.

If it's an existing group or one which has the remnants of a previous group within it, a caucus may have initiated the project, with an agenda. If it's a youth group, there are issues inherited from previous activity. 'We did a great musical last time so we want to do another.' 'We all want to do something on animal rights.' There's no necessity to follow these givens, but they indicate current expectations. An alternative direction can always be proposed, being mindful of the earlier agenda. A group of women may have issues they want to tackle, issues around abuse, alcohol, image representation. A group of individuals with learning difficulties or disabilities may want to do something to change their image in the eyes of those around them. Or they might want to create a visual piece of theatre on an issue not related to disability. If the facilitator is coming from within the group itself to take the work forward, what's required may be some distance so that individual can provide an independent leadership. If the group is to work collectively there may need to be some clear agreements about the process and how decisions will be made.

The facilitator may need to become familiar with the character of the group, perhaps even elements of personal biographies. There may be individuals who are consistently disruptive, there may be some who have previous offences which might be important to know about. More positively, biographical information may help the facilitator to key into particular enthusiasms: Vince and Margaret always work well together, Yanic opens up when family is a theme, Pedro has a passion for movement.

One of the great rewards of working in community drama is finding the uniqueness of each group and discovering how to give this uniqueness expression. So an early question is, what distinguishes this group from every other? What particular experiences can they speak to? This uniqueness will stamp their productivity with its own colours. Working in theatre is a good way to learn the secrets of strangers. The sharing of secrets can create a real intimacy which elsewhere takes years to achieve.

To summarise, a good drama session has the seeds of its success planted long before the first game kicks off. If the character of the group hasn't been assessed – through meeting them if possible, there's a danger of mismatching the exercises and the group. But with some shared understandings in place there's a better chance to develop mutual respect in the early stages.

THE STAFF

Did the project initiate with the staff? If so, what were the assumptions that drama is the right stuff? To what extent is the group behind it? Sometimes staff can have unrealistic expectations of a drama process – they hope it will silence fractious group in-fighting *as well as* give the Centre a showpiece for the Annual General Meeting. I remember a case when a youth worker expected a full-length play in no more than six sessions, rehearsed and ready to perform. The job of determining objectives really needs to be negotiated with the workshop leader(s). To be persuaded into unreasonable goals will generate anxiety all round. We need a programme which is achievable, if anything erring on the side of modesty rather than ambition. It's easier to increase the tempo of the work when it goes well than decrease it when performances have been publicised.

Being clear over likely numbers assists the planning. In institutions like prisons where things are unpredictable, clear information is sometimes hard to obtain. Staff may be welcoming you in because it lets them off for a few hours. It's not exactly unknown in schools and colleges either. I remember one occasion when colleagues and myself arrived at a prison to run a drama workshop. The warders had told the inmates, in the interests of generating enthusiasm, that they would be watching a performance. So thirty of them filed in. 'No, we wouldn't have come if we'd known it was a workshop. Certainly not if you have to stand up and act stupid.' With twenty-five fewer, we might have made things happen. Instead, we struggled.

When participants are in wheelchairs or have learning difficulties, the commitment of the staff will be essential. Perhaps they should be assisting in the session. They'll have vital personal information about group members, for example about medication or physical limitations. It may be there needs to be one carer or volunteer per participant.

Blind participants can have things explained to them. Those in wheel-chairs can be moved around the room. But there are dangers also in having non-participants present – we want to avoid a situation where they, perhaps in good faith, dominate or control their participant.

THE SPACE

Does the space have disabled access? Is this an important consideration? Increasingly venues are paying attention to these issues but carrying wheelchairs down stone steps to reach a theatre basement is still a reality. Experience suggests that sometimes disabled participants don't mind a bit of a struggle to get there but it may be unwise to assume this. Is transport necessary, if so what kind? Do participants want meeting at the door where they may have been dropped off? Are there helpers available?

My own preferred room size is about 35' by 25', rectangular (assuming a group of about 12), large enough for running around in but not so large you feel lost within it. The space needs to be used, or its lack of use turns against you. When this happens, the energies expended are not returned via the compression created by immediate walls. It's the same problem when working outdoors. It may have worked for Isadora Duncan pursuing physical liberation, but for most drama you need boundaries to help generate intensity. Smaller rooms off the main room, preferably separated by doors, are useful for allowing sub-groups to go and prepare scenes. But if the main room is L-shaped or has nooks and crannies, this can work against group cohesion. There can be spatial fragmentation. A group whose members want to test the workshop leader's patience can cause problems by using the space to hide in. I've found the worst space to be one of those large school halls with a raised stage and curtain down one end. There's a school in Nottingham which is etched on my memory along with images of colleagues constantly searching for teenagers behind voluminous stage curtains.

The floor is important for safety reasons. Stone floors are dangerous for all but chair-bound sessions. Carpeted rooms are usually OK but create problems for physical activity and movement work. Wooden or linoleum floors are best, and a sprung dance floor best of all. This will have a certain degree of suspension which allows for jumping, rolling and working out. But none is a guarantor that accidents cannot happen. Pillars can cause serious problems because they restrict the available delineation of stage space. Unwanted chairs or other furniture are difficult too because they clutter the space or can be called into use by individuals looking to ease themselves away from the work. You turn round and someone has disappeared behind a heap of chairs, quietly lighting a fag.

If a room is unsatisfactory, the option of not working may be preferable. I was once asked to work in a gym where there was a rock group practising down the other end. On another occasion, huge windows opened on to the playground where those who'd opted out could mock those who'd opted in. To begin work under such conditions may lead to a failed session. It'll be followed by a discussion at the Centre Management Committee some days later. All will agree that 'We'll have no more drama, our kids didn't like it. I don't know why, maybe they're just not artistic.' Under other circumstances they might have liked it very much.

THE FORMAT

What should be the format of sessions? Is the workshop a one-off or part of a series? What is to be the length of each session? How many will there be? What are the targeted outcomes if any? What kind of evaluation will there be at the end? The format should be agreed between the staff, the group and the facilitators where appropriate.

It may be that a tight format is chosen: Day One, Drama Games, Day Two, Masks, Day Three, Improvisation and so on. The advantage of this is a clarity and a notion of proceeding step-by-step. But this sense of 'making progress' which it gives may be illusory. The lessons of Day One may not have been sufficiently realised before we're confronted with a new set of learning tasks in Day Two. Where this more rigid format works well is in a 'taster' context where individuals are dropping in and out.

The alternative is to conceptualise the timetable more broadly by holding over decisions until the group has met and expressed its own view. At that point it may be possible to propose, say, several days for building the group, several for developing imagery, several for improvisation and several for devising. Outlining a proposed format to which people can respond is usually preferable to just asking for ideas. 'Let's do a jazz age musical', 'Let's learn juggling and do street theatre in the supermarket foyer' can be useful suggestions but are more likely to lead to a tangled web. Instead, a broad proposal of four weeks of introductory work may be sufficient. During that time, proposals may emerge. I've been running almost weekly sessions for one project for about eight years. Participants come and go, and many return after years of absence, knowing the security of the programme. Then spin-off activities are organised. For example, performance projects are developed and rehearsed at other times in the week which don't clash with workshops.

If the project is planned to end with performance, there are decisions around a timetable to be made. I find the best projects spend more time creating a group and exploring themes than staff might expect. They sometimes expect you to move swiftly to rehearsal and then spend ages refining. Such a process generally has the effect of placing less power in the group's hands, and besides, makes for a bruising schedule. Rushing ahead into any performance before a group is ready usually generates poor results. Of course performance *can* be created in a day, a week or even an hour but in a project of any length, trust, familiarity and shared learning are essential building blocks.

There are strong arguments for team-working, some of which have been given earlier. Once there is sufficient information about the group, the environment and the format – this may be the best time to decide on the composition of the team.

THE SESSION PLAN

While *preparation* is always necessary, detailed *planning* of every session may not be. There are different views on this. When I asked Keith Johnstone if he planned, he said: *'Never.'* *'So what do you do if you run out of ideas?'* *'I ask the group what they think I should do. And whatever they say, I say "That's exactly what we should do!"'* What's revealing about his answer is not so much the non-planning but the trust he places in the group. He trusts them to know themselves best. Clearly this could be a mistake with some groups. They might suggest something completely bizarre – but assuming it stays within the drama form, it may be worth trying, if only to unblock the session. By the end of it, other ideas may have come forward.

Some drama facilitators operate with quite a fixed plan in mind. There could be a number of different reasons. For example, there is a methodological training element involved. Nic Fine observes that *'The work in Feltham (prison) is highly prepared. That's partly to do with the fact we had three trainees, and we're looking at a replicable workshop. It's got various pieces which are crucial: various lead-ins and lead-outs – what's flexible is the facilitator's individual style.'* Another example might be if a facilitator is meeting a new group for the first time, and needs the security of a tight game plan. He may additionally be quite inexperienced himself and happy to trade in the benefits of spontaneity for the comfort of knowing the plot.

Lois Weaver prefers not to plan, relying instead on a bank of stock exercises. Background experience is relied on to inform decisions. This gives a tremendous flexibility and means the work can develop its own momentum. Exercises can emerge out of other exercises. Threads of content can be plucked out and woven into different cloths according to emerging priorities. As Roger Hill observes, the problem with rigorous planning is that: *'it can never take account of what happens within the exercises. You can determine forms but content which emerges can rarely be predicted. If a momentum builds, if an exercise is successful beyond anyone's expectations, the natural thing is probably to run with it. Yet to plan nothing at all requires a bedrock of confidence which only comes after several years' work.'* There is a midway strategy. Clive Barker used to begin sessions with one game only, although I know he's changed his approach more recently. This allowed for a reading of the group's responses to the first game, then a strategy could be picked. My own preference is to make a plan, then throw it away. Only you remember into which corner of the room you've thrown it. You've a clutch of ideas, some key exercises, some wild experiments, some tried and trusted games. Then you walk in, meet the group and start adapting.

Getting drawn too closely into defining objectives can be a mistake. Not that issues or objectives can't be discussed. But drama is an art not a science, and participants who seek specific, detailed answers to questions may be disappointed. And if we start flagging up objectives in a way that implies mechanistic solutions, the group gets anxious trying to achieve them and misses the point. But what you can do is have a *focus*. This allows for selection of exercises according to their relationship to this focus. It also gives the session an intellectual anchor, broad enough for digression but narrow enough for specifics. It means that you have some yardstick by which to test the appropriateness of any exercise that's suggested. Once the focus is understood, it helps in the building up of challenges during the session.

Everyone then has a 'feel' for the qualities we're exploring, which are the energies of theatre and which define its aesthetic. Here are some examples of focus: Co-operation, Emotional Impulse, Projections, Emotional Expressiveness, Status, Playing for the Other, Spontaneity. They enable an aspect of theatre language to be explored without implying an abandonment of a wider perspective. They permit an holistic approach; always relating a part to the whole, the particular to the general. So we may be working on spontaneity, but we can't do this without awareness of emotional expressiveness being part of the process.

The focus may be chosen by reference back to earlier sessions. For example, I might think about how the group needs to develop. To determine that, I hold in mind the image of that group working superbly, then set it against the memory of the last session. What's absent? What's not occurring? You could liken this thought process to imagining that someone has a sense like sight or hearing which is not being used. How to provoke it? What would need to happen to force them to use that sense? Taking sight away pushes emphasis on hearing. Working without words places stress on the image. If the participants are blocked by too much internal commentary, what would seize up that commentary so they can't 'scriptwrite' their scenes?

But planning for a session is not just about selecting exercises. It's about getting into a particular frame of mind. The best preparation involves discovering an enthusiasm for what you have to do. Annoyingly however, some of my best workshops have happened when I've felt unwell – perhaps this is because illness removes certain psychological blocks, I'm not sure. Phelim McDermott's *'way of planning is to read things that inspire me and get me excited. I plan only in the sense that I might be reading a book by a director or an artist and I think, I'd like to try that. I have an overall feeling or an atmosphere of how I want the rehearsals to be, or the shape of the workshop to be, and I go moment-to-moment . . . Generally planning is not about the workshop, it's about how you feel an hour before you do it, when you're worrying about it. And you plan to make yourself feel good in that moment . . . I'm interested in the process and the things that go wrong. The moment when you think "I should have planned" is really the most interesting moment. Because that's the moment when you could possibly discover the most interesting thing.'*

SPARKS: EARLY EXERCISES

Sparks are what you melt the ice with. I used to think *talking* would do it, *ideas* would do it but strangely my brilliant elaborations froze people to their seats. Too much stress on ideas made the work appear more daunting not less.

There is already anxiety in the room. Walking in, your own confidence often evaporates as you see how relaxed everyone else looks. Whatever games or exercises you had in mind suddenly seem inappropriate. You've brought a cricket bat to mend a car. And people aren't talking to each other. They're waiting for you. Maybe some will have hidden obsessions and all the games will be wrong. Maybe this isn't the drama group, they're from the Theatre Workshop Leaders Inspection Committee or it's the Gardening Club brought in to make up the numbers. It'll be the hardest group anyone has ever worked with and they'll break me within the hour . . .

Anxiety cycles are to drama, what petrol is to the engine. Just enough makes it happen. Too much and the system's flooded. The same is true for performers and those leading sessions. Perhaps this is because we know inwardly how powerful the medium can be, either that or we're simply frightened of being shown up. Clive Barker reckons he allows himself *'three sentences before there is some action. Once we've done something then we can talk.'* [25] He argues that the longer the chat the more anxious the group can get, knowing that *at some point* they will have to get up and do something. Meanwhile the chat is widening the gap between them and the demands of the work. But arguably there are times when a longer talk *is* necessary. What are the expectations of participants? The gardeners will only be angry later. Does the focus for the session need to be marked out? Do ground rules need to be discussed? Do the group members know each other? Lois Weaver has a rule of always asking the group if they would like to ask *her* a question.

THE WARM-UP

Warm-ups as they're known, proceed from the idea that a warm, energised body is ready to begin work. There's sense in this but it can be used as a pretext for inappropriate exercises; Martha Graham dance exercises, aerobics, ballet, yoga and even army training routines have been known to surface. But the intention is not to make ballet or war, but theatre. There's nothing worse than beginning drama work with a group that's been dragged through a series of physical exercises leaving participants exhausted, demoralised and angry. The only situation I can recall justifying this kind of approach was where the punishment related to the play. When the Living Theatre were working on *The Brig*, a show set in a marine punishment block, they used actual marine training exercises to begin rehearsals as means to inhabit the kind of mind-set which the play inhabited. More recently the National Theatre employed army training prior to a production of *Chips with Everything*.

The phrase 'warm-up' is so well established within the culture it's hard to see it being supplanted. But 'tune-up' might be more appropriate. Because players do need to tune in to each other. Everyone will arrive with a different mood, a different level of enthusiasm. Someone's come from the gym, another's been working in an office. Someone's depressed, another is behaving like an incendiarist chased by the police. The task is to bring them to a common level. '*Your first job,*' argues Roger Hill, '*is to raise the level of energy of everyone in the room to a point at which it's just above the height of whoever has the most. So that even the most energetic have to stretch. And the people who've got less have to stretch more. So we've all gone up some way. Next we have to focus in . . . And when the energy is focused in, we've got to lay it to rest, ready to be used again. So you need energising, stretching things, you need rhythmic things to control it, you need focal and reaction things so the circle is formed.*'

Alternatively, we could argue the complete irrelevance of a warm-up. Jonathan Kay proposes that the attitude of foolishness, which is at the heart of performing, must be in place from the outset. It cannot be conjured by 'warming-up' because it's about an attitude, not a physical temperature. Certainly in many cases the distinction between a 'warm-up' and 'the work' is overstated. There's no reason why the initial process can't build gradually into a more intense behavioural mode. It's possible for exercises to be seen not so much as preparation but as microcosms of the later macrocosms which are the larger challenges. This allows for a gradual acclimatisation of both mind and body. So we're always working with the whole person – albeit in a more gentle, exploratory way during the earlier period. We explore 'miniatures' of the later full-size portraits. Boal's approach is different again, it's to work consciously in the early stages with each of the different senses: hearing, sight, touch, several senses and memory. The later work then aims for an integration of these, using exercises which draw from all the performer's abilities.

However the problem is solved, we are always moving from a world of conventional behaviour into one where rules are altered. So some kind of ritual bridge is necessary. It may be a favourite game, an energy release exercise or a more meditative, imaginative journey. Peter Badejo argues for rhythm work, claiming that *'people in this country do warm-up in a stretching manner. I do warm-up in a rhythmic manner. From the beginning you get people used to using rhythm. I use live music. I can't use tapes, they don't give me the punch I need. So if you have a thirty minute warm-up you get people moving into a full rhythm beat. The head, the body. So even if they're moving their hands, the leg, they are getting used to it – for say, forty-five minutes – so by the time you get into other work, it consciously or subconsciously reminds them how useful it was . . . You don't have to be a dancer to relate your body to what you hear.'*

Interplay Theatre may set up the room so it is the environment itself which creates a starting point and generates action. *'Something is happening as the group comes in. For example, someone is lying on the floor, covered with a blanket. There's music happening, it's quiet, it's a very special atmosphere. Or there's dried leaves on the floor, which is another start point . . . Then the movement comes from what the objects gives us.'* Jon Palmer.

I would propose four qualities that a group new to drama might consider for initial foci: ATTENTION, ENERGY, IMAGINATION, and COMMUNICATION. With these, the group will get itself into a frame of mind for more difficult challenges. The first task is always to build a group which will share tasks, and collaborate. But before even this is possible, we may need to introduce the drama medium. Group members may never have been to anything like a drama workshop before, so while they're getting to know the group, they are also getting to know the art form.

At this point, games are listed. It's useful to reiterate that none of these can be set in stone, their titles and modes of play vary enormously. They're given as examples which can be drawn from or altered to suit the context. There is no attempt to be comprehensive in selection or present them in a preferred order. They are often transferable across categories – a concentration game might also be listed as a communication game, a movement exercise for devising. Further games under these headings are given in the appendix.

A. ATTENTION

This quality is about concentration. It implies watchfulness, a quality of being awake. It means giving someone else your full attention. To do this, you need to come into the present tense, to leave aside those preoccupying thoughts you carried here and just be spontaneous. There may be distractions – either internal or external – inevitably everyone's head is a babble of voices but through engagement with the exercise we're hoping to transfer that energy into play.

WALK, CLAP, FREEZE stands for any exercise which involves the facilitator giving instructions to the group who move freely about the room. It can be as simple as this instruction suggests or as complex as you wish to make it. The exercise usually begins with individuals separate from each other, perhaps coming together during the exercise so everyone can be given instructions 'as a group'. If played early in the session, it can help the group begin to disassociate themselves from habitual perceptions. For example, the group can be asked to walk about and name the objects in the room, then later, walk again and start wrongly naming them (so they point to a table and call out 'chair'.) This can lead to exercises which ask players to alter or 'invert' reality, perhaps using props.

Some groups benefit by being kept together in a circle during the first half hour. If everyone can see everyone, this helps the development of familiarity and trust. To encourage the learning of each others' names, Ali Campbell uses NAME CHECK and finds it breaks the ice with humour. Essentially it's a challenge game. It can be led by the facilitator who perhaps chooses not to be specially good at it. FRUIT BOWL, another circle game, has some of the same characteristics.

WALK, CLAP, FREEZE

The group walks around the space at will. Their task is to respond in different ways to different commands. The commands are given by clapping or verbal instruction. One clap might mean 'walk', two claps 'stop'. Three, 'reverse direction'. The purpose is to fulfil the commands with speed and discipline.

Extension: Invent your own variations, adding different sounds for different commands, or different verbal instructions, e.g. give instructions to influence the walking. 'Walk faster, walk in slow motion, run in slow motion.' And maybe open the group up to awareness of each other: 'Look shiftily at other people, then look away quickly. Catch people's eye and look away. Then hold the gaze for a short time before looking away.' Such an exercise can go anywhere. 'Discover you have jet-propelled shoes', 'Be on a journey together, pitch camp, climb a cliff face.'

NAME CHECK

The group is seated in a circle. One player is in the middle. Her task is to say the name of anybody in the circle three times before the owner of that name has a chance to say it once themselves. If she manages it, then that named person has to come into the centre and do the same with somebody else's name. If she fails, she must try again with another name.

FRUIT BOWL

The group sits in a circle, except for one who stands in the middle. There are no spare chairs. Each player is given the name of a fruit, either apple, banana or pear. The player in the middle calls out the name of a fruit and all those who are of that fruit, have to find another seat – including the player in the middle. Someone will fail to get a seat – that person calls the next fruit. If they call 'Fruit Bowl!' everyone has to change.

Variation: 'Anyone Who ...' Central player calls out distinguishing characteristics: 'Anyone with a white shirt / blue socks / who was drunk last week ...'

I find it useful to change the format of games quite frequently in early sessions so the group never gets a chance to settle for too long with any particular one. Essentially there are only a limited number of ways to organise the group; Pairs, a Circle, Shattered Focus (people moving freely), a Line (or two lines) or the Stage (people facing an open stage). If the format is changed frequently, the participants find themselves having to give up some internal controls over their own behaviour – because there is seemingly no standard *modus operandi* to which we always return. What is expected of them is always changing so it's hard to 'teacher-please'.

Still in a circle, DRACULA depends on knowing people's names. It involves tasks which appear simple but are surprisingly hard to master – so the playing usually generates laughter. It becomes less successful if participants try to turn it into a challenge game which fundamentally it's not. They may for example run to 'strangle' or 'stab' a victim before that player has any reasonable time to organise a rescue. At root it's a co-operation game despite its pressures and penalties. One way to avoid it becoming a challenge game is having the Dracula figure count to ten or twenty before being able to 'kill' the other player.

Pairs games give people a chance to get to know each other on a one-to-one basis. Inevitably some pairs drift off into general chat during the exercise but this is usually not disruptive of the process. HYPNOSIS is from the Boal canon and like several of his exercises, keys in to important areas. Like much pairs work, it is a power game – one partner has power over another. But the power is held conditionally. If the leader demands impossible physical manoeuvres of the follower, the follower loses trust and gives up playing. Again, some may try to turn it into a competition and may need to be watched.

The value of the exercise lies in the physical fluidity which it hopes to engineer. If played well, the follower is gently coerced into shifting weight while relaxing certain muscles. Other muscles get used which ordinarily might be neglected. It encourages body postures and movements which are unfamiliar. I encourage leaders to take their partners through 'the balance point', the point at which the follower has to shift weight and change balance. The body restructures its weight in that moment. So if the player is prone to 'fixed' postures, this shift encourages them to become dislodged. Preferably the follower should relax as much as possible, only calling into attention those muscles which are required to accomplish the movement. The person leading should be consistently inventive using different heights, speeds and levels so that no rhythm is ever fully established. Afterwards it's useful to ask participants what they felt. It could simply be 'Who

DRACULA

The group stands in a circle. One player is nominated to be Dracula; their task is to find a victim. Dracula chooses someone and slowly walks towards them. Before Dracula arrives, the 'victim' must catch someone else's eye. This 'rescuer' must then rescue the victim by calling out their name. Assuming the rescue succeeds, Dracula goes in pursuit of another victim. If it doesn't, Dracula bites their neck or 'strangles' them or uses a mimed knife to 'kill' them.

Variation: the Dracula role changes whether or not the bite was successful.

HYPNOSIS

In pairs. The leader holds a hand in front of the face of the follower so the tops of the fingers are on a line with the hairline. Then the leader moves the hand around, and the other has to follow, keeping the head in the same alignment with the hand all the time. It's then a question of leading the follower around the room, avoiding other players.

prefers leading and who prefers being led?' Or the question could address any feelings that were aroused during the exercise. It may be useful for players to start paying attention to their own feelings, and to share observation of these. This helps to establish the idea that 'what you feel' is part of what we talk about in the workshop.

If the group has difficulties concentrating because of their age or situation, it may be a strategy to take the work in short, focused periods. If there is resistance to any organised coherent activity, discussion or referral back to staff may be appropriate. Some groups may be willing in spirit, but have blocks around use of the drama language. In which case, challenge games may offer a different way in. These, like RACE FOR THE KEYS are inevitably about individualism and winning but they can get a difficult group off their chairs, and once active, they may be more open to co-operative exercises.

B. ENERGY

Running challenge games is an easy way to precipitate energy release but may set an unhelpful precedent. Other release games can use a competitive edge but are more about fulfilling tasks or avoiding

---

BOMB AND SHIELD

The group is asked to listen to instructions, then move freely about the room. They're told to each choose someone else in the group (excluding the facilitator) who, for them, is a bomb. And another person who is a shield. Once they've chosen – silently – these two people, the task is to get into a position in the room where they're safe. In other words, where the shield is between them and the bomb. After it's run a few minutes, the facilitator can count down to the bomb's explosion.

Variation: I once adapted this and asked each player to choose one person they wanted to say 'hello' to. The task was then to make contact with your chosen ('hello') partner and get as far as possible from anyone who wanted to speak to you, only offering them a 'sorry' in return.

---

penalties. TAG is one of these and there are any number of variations. It may be that after it's been run once or twice using different variations, the group is invited to invent their own rules. It's surprising how quickly this invitation can be taken up and how insightful the suggestions sometimes are. It's as if playing the game gives participants an inside knowledge of the game's potential. Such a tactic also helps participants to see the structures of games as changeable, not as sacred or immutable.

BOMB AND SHIELD is presented as an adult game but inside there's a children's game trying to get out. Ironically, the only time I've known it fail was with children aged 11-13. They merely stood around trying to work out the purpose of it all. Exercises which break up cliques and factions are useful with older teenagers. A particular example is WIZARDS, GIANTS and ELVES. It involves the forming and reforming of teams each time a round is played. Although it takes a while to explain the rules, it generates a heady excitement and can run for ages with the right group. PEOPLE TO PEOPLE can serve a similar function. Such games help eliminate rigid, personal space boundaries – for the energy expended in pursuit of objectives involves forgetting conventional codes of conduct. Taboos around touch may begin to be broken, and often rules can be imposed which *insist* the game is played with some measure of physical contact. Participants get used to the idea that touching within a game does not carry the same

WIZARDS, GIANTS AND ELVES

Wizards beat giants because they put a spell on them. Elves beat wizards because they can run up their cloaks and strangle them. Giants beat elves because they can tread on them. Once this supremely logical set of impartial and politically incorrect truths is mastered, the group divides into two equal teams. Each goes to an opposite wall. Each team secretly confers and chooses one identity. All in each team will be either Gs, Ws or Ds. Then on a given signal from the facilitator, the two groups advance four paces – on the fourth the teams reveal who they are by going into the pose of their character. Giants are shown by holding arms up in the air, elves by crouching down and wizards by holding the arms out front, as if to spell-bind. Both teams should declare themselves at the same moment. The team in a winning position has to touch as many of the others before they can reach home base. The losers have to run like hell. If it's equal, all mutter mutter and return to the start. If there *is* a winning/losing combination, the losers who are touched have to join the winning side. So the losing side is depleted by the number who haven't made it home. Then the two teams confer again separately as before, and play another round. The aim is to go for a wipe-out by one team of the other.

PEOPLE TO PEOPLE

The group moves about at will, in response to commands. One person is 'out', their job is to call out 'People to People'. At this point, the players – including the caller – have to find a partner. Someone will be left out. That person then names two body parts and all the players, in pairs, have to join e.g their ear with the others' elbow. The new caller calls 'People to People' and the process begins again.

Variation: The caller may call out two sets of body parts to join up.

signals that it carries outside. Touch doesn't have to signal a sexual or antagonistic message.

PUSHING is another Boal exercise which has resonance beyond its apparently simple dynamic. Once the group has been divided into pairs (initially it may be more suitable for partners to be of similar weight and size) it may be useful to play the exercise badly. (Playing exercises badly is always an option (a) to help identify the mistakes, and (b) to reduce a fear of 'getting it wrong'.) So the first pair might be asked to push against each other shoulder to shoulder and try and push the other backwards. So it's a competition. It's a struggle and the resulting sweaty desperation shows clearly what we hope to avoid. Then the players are asked *not* to think about winning but instead to tune into the other's strength, and negotiate with it. The task becomes about paying attention to the other person, thinking about what they need as a resistance. This means registering the energy coming through then filtering one's own energy accordingly. The player must generate enough energy of their own to draw out the strength of the other. Usually this means an adaptation, because one is likely to be stronger than the other. So each is using enough strength as is appropriate for that partner. What we should get is a playful exchange of energies. It's still a pushing exercise and requires genuine effort but the point of concentration is to bring out the best from the other person, not from yourself. After it's been played, the partners should feel revitalised rather than tired. This exercise serves well as an introduction to improvisation where success lies in constant receptivity towards one's partner.

One extension of the PUSHING exercise involves the pairs transferring energies into an emotional dynamic. This might begin by continuing to play the exercise but starting to use emotional as well as physical means. It's easier at this point if the roles change and one is clearly pushing, the other resisting. So the one pushing will start to cajole, pressurise, plead with, tease, etc.,using words as well as physicality. Perhaps they try to get their partner to cross the room. The exercise can be run into a third stage which involves no physical contact at all but *only* verbal/emotional pressure. Here one player has to bring the other across the room while their partner provides a resistance. Each will continue to be sensitive to the other's feeling state.

C. COMMUNICATION

For some, the hardest thing is an equality of communication, both listening and expressing equally. Everyone has 'blind' and 'deaf' spots and the tendency to forget what was said – or not see what was meant – is often in evidence. Of course some groups may have genuinely impaired hearing or sight; in these cases the facilitator needs to select the appropriate mode of communication so participants can play from strength. Exercises can be adapted with this in mind.

Exercises such as INTRODUCTIONS help to gauge the attention levels in the group and, too, levels of ability. GIBBERISH

PUSHING

The group divides into pairs. Each pair lines up shoulder to shoulder, and pushes against the partner. The aim is to draw out the strength of the other person, through an interactive give-and-take. Later, other positions can be tried; hands to hands, backs to backs, etc. *Variation*: add a third player, and explore the balance between three. *Extension*: explore how the physical dynamic could be slowly transferred into a verbal/emotional dynamic with each player trying to bring their partner across the room.

INTRODUCTIONS

The group sits in a circle. Each person introduces themself with one piece of information about themselves or about how they're feeling today. The second person introduces the person who's just spoken, gives that piece of information then introduces themselves. The third speaker introduces the first two, then themselves. The fourth follows the same pattern. It can get a little awkward, and time-consuming, with a large group . . .

GIBBERISH INTRODUCTIONS

While the group is seated on the floor or on chairs, player A turns to player B on their left and makes a statement in gibberish. Perhaps the facilitator has asked a question, for example, 'Tell Terry on your left how your journey was today?' So Janice tells Terry in gibberish and Terry has to interpret back to the group. Having no idea at all what Jill is saying, any description involving camels or kidnapping is of course perfectly acceptable. The statements and interpretations can then move round the circle. If necessary the facilitator asks supplementary questions of the speaker, who answers these in gibberish.

INTRODUCTIONS will show who is and who isn't comfortable with a more theatrical form of self-expression. If this is found to be awkward, an exercise using shattered focus, everyone walking freely and interacting with everyone else, might allow gibberish to be explored more easily. A situation can be invented such as the RUSSIAN FEDERATION OF SHOE MANUFACTURERS CONVENTION. The Company Directors are meeting in the reception hall of the Annual Conference, and pleasurably observing each others new shoes, in Russian of course.

The NEWSPAPER GAME is an exercise calling for lateral think-ing. The first couple of rounds lure the group into a false security that the answer to each challenge lies in physical strength and agility. When this proves inadequate someone realises a different approach is called for. WHOSE STORY IS TRUE? works for most groups who can handle story-telling. It's an excellent introduction to creative lying, and therefore a fair introduction to acting. For those who feel uncomfort-able being in character or going in front of an audience, this exercise propels them gently into performance, albeit a commentative, story-telling mode of performance, without pressure. It also nicely reveals to participants how rich their pre-existing 'acting' skills are – it's very rare for the truth-tellers to be easily spotted.

If the group is resistant both to the performance idea and to organised structure, a question and answer process initiated by the facilitator may bring the group into play. At its most formal this would be INSTANT STORYTELLING where every answer given to a structured formula of questions are accepted. And so the story builds, for later acting out if appropriate. For more details on this, see INSTANT THEATRE. A more informal approach might be similar to DRAMA NEIN DANKE developed by Roger Hill where the work starts to build from the group saying 'no' to things. *'Obviously if you can't get people to sit down with you and try something out, then you've got other work to do – and not just you but the youth leader as well. But once sat down, I'm going to point at someone and say "It's you". Then that per-son must take the attention away from themselves and point to someone else in the circle. (Later) when someone points at you, you invent an excuse why it wasn't you. For example you fabricate the existence of some event for which someone must be held responsible. A party that went wrong . . . Of course one or two of them are a bit mad: "I was fucking my girlfriend." "I was on the moon at the time." And all the time you're shifting the blame . . . and what we've done is we've been demonstrative, we've been responsive, we've been inventive. "What's this got to do with acting?" "That's what you've been doing – in a rudimentary way."'*

Then it may be possible to move, for example, into creating the actual party which went wrong. After all, we've accumulated quite a lot of information about what happened. A different approach might involve beginning the session with the creation of a dramatic scenog-raphy. I might simply place a closed shoebox on the stage, then say, 'Someone finds this box in the first scene of our play. Who finds it and

THE NEWSPAPER GAME

Chairs are put away and several sheets of newspaper are placed on the floor. There is an instruction given: 'Everyone must be touching the newspaper, nobody must be touching the floor, the walls or the furniture.' Before long, everyone (probably) stands on the newspaper. Next, the amount of newsprint is reduced. It keeps being reduced until the group has found a way of solving the problem without everyone standing on the paper or each other.

WHOSE STORY IS TRUE?

The group, which needs to number six or more, is divided into sub-groups of three or four. One person in each sub-group needs to remember a true story that happened to them. It might be something involving a minor misdemeanour which they committed as a child. They tell that story to their sub-group so that each listener can adopt it as his or her own – and tell it as if it were their own story. Then everyone comes together and one team is invited into a stage area. Everyone in that team – in turn – tells the story as if it happened to them personally. Of course only one person is telling the truth. And it's the task of the audience to find who is the truth-teller.

Extension: The facilitator can ask the audience if they would like to ask any of the story-tellers questions about their story, about events or characters in it.

Variation: The group divides into two sub-groups. One half is a group of detectives. The other is a group of friends, one of whom has committed a theft, for example from a shop. (You need at least one person willing to admit to shoplifting for this to work.) The friends all learn the true story. Then they each take a chair and go to a different part of the room where they sit down. The detectives have to investigate by moving round and questioning the suspects. Each suspect claims they stole the item. In other words, they all 'confess'. Afterwards, the detectives go into a huddle and decide who they think is the guilty party.

what do they do with it?' We know at some point, somewhere down the line, we'll open it and discover its contents – but probably not yet. The group having made these early decisions, we play them out. Then we simply follow the path of 'What happens next?' with the facilitator looking to select all the answers which can reasonably be accommodated within our simple narrative structure. Participants get up and play roles accordingly.

D. IMAGINATION

An early task is to help participants use their imaginations as valid sources of inspiration. If possible they should be discouraged from feeling responsible for their imaginations. Instead the imagination should be viewed as a source of material which has its own, unreachable logic. It's no good trying to insist that the imagination be always correct and proper. The second stage involves accepting the imaginations of others, acknowledging that what others have created imaginatively *is true* within the fiction, as much as anything *you* might have invented. This stage is harder, and some players find it difficult to give up their own inventions in favour of others.

Keith Johnstone argues that *'It's possible to turn unimaginative people into imaginative people at a moment's notice.'* This is true, but it is sometimes difficult to get them to admit the change has been made. Generally, people have learned that being foolishly imaginative gets them into trouble, so they maintain a careful watch over themselves. They learn to be comfortable with a much more matter-of-fact approach to communication. They habitually shut down any offer that comes their way like a caretaker throwing down a grille, and they expect others to do the same. If a participant has difficulty here, it may be appropriate to work with them one-to-one. I might simply ask them to say 'what they see' when I open my hands. There's going to be something there. What's the first thing they see? Or else my hands become a book and when I open them, they see a word. What's that word? And what is the following sentence?

Having colleagues putting pressure on an individual offers a different approach. The participant sits down on the floor beside an imaginary box, and pulls imaginary objects out of it, one at a time. The other two are there to urge the player on to get faster and be more precise, and not to make extraneous movements. CHANGEABLE OBJECT uses an actual object as an imaginative trigger. Imaginations are sparked by looking at the object and speculating 'what else' it might be. It may be a hammer or a rolled up newspaper but our perception of it changes when it's used as a strapcord or a cricket bat, a gun or a contraceptive. We're endowing this object with other properties which allow us to 'see' it as something different. As the exercise runs, quieter

CHANGEABLE OBJECT

The group sits on the floor in a circle. In the middle is placed a neutral object, a rolled up newspaper, a tray or a box. Group members are invited to pick up the object and use it as if it were something different. Participants get up as they choose, on impulse. They 'use' the object, then sit down again. The group should only call out if they don't understand the transformation.

Extension: One players uses the object, as before. A second player enters the scene and interacts with the first. During the interaction, the object must pass from the first to the second player, but without it being 'asked for.' Then the first player sits down. Then the second 'transforms' it into something different, allowing a third to step in.

ANTIQUES

The group again sits in a circle on the floor. Everyone in the group is a highly intelligent professor of antiques. The 'antique' is passed around. Every expert disagrees politely with the previous one, and has a different interpretation as to its original function, its country of origin and its value. The facilitator mediates.

members may gain in confidence from the ease with which others are joining in. If there are individuals who never get up, there's always the option of passing the object around in a circle. ANTIQUES works in a similar fashion but draws on television panel games. A group of 'experts' pass around an object and speculate about its age, value and purpose. The temptation is to plan an amusing anecdote as you wait for your turn to come: the temptation should be resisted. Planned ideas always feel slightly dishonest.

COMPLETE THE IMAGE offers an excellent way in to image work. After running this successfully, any of the approaches documented in the later chapter under Imagework could be picked up. Played as described here, the momentum is impulsive so there is minimum pressure to 'perform', at the same time, if *no one* contributes, which never happens although the exercise can slow down rather seriously, then there's no play. Initially when it's played, the action tends to follow a pre-ordained pattern, certainly with male groups; there are images of violence and mimed objects keep appearing. So rules can be imposed which coerce the players away from these easy solutions. Alternatively, rules might insist on some physical contact between the players, or on eye contact.

An obvious stage forward is to add a third player to each image or invite repetitive movements instead of still images. Or phrases could be added as well as movements. Once a few movement/phrases have been accumulated, you might break the group up and have them move around the room at will. Then each time they meet with someone, they use one of the phrases and build a dialogue, using just these phrases. It may be worthwhile recalling them as a group first and selecting half a dozen of the best phrases for them to use. After the exercise, improvisational work can spin off in a number of directions. It may be that the facilitators have a specific brief to work on, so specific images or phrases could be selected and used as the basis of scenes.

NARRATIVE GAMES work by 'stopping' traditional thought patterns and insisting on digression. An invented story is really just a digression into an imaginative sphere. The player is encouraged to 'corrupt' reality by lying about what happened. This involves going against what we've learned and some may complain it feels unnatural. The point to make is that dramatic material inevitably distorts or alters what is 'true' and this exercise only makes a point of it. Breaking our habitual patterns of dialogue may be a necessary part of opening up our imaginations. If participants find the exercise irksome, it may be worth chatting with them about the difficulties.

The willingness to be 'knocked off centre' is vital for engaging with an unfamiliar imaginative territory. Although we cry out to act, perform, speak about *what we know*, the territory of *what we don't know* is more interesting and exciting. If we forever remain within the parameters of the familiar we can less easily push back our personal boundaries. Working in an area of *don't know* is difficult, because we feel lost there; but the longer we can stay there, the more likely we are to find a wave to ride on, if necessary pushing out from the familiar, on a journey which will inevitably take us somewhere.

A NOTE ON ENDING SESSIONS

More often than not, a feedback period at the end of early sessions is necessary. The facilitator can get responses from those who may have withheld them. Opinions about future directions can be gathered. Compliments can be given. It's especially useful for participants to say

COMPLETE THE IMAGE

The group sits in a circle. (The exercise can also be played with the group in a line, facing a stage.) Someone comes into the circle and strikes a pose/makes a shape. The image can be abstract or representational. Anyone else can then jump in to 'complete the picture' by adding themselves in a different pose. So the two shapes together create an image with a meaning which was not necessarily present when the first pose was struck. The image is held for a moment, then the first player sits down. A third player adds themselves to the second, thereby creating a different image again. Then the second player sits down.

Extensions: Different rules can be applied. For example, 'no violent images' or 'no miming.' It can be extended by having three players on stage at any one time. Additionally, the player who gets up can be asked to create not just an image but a gesture, which repeats. Phrases can also be asked for.

NARRATIVE GAMES

The group divides into pairs. Partner A is asked to tell a story, something which happened to them. Every so often Partner B interrupts and denies the truth of what happened. A then has to accept the contradiction, and accommodate it into the story.

Variation: Partner A tells a fictional story, and this time the interruption asks for an explanation of a word. A then has to spontaneously explain what 'blue' means or 'pigeon' or 'dogdirt' but giving an entirely imaginative explanation, one which runs contrary to the accepted meaning of the word.

what they feel about what happened and articulate any new perceptions. There may be an incident which caused friction – does it need to be talked through?

If open discussion is inappropriate – because of time limitations or the group is falling into fractious argument – more formal techniques can be used. For example, participants may be asked to sum up what the previous participant expressed before she can make her own point. Or the facilitator can ask everyone present, in turn, for their responses in a few words. The responses go around in a circle and no one is allowed to interrupt. However this feedback session runs, we hope to end on a note of positive affirmation, looking forward to the next workshop.

BUILDING A GROUP: TEAMWORK

Once the group has accepted the idea of working together, joining in, following the rules of the game, accepting drama conventions, it's time to re-introduce the idea of teamwork. This allows the group to move into areas which require a greater degree of mutual support. They start to perceive themselves *as a group*, with their own identity and responsibilities. Keith Johnstone has been known to start a workshop with a simulated tug of war. No rope, just two teams and some mime. Inevitably the two groups heave away, straining and struggling, neither side willing to give an inch. Then he stops it and asks the participants what they're doing. 'Trying to win', they might say. 'But there's no rope. How can you possibly win?' It's an adept ruse to highlight the difference between staged and actual conflict. Certainly the tug-of-war players are in conflict, but why should the actors be so? Why can't one team of actors be prepared to lose? If neither group of actors is prepared to lose, perhaps they misunderstand the nature of their fictional conflict.

What are the constituent elements of teamwork? How do you create it when it's absent? In the army it's achieved through shared physical peril. Even in peacetime, swimming across icy rivers, abseiling down mountains and sharing inedible canteen food is generally considered the best way to bond. In theatre work, we place less value on Great Heroics but nevertheless need to explore a parallel universe to achieve comparable solidarity. No physical danger necessarily but acclimatising ourselves to danger and risk, certainly. Fear of failure is partly relieved by learning to adapt to others: you no longer feel so much 'on the spot'. Paradoxically, by taking this attitude, you benefit your own performing. If we don't sign up to the group ethic, no one will succeed individually. So if we split to create two teams playing tug-of-war, *as actors* we need to be still pulling together. The rope is not the means by which to compete but the means by which to collaborate.

I would propose four elements of teamwork: SUPPORTIVENESS, SPONTANEITY, ADAPTATION, EMPOWERMENT.

KNOTS

The group forms a circle, and holds hands. Then the hands are released. Now everyone puts a left hand into the centre and finds another hand. No one should be holding more than one hand. (It's possible there may be a hand spare – they have to just wait until the next stage.) Then everyone puts a second hand in, and again finds another hand, one only. Both times they should avoid taking the hand of the person to their left or right. Now everyone should have a hand in each hand. The group has formed a knot. The purpose is to untangle the knot by any means possible, without letting go of any of the hands. If the group fails to make progress, an allowable concession is to release and rejoin one or two pairs of hands.

A. SUPPORTIVENESS

Trust is only possible if group members are looking out for each other. If anyone falls over, trust means they'll be caught. So the next stage is; you fall over deliberately. The falling over becomes fun. Observation and empathy are essential qualities. If I can't see – or sense – how you're getting on, I can't help you. And once I've seen you, if I can't feel for you in your predicament, I can't find an emotional impulse to carry out an action on your behalf. I need to connect to you. I need really to connect to everyone in the group.

Exercises like KNOTS are about learning to negotiate with others. You're in a tangle with them, and there's always the possibility of someone getting bruised. The removal of personal space boundaries means you're all in it together. There's a lot of unforced physical contact. It's interesting to observe participants' behaviour during the exercise, and important not to intervene. Someone may try to take control but the likelihood is, they won't manage it for long because they simply won't be able to see enough of what's going on. Hopefully the group will untangle themselves and form again a new circle. Now it may happen that we emerge with two interlocking circles. It may also happen that the group can't manage it, get dispirited and need concessions made, but they can still solve the puzzle. We can discuss afterwards: who tried to take control, who preferred to leave it to others? Are participants aware of their choices? Is that how they operate in social situations generally?

LEADING BY SOUND

In pairs. This time, one player is blind. The leader has to lead them about the room by means of a small sound, avoiding furniture and the other players.

Extension: A lone player can try and 'steal' blind partners away by imitating the sounds they're following.

THE DIRECTOR

This exercise is run in pairs, one pair at a time. One partner is blind, the other directs their movements. In the space are placed a number of physical objects and other members of the group, as obstacles. The purpose for the director is to steer their blind partner through the maze to the other end, without their falling over anyone or anything. The exercise might be run with several directors guiding several blind partners simultaneously.

The exercise encourages participants at a simple level to be aware of looking after each other. This can be extended through exercises which involve a blind partner, for example LEADING BY SOUND or THE DIRECTOR. Here, the blind partner should be encouraged to say as much as they can about their feelings during the obstacle course, so their apprehension or fear can be fed back to the director and she can take steps to reassure them. SUPPORTED STORY-TELLING also hopes to create empathy between players. This time the group is instructed to watch the storyteller carefully to see when he might be getting into trouble with the exercise. They have to read the teller's body language and listen to their words to determine whether or not confidence is flagging. Has the storyteller lost the plot? If so, someone needs to jump up and replace him. Afterwards, we can compare notes. Who was left up there for ages without anyone coming to the rescue? Why couldn't we see they were in trouble? And was Jane really in trouble, or was she substituted unnecessarily? If so, what was she doing that was 'misread?' We're less interested in the content of the story than in reading each others' body-language and learning about the actor-audience relationship. A similar exercise makes this actor-audience contact the main focus; its purpose is to encourage good eye contact. This time the storyteller continues uninterrupted, but if any spectator feels inadequately included, they raise a hand. They may feel they're

SUPPORTED STORYTELLING

The group sits in a circle. In the centre, one player tells a story – one they know or one they invent. The audience listen. At any time the storyteller should be replaced by a spectator if that spectator thinks the storyteller has lost the plot, or needs rescuing. If this happens, the storyteller has to sit down and is replaced by the rescuing group member.

THE COWBOY AND INDIAN

The group divides into pairs. Each pair decides on a situation which involves two characters, and has some scope for action. One player begins by saying what the other character 'does'. 'The Indian walked into the restaurant, looked around and sat down in a chair.' The other actor, playing the Indian, then acts out what has been described. On completing this action, the actor playing the Indian describes what the Cowboy does for the other actor. 'The Cowboy, who was employed as a waiter, swaggered over to the Indian, and began to wipe the table, showing his gun as he did so . . . ' The scene continues, each actor maintaining responsibility for the other's course of action. Giving exact speeches to the other actor becomes clumsy, but some guidance on speech may be useful – for example: 'The Indian went ahead and ordered everything on the menu.'

not getting sufficient eye contact, for example. If they feel completely abandoned, they start waving. These signals alert the storyteller not to neglect their audience.

THE COWBOY AND THE INDIAN is more of a performance improvisation, but can be played by pairs on their own. Again, it's about looking after your partner; this time by controlling their script. (It's a simplified version of a Keith Johnstone game called HE SAYS, SHE SAYS.) Each actor is responsible for the dramatic momentum of their partner, if not for their exact words. This makes them super-conscious of how different ideas are helpful or unhelpful to the acting out. Each actor has to concentrate on their partner rather than themselves. One benefit is it helps to reduce self-consciousness. After all, if they're left adrift in the scene – it's the other person's fault! In feedback they can discuss which instructions were easy and fun to carry out, and which felt awkward. What you tend to find is those instructions which impel action are easy to play while those which instruct attitude or feelings are not. 'He went to the till when the waitress was distracted and rifled it' gives the other actor plenty to do. But 'he thought for a bit, then got very annoyed' will prove almost impossible to play.

B. SPONTANEITY

The exercise of spontaneity is linked to use of imagination, since it's really imagination-in-action. 'Be what you see' is how Jonathan Kay expresses this responsibility. By cutting down the time between the thought – the mental idea – and its physicalisation, we become increasingly spontaneous. If the performer is fully engaged, there is no 'gap' between idea and expression; everything is immediate. The 'ideas' express themselves as they are formed. (A sub-heading of 'Spontaneity' might be 'Positivity' since we're discussing a quality of spontaneous acceptance, not the egocentric impulse of denial. Spontaneity should be directed towards developing the play, not destroying it.)

This avoidance of self-censorship can disarm newcomers, as it contravenes learned behaviour. But if the newcomer starts to take risks, the sensation of spontaneity will become less foreign. They can also take comfort from seeing how others aren't penalised for apparently bizarre contributions.

Exercises are given which explore spontaneity through physical, verbal and emotional means. The best exercises engage all aspects of the performer's psyche. DANCE DIALOGUE can be seen as a direct extension of COMPLETE THE IMAGE. It operates through physicality. Instead of a group creating imagery together, now just two players interact with each other alone. This means that the responsibility is always there to respond imaginatively to the offer made by the other actor. There's less time to think, and once the exercise gets into a rhythm, the player soon gives up planning altogether, it's not worth the effort. The exercise becomes something akin to contact improvisation, or a piece of unstructured dance.

Keith Johnstone's YES, AND explores verbal dialogue. The inbuilt structure of the exercise prevents the actors from blocking each others' contributions. If the players work together well, their dialogue tends to build to a natural crescendo in which the players, having become Gods, blow up the universe and eat the remains for lunch. Having written that, I'm reminded that good improvisers will never stop at lunch . . .

DANCE DIALOGUE

The exercise is played in pairs or with one pair performing to the rest. Player A strikes a pose/makes a shape. The other responds to it with a pose of their own. The shapes can be abstract or representational. Then player A responds to what B has done. They have to find the impulse from *inside the image they're in,* rather than by standing outside and looking at the other player.

Extension: the players can reduce the time they give themselves to respond, then start to move before the other player has finished moving. This begins to give the impression of a continuous dance.

YES, AND

A dialogue exercise. It also can be played by pairs on their own, or in front of a group. The players stand opposite each other, and are encouraged to move physically, to keep light on their feet as the exercise progresses. Player A says 'Let's . . . (do something; go to the beach, steal a car.) Player B must reply with a sentence which begins 'Yes, And – (– we can swim! – drive it to America!) Player A then follows the same rule, replies with 'Yes, and – ' and every response is the same from then on.

Some common mistakes with this game are: to turn the dialogue into a list of 'things which will be done' rather than building on, or over-accepting the previous offer. Secondly, to bring no emotional dynamic into play. The exercise is about enthusiasm and positivity; it needs to be played with both. Thirdly, to ignore the other's inventiveness and determinedly go off on your own track. It's important to listen to – and key in to – the other person. Lastly, it's a mistake to cunningly twist the 'yes' into a negative so it becomes 'no'. This tactic goes something like 'yes – and then we'll be so depressed we'll probably commit suicide.' Again, the point is to think about what will be useful for your partner. Does your contribution help them to build the speculation or not?

REACTIONS might be used if a group has grown lethargic; it's about reacting spontaneously to provocations. It can also be used towards the end of a session when a group know each other well and can send each other up. They can use it to tease, dig or satirise what they know of each other.

In his book *Impro* Keith Johnstone explains his own way of working with BLIND OFFERS. My version represents a shift in emphasis, but the central idea is the same; using visual stimuli created by partner A to trigger the imagination of partner B. *'When you make a blind offer'* Johnstone argues *'you have no intention to communicate at all.'* [26] In other words, you simply make a shape. But the partner 'reads' the offer as if it was intended to communicate. Put another way, the partner 'projects' on to that neutral shape a quality which was not in the creator's mind; he or she makes an assumption about it, which is then accepted by the image-maker. If partner A makes the initial shape with the intention of communicating a *specific idea*, the partners get into trouble. If I make a neutral physical shape but think 'guitarist' and my partner accepts it as 'hobgoblin' and starts to improvise to that, we're at odds with each other. I'm likely to block his subsequent offer as I'm still stuck in 'guitarist.' The two actors need to tune into each other otherwise they're not in the same play. Newcomers have to learn to 'give up' their cherished ideas, or 'murder their darlings' as GK Chesterton put it. This gets you into a 'don't know what's going on' territory where you have to learn to feel comfortable. In 1996 Keith Johnstone gave a talk in London, and pointed out how spontaneity relates to group playing. *'The further ahead an actor plans, the less able they are to work with anyone else on stage.'* This is precisely because of the heavy bags they are carrying around with them which they think are 'good ideas' but are really just heavy bags.

There are steps that can be taken to discourage planning ahead, one of which is giving instructions to players during an improvisation. Such instructions 'knock them off centre' a little, and shift them into a 'don't know' / uncontrolled area. Playing BLIND OFFERS can be a jumping-off point into more elongated improvisations. And in longer impros, there's more scope for directing actors from the sidelines, what Viola Spolin calls 'sidecoaching'. For example, why not establish the precedent that during improvisations, the facilitator can ask the actor to swap parts with another actor? Or the actor might be told to play an animal or an inanimate object. Or the actor might play two parts, and start flipping between them? Or the facilitator may give the actor a line to say, to push the scene on. A line might be offered like: 'You don't recognise me, do you?' or 'I have to tell you something difficult" or 'What the hell's that?'

REACTIONS

Is played in a circle. One player comes into the middle. Other players can jump into the circle, no more than one at a time, and give the first player a piece of news or information. 'I'm afraid your dog has just been run over' or 'Your numbers came up on the lottery!' to which the first player must react without thought – spontaneously and with great energy. The reaction should be unplanned; the aim is to identify what is 'felt' and to communicate that feeling. The first player then finds an opportunity for this impulse to take them offstage, leaving the other player. Then another steps in. (Note that 'I fancy you' or 'I've brought the socks from Planet Zog' are probably not helpful pieces of news.)

BLIND OFFERS

Can be run by pairs privately, or in front of a group. Partner A strikes a neutral pose. Partner B responds to it 'as if' it were an offer to an improvisation. (An 'offer' is simply a gesture which invites the other actor to enter into a collaboration around the substance of that offer.) So Partner B starts to improvise. For example, Partner A stretches an arm out ahead and a leg out behind. Partner B becomes another 'skater on the ice rink.' (An instruction can be given to allow, or disallow talking.) After the scene has run a short distance, the actors stop and Partner B makes a shape which Partner A responds to.

Extension: After working separately, pairs can be brought together in a circle and each pair can perform in front of the group – not to repeat what they've done already, but to develop new material. At that point there may be scope to extend the improvisational ideas and give directions to the actors accordingly.

THE CAR

Again the group divides into pairs. One partner is a car, one a driver. The car is driven through touch on the back of the blind partner. A series of touch signals is worked out. For example, touching left shoulder means turn left, centre back means stop, etc. Sighted drivers can always be sent into the arena to increase the dangers. The purpose for the driver is to steer their 'car' safely, avoiding contact with all other cars.

THE YES GAME

The group stands or sits in a circle. A minimum of about six players are needed for this. Each player pairs up with a player opposite. If any player steps into the circle, her partner has to step in also. At first, players are asked merely to cross the stage area and acknowledge each other, returning to each other's place. No more than one pair should be in the circle at any one time. Then new conditions are introduced, becoming progressively more challenging. For example:

1. The players cross, but one must ask the other a favour, to which the answer given must be 'no'.

2. This time the answer given must be 'yes'.

3. This time we briefly explore what happens after the answer 'yes' has been given.

4. The players cross, and anything can happen or develop between them. Players try not to block each other's offers.

Variation: When players cross, they are characters meeting each other and each time they contact, different conditions apply. The following characters might meet:

1. Two friends who are glad to see each other.

2. Two friends, one doesn't remember the other.

3. Two former lovers, one who wants to get back together, the other is horrified at the suggestion.

4. Two meet; one has carried a grievance against the other for some time.

But before we get to these possibilities, there may be more fundamental problems. Actors may be avoiding a commitment to the playing, so they give themselves 'outsider' roles. 'I'm in the improvisation but I'm a teacher, telling you what to do.' 'I'm a sculptor and you're the model.' 'I'm a fencing instructor' or 'a doctor'. This allows me to make the other actor the 'subject' of the scene – while I'm on the edge, controlling. So a facilitative response might be to encourage them to be *inside* the same reality as they perceive the other actor inhabiting. If Player A does a shape and Player B's' immediate perception is 'sick man', then don't be a doctor, be a sick man too. Another tendency is for the actors to put *both of themselves* outside the action. So for example they

INSTANT IMAGES

The group sits facing the stage area. The facilitator asks for players to individually imagine themselves on the stage, in a certain pose. They merely have to get up, take the shape for a moment and sit down. People then get up in their own time. The next challenge might be to get up without planning your pose: so you have to make it spontaneously, only planning where on the stage area you're going to be.

Variation: During either stage, the facilitator may ask the players to stay on stage until they're released. Then she may thank them and send them back, even before they've reached the stage. This also allows the facilitator to monitor and build the onstage images as more players get up.

Variation: Themes can be proposed, for example 'family' – e.g. 'an angry/happy/disfunctional or alternative family' – in which case players get up to be part of such a family.

end up 'looking at someone' – falling off a building or coming out of a spaceship. Then the facilitator might suggest to one or both actors; 'Why not be that person falling?' or 'Why not be that alien?' You have to go to where the *action* is, then later you can flip out to be an observer.

But even this may be rushing ahead. Some participants may still be having difficulty with just getting up from their seats. If so, we have to take a step back. There's no point exploring more advanced impro when the group is still struggling to sustain concentration. THE YES GAME and INSTANT IMAGES may ease the shift into impro. The former simply demonstrates how saying 'yes' and saying 'no' can have different consequences. It may also be an appropriate time to talk about the actor/character distinction. The actor is always saying 'yes' to everything, but the character is perfectly entitled to say 'no'. 'No' sometimes better helps develop the action. 'You'd walk out if I tried to kiss you, wouldn't you, Simon?' Even deliberate blocking may be fine if it creatively provokes the other actor. Because THE YES GAME can so easily be stopped and restarted, the facilitator can work on a range of different kinds of interaction; argumentative, regretful, excitable, lustful. INSTANT IMAGES is a simple image exercise, but its value lies in cultivating spontaneity. It helps to reduce the fear of getting up by making 'getting up' or 'moving on to the stage' more habitual.

C. ADAPTATION

This quality is about learning to give way, and co-operate. If we're too stiff and resistant to others, we can't co-operate with them. It's our emotional and physical flexibility which allows us to do this. Physicality and feeling are linked; emotions surface in, and suffuse the body. By becoming sensitive to inner feeling, we can change our physicality. We have to be prepared to enter into a feeling territory, otherwise there's no play. Without emotional engagement, the play remains demonstrative, mimetic or an act of storytelling.

BOXING opens up this area. It's principally about physical co-ordination but emotions tend to enter in. When pugilists box, they try to avoid this. They want to knock hell out of each other – so try to stay cool-headed and focused entirely on winning. Aggressive feelings are found and directed. Playing the game in a drama context means unlearning this and doing the opposite. You have no interest in winning: instead, what's important is playing, co-operating. When John Wayne threw a punch in the movies, he drew his arm well back before striking. This not only prepared the other actor but told the audience that he was mighty powerful. The same principle applies here, we work together to create an effect. Instinctively people *want* to play by the rules of traditional boxing, they *want* to catch the other by surprise, they *want* to avoid their punches. So the instruction is: 'Get in the way of their punches, be happy about losing. After all, you're not *really* losing.' If we can get to the point where winning and losing are equally irrelevant – can 'look those two imposters in the face' – the exercise becomes creative and the players can move from there to create scenes. If in addition they can allow themselves to show emotion, then the emotions 'light up' their playing.

MOVING AS ONE starts to cultivate shared feeling states in the group as a whole. It's about finding a common physical tempo. There are many such exercises. (Sometimes they work so well players find it hard later to define an individual tempo – of a character for example – which is contrary to others on the stage.) This exercise can also move into group work where all the characters on the stage share the same fate. For example, they're all prisoners in the Bastille, or a crowd at a football match. But groups at an early stage of development will find these extensions difficult; the issue of leadership may still be

BOXING

The group divides into pairs. Each couple has a boxing match. Only there are two simple rules: all movement is in slow motion, and there is no actual physical contact. However, the players behave *as if* there were physical contact. So punches which are thrown, are reacted to as if they hit. Queensberry rules don't apply. Players should not attempt to win but concentrate on developing a fluid exchange of punches between them.

MOVING AS ONE

The group stands together against a wall, or sits together on the floor. The instruction is to perform a sequence of movements – together – without any one individual obviously leading. For example, to move away from the wall, sit on the floor, get up, sit on a row of chairs, etc. The facilitator gives no verbal instructions except at the beginning. Then in feedback, we assess whether the leadership really was shared. How much awareness did people have of each other? Was there genuine co-ordination?

Extension: The group can all be people sharing the same fate; a crowd at a hanging, lost in a desert, etc.

problematic. In particular, players may find it hard to shift between leading / not leading. However, the challenge of completing tasks 'as a group' – through keying in to each others' movements – often generates a collective determination to 'make it work'.

SOUND AND MOVEMENT must qualify as a classic exercise, echoing patterns of ritual behaviour. It's used by theatre companies throughout the world. It's a copying exercise; it appears banal on the surface but when played with commitment, it challenges participants to push back personal boundaries. For in sharing each others' rhythms, the participants stretch their individual capacities for expressive movement. Individuals who are natural giraffes become Yorkshire terriers. Individuals who are small birds become tigers or wolves. The exercise pulls you away from your natural centre into another's rhythm – there, you can learn another player's quality whether aggressive, camp, nervous or whatever. It's a hard exercise because it requires sustained energy and concentration. Sometimes participants prefer to play it mechanically, ducking the emotional challenge. They just go

SOUND AND MOVEMENT

The group stands or sits in a circle. One player is in the middle. She begins a sound and movement, which repeats. Maybe she takes a moment to find a pattern which they like, but once found, it should remain constant. The group picks up that sound and movement and copies it simultaneously. In this way everyone's impulses are co-ordinated. After a while, when the central player feels those on the circle are all sharing the movement, she goes to change places with someone. The new player then comes into the centre. Everyone still repeats the same pattern, however they now follow the adaptation which is made by the new central player. That player doesn't stop and restart the movement but adapts it to a pattern they prefer. Everyone on the outer circle follows them. The second player then finds a third.

Variation: Rules can be less strict according to the ability of the group. For example, we could all stand in a circle and the leadership pass round the circle.

through the motions not the e-motions. So there's some value in the facilitator leading from the inside, setting a benchmark. The disadvantage is, there are restricted opportunities to give specific instructions from inside. FOLLOW MY LEADER continues a similar idea, but the circle is broken and the group moves around the room. We know it by its association with traditional children's games. As long as the adults can avoid thinking this is stupid by inference, it can get them into surprising areas. The changeover between leaders happens differently from in the children's game. It must happen spontaneously rather than by design. Whereas in SOUND AND MOVEMENT one leader goes through a transformative process in the circle, this time an individual breaks away spontaneously from the pack and defines a different movement straight off. Again, some individuals will resist 'accepting' the new leadership: we all instinctively want to stay with our preferred patterns. But, if we *can* shift into another's pattern, we're helped towards becoming actors capable of transformation.

MAKING LETTERS AND NUMBERS is more mechanistic but in the early stages does involve some lateral thinking as participants figure out how tasks can be fulfilled. There may be several wrong attempts, and it's worth refusing to modify the rules. Once the exercise

FOLLOW MY LEADER

The group moves around as a swarm, with one person leading. That leader walks with a particular rhythm, a particular mood. Everyone has to follow, keeping together as a group, a bunch rather than a line. After a decent time, anyone can break away with a contrasting walk/run/rhythmic movement and then all must follow this new leader. After a while someone else can strike out again and everyone follows as before. The person making the change, should aim for a contrast with the preceding attitude.

MAKING LETTERS AND NUMBERS

The group moves about freely in the room, and meets the challenges offered. For example, to keep stepping into all the 'gaps' on the floor, moving about so the floor is equally 'covered.' They go back to this task in between the separate challenges. While meeting these, talking is forbidden.

Stage One: the group is asked to divide into groups of twos, threes, fours or fives. When completed they move on.

Stage Two: the group is asked to create e.g. three cubes, five triangles, two spheres.

Stage Three: the group is asked to create a letter, say the letter X. Then a word, e.g. cat or catastrophe. (The only way this is really achieved is by the group forming the letters with their bodies on the floor, in 2-D.)

Stage Four: THE TRANSPORT MUSEUM. The group is asked to create a number of forms of transport in a museum, which are still able to travel if required.

Stage Five: the group creates images, e.g. the court of Louis XIV, or a scene at the guillotine, or a McDonalds on Saturday night. All challenges should be met as quickly as possible, without conferring.

has 'taken', the number and intensity of the challenges can be varied. The exercise helps participants to see how their role on stage is valuable not by *what they do*, but by what they do *in relation to others*. For example – in the image-making stage of the exercise – taking the role of the slave may be right *or* wrong. It might be right in one exercise and wrong in another. In the first, being the slave fills that space where the slave ought to be, so it completes the mosaic. It fills out the image in a way that's complementary to the other elements. But in the second case we already have three slaves – another simply clutters the image. Maybe a better choice is the queen's husband or the dead tiger. Participants sometimes think that to 'change your mind' is a weakness. But those who do – in favour of strengthening the overall composition – should be complimented. MACHINES explores a similar idea, but is difficult for groups not already committed to developing their group mechanics. It's not about spontaneity, it's about interlocking. Why is it hard? Perhaps because our desire to impose ourselves is so strong we have no energy left to be imposed upon. MACHINES makes causative behaviour our focus. The atmosphere around the exercise is quite reflective sometimes, because it requires careful observation. How can you construct repetitive physical movement which is reactive, which is built on interdependency? When a machine finally does get constructed harmoniously, it 'feels right' and 'looks right'. At that point the group can extend the exercise. But if you jump to these more obviously 'entertaining' areas too quickly, the basic idea might not have been mastered. But once we have moved on, there's real opportunity for social observation and social critique.

Exercises like THE TRANSPORT MUSEUM are similar wherein participants combine to make animate or inanimate objects. Unless there's understanding of how each person functions within the whole, the exercise runs into difficulty. Within the Lecoq canon there are various exercises around cooking, exercises which involve actors playing the parts of eggs, butter and pans in the act of omelette-making. The application of heat completely transforms the central characters!

For those who find it difficult adapting to others, two exercises place a focus on yielding and humility. WHERE'S MY RADIO was devised specifically for working with young men who were stuck inside machismo and self-assertiveness. Essentially it's a contrivance to *encourage* attitudes which they try to *avoid*. Later I discovered it has particular application in prisons where radios form a currency. There are tasks to be completed, but it's more about observing and discussing how the challenges are met, than completing them. So the facilitator needs a clear head on the purpose of the exercise otherwise it can drift off meaninglessly. At the outset it should be made clear that the person

MACHINES

The task is to make a machine in which all mechanical parts are integrated. Participants take the role of the parts. One person starts by doing a repeating sound and movement with their whole body. Others then join in to extend the machine, being 'activated' by parts already present. The machine should aim for a sense of completeness.

Extension: Social Machines. A theme is chosen, e.g. monarchy or the law or drug culture. The first player takes the part of a social role; the queen or a judge or a pusher. They give us a gesture and a phrase. One by one, others add themselves as other social roles linked to – and affected by – those already present.

WHERE'S MY RADIO?

The group stands in a circle. One player moves across the circle to another player and asks for their radio back. He or she loaned it out and they need it back now to hear a particular programme.

The person who borrowed it however has lent it on (without asking permission) to someone else. So the borrower's task is to apologise and agree to get it back as soon as possible. They should be genuinely humble and apologetic. The radio owner should be angry. Next, the borrower moves on to the person they lent it to. Now they can be demanding and aggressive. They move from playing low status (humble) to high status (assertive). However, the person they lent the radio to has also lent it on . . .

who has borrowed the radio and loaned it on, is in the wrong. He has no defence for his behaviour. So it's not even worth making excuses. Instead, the challenge is: can he apologise and remedy the situation? If he avoids doing this, it's for the observers to notice *how* he does it. Often players are unaware of just how they try to avoid being in the wrong. They might subtly place the blame on someone else, for example. So the rest of the group is encouraged to observe the interactions and comment on what they see. How does the player deal with the situation? What tactics are used? Individuals who naturally play high status in life, find this exercise especially hard.

RADIO is clearly more of a social skills and communications exercise but all of us need to be able to change our mask according to situation. We need to adapt to circumstances, and allow different feelings to inform our behaviour. Playing an exercise like RADIO encourages self-perceptions around these issues. MOODS is another exercise to explore emotional qualities, but is more purely theatrical. Like SOUND AND MOVEMENT it's about emotional sharing but without the stress on rhythm. It can serve as a springboard into devised work where emotional states of characters are sharply contrasted.

D. EMPOWERMENT

This section is about playing with power relationships and learning different status practice. Often individuals 'get stuck' in high or low status profiles. Perhaps they were learned early in life and now they can't get out of the habit. Person A complains that he always gets taken advantage of by girlfriends. Does he ever play high status with them? Is he ever assertive? Person B will never admit to being in the wrong. Why should she? Better to brazen it out than get taken advantage of. To be better players in drama or life, individuals need a versatility with status. Within these exercises we can ask participants about the status level they think they naturally play, then confront them with spectators' observations. Perhaps they're asked to play against their natural inclination. Initially, we could create an imaginary dialogue and play around with status combinations. One player goes to ask another for: a pint of milk / the loan of some money / to come to a movie. Each time the scene is played, the status levels are different for each player. How does the difference feel? What's the status gap? Does what the players see as the status gap, correspond with how the observers perceive it? Or we might begin by playing what is sometimes known as THE POWER GAME. The group sits facing an open stage. Someone is asked to go and take a high status position in the room. Maybe someone stands centre stage looking at the audience. Can anybody find a higher status? Can you make the first actor 'appear' low status? Maybe someone takes a chair and sits, and 'inspects' the first actor, reflectively – and so on – it's surprising how many times the status can be lowered. The other approach involves working from low status positions. The low status 'competition' usually ends with someone's head in the waste paper basket.

Status is a powerful but invisible factor – for in everyday exchanges, our status profile is so habitual we're often unaware of it. But it's tremendously influential in outcomes to conflict as audiences can witness.

MOODS

The group sits on the floor, in a large circle. One person gets up and moves into the stage area. They move around the circle. They are asked to inhabit a particular mood, which should be clearly expressed. For example, they're very impatient and nervous, always looking at their watch. Or they're angry with themselves or they're happy, skipping. A second player must get up and joins in with that mood. They share it, picking it up osmotically, doing the same actions, moving in the same way. These two players acknowledge each other and relate, but don't speak. Then a third player gets up – their job is to bring a mood which sharply contrasts the prevailing mood. They also move around the space, being aware of the others. The first actors then have to adapt to the newcomer, slowly. They allow their mood to change and to 'feel like' the new-comer until all three share the same mood – happy or frustrated or sad. Then the first actor sits down and a fourth enters. The cycle begins again.

Extension. To ask the audience after (or before) the exercise is run – whether any combination of moods which they see, suggests a particular encounter. Then that scene could be run, initially without words. For example, two angry people joined by a nervously excited person might suggest three people in the waiting room after they've all interviewed for the same job. This scene is then run.

Playwrights construct plays accordingly; plays from *Macbeth* to *Waiting for Godot* use status conflict to hinge key plot lines. Macbeth can't cope with the high status demands made of him by his wife while the two tramps *perceive* a life outside their low status predicament but are unable to break their enslavement. We can play endlessly with status to explore our aspirations. THE KING GAME works on status interactions by establishing one extremely powerful figure and some powerless fools. If the fools can live comfortably with their power-lessness, their lack of status becomes fun, an excuse to break rules. If they can't take this step, the game is always a struggle. The exercise can be played in different ways, for example to explore low status tactical play – here the emphasis is placed on how 'low status experts' use cunning and flattery to get their way. Or it can be played to learn about use of space in status interactions. What behaviour (and use of space) does a high status player expect from everyone else? It can also be used to build scenes based on hierarchical behaviour. I've even known it used as a game which explores performers' fear of the audience. In this case the 'king' – maybe the facilitator – represents the audience. The participant is the performer. If the latter can learn to improvise in front of the former without fear, that's a step forward. Finally, the exercise can simply be used to induct participants into structured improvisation via an easy route.

Children enjoy it because they can show off their imagination, cleverness and versatility. Adults enjoy it because it throws all their fears into one basket. It's releasing to accept the challenge, to 'be killed' and live again. As it runs, it may be useful to ask participants, 'observe what works and what fails'. What is it that makes an intervention succeed or fail? For anyone who plays the king or queen (or Godfather or Tribal Chief or Head Dalek) it's also great fun just having that power of life and death. And especially with children, it's not unusual for the quietest member to volunteer to be king and then hugely enjoy being a complete tyrant. Their decisions about killing will often be quite revealing – it's worth asking them just why they killed people when they did.

ABSOLUTE POWER works in pairs. It gives one player complete domination over the other, only takes away the power of speech. So each player can exploit their partner only to the extent to which they can communicate. It's a kind of master-servant game through a physical medium and can be used as an introduction to exploring power relationships. MASTER SERVANT EXERCISES are useful because once again, there's this double reality; that of the two actors co-operating and that of the master and servant in conflict. Master-Servant exercises can take any number of forms, for example:

1. Servant tries to please master, who finds tasks for them to do. (Contrary to expectation, players find it hard to be the master because of constantly having to invent tasks. So a question for them is – what would you *genuinely* enjoy, that the other could do for you?)

2. Servant tries to subvert the master's position, while at the same time appearing to carry out all the desired tasks (this is hard for the master again – this time they have to learn how to 'unwittingly' encourage the other's subversions.) A simple way to play this version is by having the master sitting on a central chair and two servants either side. The three of them face an audience. The master questions

THE KING GAME

A king or queen is called for, and someone volunteers. That person sits in a chair at one end of the room. The rest of the group sit in a line at the other end, facing the king.

Version One: The king needs people to become members of the court. Each participant gets up in turn and tries to please the king, using any means they choose. If the king is pleased by what they say or do, that individual is allowed into the court. They come and sit with the king. If the king is displeased, the king may kill them. This is done by a click of the fingers and the player must fall down dead, where they are. The king is not obliged to explain or justify their actions. It's important they are quite ruthless.

Variation: The king is a mafia boss, gang leader or tribal chief. He is looking for villains or warriors to join him. But as before, he is under no pressure to accept anybody.

Version Two: The king is played by the facilitator who represents the audience. Each performer may come and entertain the audience, but will always get killed in the end. The facilitator kills to communicate something about where the player is going wrong.

ABSOLUTE POWER

In pairs, one player has to give instructions to the other through physical directions and gestures only. The other is effectively their slave. The slave has to carry out all movements as directed. Then the two switch roles.

them both, only each time he turns away to face one, the other servant makes faces.

3. Servant confesses a sequence of mishaps to the master – or mistress – when they arrive home. The mistress gets incredibly angry but always just manages to reconcile herself to the disaster. BUT the servant then reveals yet another mishap and the cycle turns again. (This is what Johnstone calls 'over-confessing' – each reported mishap was in fact the cause of another, even worse mishap, which is also confessed.)

4. Servants are given servants, so that orders are passed down the hierarchy. Perhaps the servants are given numbers – One, Two, Three and Four. Rolled up newspapers are given to One, Two and Three to

enable them to help things along, i.e.beat hell out of the person below them in the hierarchy. One speaks only to Two, Two speaks only to One and Three, while Three speaks only to Two and Four. The most unfortunate appears to be the one at the bottom of the pile but after running it, it's often observed how the two in the middle have to work the hardest. This is because they get all the pressure from the top but can't actually guarantee that the tasks are completed. ('I'm sorry, Number One, I really can't explain why the chairs haven't been stacked in a pyramid yet!') Probably Number Four has given up worrying, and is dossing about. The exercise is best played with tasks sent down the line that can genuinely be fulfilled – there's little point asking for a three course meal in a rehearsal room.

THE SELLOTAPE GAMES and CLINT EASTWOOD are constructed around the observation that we often take on the status that is given to us. If we're treated like a child, we tend to behave like one after a while. We may start to unconsciously accept others' negative projections about who we are. These exercises theatricalise that social process. We set it up so that each player's identity is determined not by themselves but by the other players. CLINT is derived from Eastwood's technique of making his character look dangerous by having all the *other* characters in his scene behave *as if he was* dangerous – diving under tables when he walks in, trembling with fear, moustaches quivering, etc. He becomes dangerous not by anything *he* does but by *their* projecting on to him a high status, dangerous quality (he can choose whether they live or die). The cheroot or the spitting heightens this effect by showing his contempt for their servility. CLINT is a good scene to run if, as in the Johnstone anecdote given later, a participant is having difficulty experiencing different emotional states. For during the exercise, the participant experiences the full force of the group's projections. This not only tends to provoke feeling (heightened because the actor doesn't know what's coming and so can't anticipate), but also demonstrates how powerful a group's behaviour can be. It's important to ask the central actor afterwards about the experience; how the different group behaviours were *perceived* and what was felt in response to them.

THE SELLOTAPE GAMES by contrast don't have a central character but run as a kind of role play with everyone participating simultaneously. In THE SELLOTAPE GAMES nobody knows 'who they are' – only who everyone else is, or so they believe. This allows

CLINT EASTWOOD

Some of the group make up an audience. The rest are drinkers in a bar, just chatting and drinking. There is an established sequence which is followed each time the scene is played. They chat – the single actor walks in – and everybody reacts. Their reactions are rehearsed, and are set by instruction rather than by 'how the actor walks in.' For example, the first time the actor walks in, everyone hides under the table and the barman is very nervous asking the actor what he wants to drink. The second time everyone treats him like a pariah, whispering and pointing. The third time, they salute. Different variations can be invented. The single actor should try to understand their role, and play along.

THE SELLOTAPE GAMES

A social situation is devised where a group of people are going to interact. For example, it's a party or a conference of some kind. The facilitator writes out a number of labels which will be attached to the foreheads of the participants. This will enable others to see the label, but the wearer will not know the content. For example, the labels might simply be marked with a number between 1 and 10, to designate a status. 1 is high and 10 low. Or they may be given 'social' labels such as 'Bully', 'Flirt', 'Failure', 'Alcoholic', 'Star' or professional labels, 'Doctor', Rock Star', etc. Then the role play is begun and the party or gathering commences. The players should not indicate to each other what they observe, but treat people in the manner of their label. It is for each participant to discover what their label is, through others' reactions. Once discovered, they should play along with their 'typecasting' (or they may choose to play against it.) The facilitator can choose to issue instructions – e.g. asking participants to team up with those who they feel an affinity with towards the end, or acting out 'to the full' their characteristic.

individual players to find their characters not through working up an idea internally but by studying others' reactions. You find out who you are by observing and listening. You accept these projections and build a character accordingly. In feedback, it may be useful to ask people *before* they take the sellotape off how they arrived at their interpretations. It may be useful to ask questions like: 'Who – or what status – do you think you are?' 'How did you feel when you realised you were high status/low status?' Natural high status players in life may have resented discovering their status was low. Low status players will tend to guess their status level to be lower than it was because they interpret deference as people being tolerant towards them. There's scope for the facilitator to cast against type to provoke these disjunctions. Follow-up impros might transplant these newly discovered characters – with their appropriate statuses – into different situations. So the addict can be sent to visit his friends in Needle Park or the pompous doctor invited to give a lecture to the rest of the group.

In the situation of someone getting seriously stuck – i.e. they find they just cannot move outside their habitual status – they can be coached in a more technical way. For it may be they are blocking certain inner feeling. So they're told where to look or how to stand. Johnstone, a great status expert, records the following: *'Another student refused to play high status in anything but a wooden manner. He said that he lived in a working-class area and that he didn't want to be stuck-up. I explained that I wasn't trying to remove his present skills, but only to add a few new ones . . . I asked him to play a scene in which he was to tell his father he had VD. I chose the scene to stir him up and involve his real feelings . . .* (Johnstone describes how the actor tries – and fails – to engage. Finally Johnstone 'choreographs' his movements.) *I stopped him. I explained that if he turned from the window, looked at his father and didn't move his head, then he'd experience exactly the sensations he was trying to avoid. I said that he mustn't try to suppress the head movements but to be aware when he does them.'*[27] This approach worked because the teacher dislodged the student's habitual pattern. For such habitual postures enforce a control over internal feelings. By changing the posture of the student in a very deliberate way, the teacher triggered a feeling response which normally would have been repressed. With the control mechanism – the old posture – no longer in place, the body opens to new sensations. At an earlier stage of life such postures were perhaps functionally defensive – but now they won't shift even after the need for defence is gone. So it takes that mechanical, deliberate manipulation to 'open up' to the present. Some may complain this approach to drama is inauthentic because it works by fixing the 'outer' to influence the 'inner' but validation may lie in the fact that it can work where other strategies fail.

BULLY-VICTIM-SAVIOUR can also be played as a role play with everyone interacting ad hoc. If preferred, it can also be run in smaller

BULLY / VICTIM / SAVIOUR

First stage: The group members are given an attribute; to be bullying, victimised or rescuing. They move around the space as per their social role. Sometimes they team up with others, or else they pursue their vocation. Bullies look for victims to bully (it may be appropriate to make a rule of 'no physical contact'), saviours look for victims to rescue and victims wait around looking for support.

Second Stage: The group is divided into sub-groups of three. Each team is asked to invent a scene (or is given a scene by the facilitator) where there is victimisation. For example, the car has broken down just after the family set off on holiday. There is Dad, the daughter and her boyfriend. In their own space, the team explore all the different roles. Firstly the scene is cast with Player A as the Dad, B the daughter, C the boyfriend. Secondly, they decide the variation to play first. For example, Player A (Dad) is the bully, Player B (daughter) is the victim and Player C (boyfriend) is the rescuer. They improvise the scene. Then they swap roles – but not their parts. Player A is still the Dad, but this time he's the rescuer while the daughter victimises her boyfriend. She blames him for the breakdown. The last variation will be Dad as victim, boyfriend as bully and daughter as rescuer. Each therefore has had a chance to try each social role.

Extension: one or all of the different scenes is brought back for the rest of the group to watch. Which role did you feel most comfortable in? And which role did you feel least comfortable in?

groups. It deals with a particularly negative but not especially uncommon cycle of power relations. I don't believe it's a great deal more prevalent in one age group than another, it may be that adults tend to find more sophisticated guises for it. Running it with teenagers, for whom it's often appropriate, it can stimulate discussion and learning around issues of bullying. Questions to be asked might include 'Which part did you play most comfortably?' 'Did the audience make the same observation?' 'Where have you seen this kind of bullying behaviour in everyday behaviour?' As with many exercises, BULLY can place the emphasis on social skills learning, or on performance.

NOTES ON DEVISING IN SMALL GROUPS

A common practice is for the group to divide and sub-groups to go off to prepare short scenes for performance. Usually the group is given some kind of starter instruction: a theme, idea or narrative structure. Dorothy Heathcote always argues for such thematic catalysts to be expressed in sentences which are grammatically exact. They must, she argues, be shaped precisely to stimulate the imagination. If this isn't done, you can find yourself calling everyone back a few minutes later. Of course not all ideas are appropriate for this kind of devising; some are essentially filmic or literary. Some suggestions to avoid might include:

Themes which are too broad: slavery, the House of Commons, youth culture, street life, old age.

Themes which are too remote: the Potsdam Conference, the Battle of Hastings, obscure diseases of the seventeenth century, hare coursing.

Themes which belong in a different medium: loneliness, alienation, the pain of separation, the dreams of a young farmworker.

Dramatic situations which are given in such detail there's little scope for interpretation. 'There's a mother and her son and the son's girlfriend. Do a scene where the girlfriend comes in unexpectedly, so the mother gets angry . . . '

What is required is a stimulus to the group's imagination which provides both an anchor and scope for invention. We need a combination of something that's fixed – which gives security – and something that's free – to provide expressive scope. The stimulus could be a theme, a narrative outline or a title. Here are some recent examples of stimuli which I've found effective:

The theme is Accusations. In this scene, someone must accuse someone else of something. But because of what happens next, the accuser has to back down. The context is domestic.

A title: 'The Unexpected Guest.' Explore firstly why that person has arrived unexpectedly and what the reactions are, of people who are present.

The theme is Status. In this scene, someone should start 'high
status' and end up 'low status', while the second person in the
scene moves in the other direction. What causes this to
happen?

The setting is a beach. A couple arrive and separately, a single
person. By the end of the scene, the single person leaves with
one of the couples. How could that happen?

Some titles: 'The End of the Party', 'Cowardice', 'The Straw that
Broke the Camel's Back', 'This time she said "No".'

The second area where we can get into difficulties is what happens
within the sub-groups. There's no facilitator present to monitor and
supervise so the more confident may bully the diffident. It's done with
a 'my idea is better than yours' argument, and perhaps the better idea
gets short shrift. Or group members can try so hard to please each
other that they end up with a poor compromise. Nevertheless, it's
probably a mistake to intervene. It's essentially and necessarily an
unsupervisable process. This is the group's opportunity to make
decisions away from the facilitator's prying curiosity.

Having said that, it's necessary to monitor progress from a distance.
If a sub-group has reached an impasse or they're having a row, the
signs are usually evident. If I do intervene, I might sit on the floor. I
have to listen to all the conflicting ideas before I can make suggestions.
Then I look for a possible *linkage* of any competing ideas. Let's imagine
it's going to be scene in a park. Someone wants a knife fight. Someone
wants an old person to get chatted up. Is it possible these two ideas can
be linked? If not, it may be necessary to choose between competing
ideas. Which idea fulfils the brief more effectively? It may be that the
quietest person in the group has the best idea, and what's required is
she needs to be given support. So the facilitator's job is to argue her
case and help others see its potential. The idea of a tea party sounds
boring but if it's about trying to find tea bags in house rubble after a
nuclear fall-out, it might be worth a try.

Or the sub-group might be having difficulties because they can't
take the plunge. They have a brave idea but are hesitant. So advice
on how to make the idea dramatic may be useful for although the
scene will be 'exposing' in some way, this may lend it a real energy.
Finally, a few questions. Does the idea fit the brief? Does everyone have
a part or some role to play? Is the idea dramatic? It isn't essential

for everyone in the sub-group to perform if extra performers weaken the piece.

The third area of difficulty is around 'rehearsals'. Generally I find that rehearsals in this situation are counter-productive. They mimic the traditional rehearsal without allowing time for reassessment. They siphon off initial spontaneity without allowing for discovery of depth within the scenario. We want the key discoveries to be made in front of a live audience. If it goes horribly wrong, we can always stop and start again. But if it's been rehearsed, the temptation may be, if it went well, to try and repeat that rehearsal. Or if it went badly, the group panics and wants to start all over. Better to spend the time marking out your stage area and maybe walking through the scene. Not acting but establishing that, for example, 'Bet enters here as the mother, Kathy as the daughter is sitting in this chair and Paulo is lying in bed over there. Then he gets up and – hey, where's the blanket, we need something for a blanket?' Community actors often resort to mime, but lack the skills. Better to find something which can serve for the blanket. 'Oh yes, and we need some lead piping.' So let's use a rolled up magazine. So rather than rehearse, think instead about stage management, cues, entrances and how the action moves forward. In other words, think objectively about what you will later perform subjectively. It will also be necessary to decide how the piece is to be staged: whether in-the-round, traverse or proscenium. It's often a strong move for the facilitator to give an instruction on staging at the very beginning.

Come the performance, the actors can take liberties with their material. Hopefully they will have built an infra-structure which provides enough security for them to commit to the scene emotionally. It's about the body's nervous system responding openly to the stimuli for the first time – that's what we want to capture in front of an audience. Emotions are triggered which can never be shown again in that way. If the player is emotionally open, there's an honesty in the playing which lends an unforced, theatrical quality. Of course, it can still fail horribly. 'Oh God,' someone will say, 'if you'd let us rehearse . . . '

But time permitting, it's possible to look at the problems. We can deconstruct the scene so the learning involves everyone. In this way, the apparent 'failure' may be a great opportunity for learning something about how theatre operates: character dynamics, tension, conflict. These are some questions that might be asked about why a particular scene 'didn't work':

Was the original idea *playable?* Did it have potential for conflict and action?

Would it work better in a different *location?* Or at a different *time?* Given the narrative line, are we seeing the most dramatic moments?

Are the group members playing to their strengths? Or have they been over-ambitious in *casting* themselves against type?

How did the group members *work together?* Are they fighting each other? Are they blocking each other? Are they allowing each other freedom of movement?

Is there *narrative development?* Does the scene move, does it travel, do the characters make a journey however small, or are we at the same point at the end of the scene as we were at the beginning?

Is there *tension* in the scene? Were there colours, moments of stillness contrasting with moments of energy?

How was the *space used?* Has any thought gone into the relationship with the audience? Is there any direct address which can lift a scene?

A common mistake is for players to rush their scene so it lacks tension. They over-talk, thinking the space must be filled by words, words, words and more words. So we might look at how spoken words can either contribute to or diminish dramatic tension. Let's re-run the scene without words.

Or there may be too much movement. Let's place the actors in a fixed tableau and have them play the scene 'still'. What if we take out some of the characters, those who may be surplus? What if the scene is played much, much more slowly? What happens, how does it change? What if someone steps forward and gives a commentary to the audience beforehand? Or even just a title?

Probably the spectators have been involved in this analysis. They are likely to see unfulfilled potential in the scene that the actors have missed. But we don't want negative criticism, this would be too easy. The spectators – as well as the actors – need to be challenged during this process of assessment. 'If you were directors', one might ask, 'what instructions might you give to the actors before we run the scene again?' 'What would you like to see more of, in the scene?' Such questions prompt the audience towards more constructive contributions.

Some scenarios perform well straight off. Everything seems to fit together. There's passion, co-ordination and intelligence. After scenes like this, there's applause then a silence. But perhaps we should discuss the scene anyway. What made it work? What were the actors doing together to help each other? What made the fireworks soar?

FOUR VOCABULARIES:
MOVEMENT, IMAGE, PLOT, NARRATIVE

This section assumes the group is now working well together and is ready for more serious challenges. The new block is divided into four areas, four different vocabularies or perhaps dialects within the same language. These are not hermetically sealed from each other but instead each one places stress on a different aspect of the performer's capability. Movement is rooted in physicality while Imagework draws from imagination and memory. Plot relies on enacted incident and Narrative places emphasis on storytelling. In complete expressions of performance, all these elements cohere together, but for training purposes there are benefits in examining them separately.

MOVEMENT
Of course all drama work requires movement, but these exercises *begin* with the physical impulse. The body houses all our capacities: intelligence, memory, fears, imagination. It has its sectors, its departments, its animate peripheries as well as its unreachable centre. Too often the body is simply 'lived in', a host which is more feared than understood. It's viewed as an unruly possession which needs to be kept in line rather than as an associate with its own intelligence. This idea of a body with an intelligence which requires respect and needs to be understood is conceptualised by Arnold Mindel as the 'dreambody'. Mindel argues that the dreambody cannot be seen as the physical body can but its effects can be seen – *'in body images, rituals and physical therapies'.*[28] It is that body which is mobilised by our inner, psychic dreaming. Its movements are unconscious but they can be brought into consciousness by specific techniques. Through the application of these, which involve placing a brake on our conscious, directed intelligence, we can begin to release physical movement which is characteristically impulsive, fluid and ambiguous in meaning.

The techniques to stimulate movement of this kind are not necessarily complicated. Copying for example, cedes control over our movements to others. When we copy, we give ourselves over to being directed so the body relaxes. It gets time off from constantly supervising its action regime. We're released from decisions about how to move and what to say. Part of our psychic space is, as it were, freed up, and in the emptiness created movements which are not consciously organised may be allowed to emerge. After copying, we may be more open to inner impulses. It's as if the long-distance lorry driver, after driving non-stop for twenty-five years, finds he can hand over to automatic pilot at last. The effect is enormously liberating. He rediscovers something of his true feelings and aspirations in the subsequent relaxation.

As we know, copying is at the heart of our learning culture, children discover their rules and language this way. Charlie Chaplin's man/boy copied those around him – the effect is comic because physically he's no longer a boy. Woody Allen's character Zelig, lacking an identity himself, became like others around him, grew a beard with the Orthodox Jews, became Hitlerian with the Nazi Youth. Copying is an emblematic consequence of our need for identity. Our porous nature means we constantly absorb gestures and mannerisms from each other. So by consciously copying in a drama context we open ourselves up to learn from each other more quickly, it's a way of casting off the baggage of our individual identities and leaving ourselves open to the group spirit. We become more receptive to different sensations and feelings.

The simplest way to start is by creating pairs then walking the space, a leader and a led. First, the leader – Sue – just walks, the other – Dane – copies. Dane tries to find Sue's walk, her pace, her rhythm. Then different instructions can be fed in. For example, the leader might be encouraged to explore different movements. Or the follower can be asked to improvise on what they see or to exaggerate what they see. Guy Dartnell says about copying that it's *'an easy source of inspiration . . . It gets people away from "What am I going to do?" It also starts people thinking physically because they're observing a physical action. So it gets people aware of what bodies can do. From the point of view of the person who is being copied, my only instruction is only "Do whatever you feel – the only thing you* don't *have to do is make up any words or make up any story." What's also important if you're to link into* emotional *inspiration is to take them away from the notion they have to make a story, which would take them into their heads. Don't think about "what would happen", just move and make sounds. Then I stop them at any point and ask the followers what it is that makes it easy and what makes it difficult to follow. What you tend to find is that leaders only do things for a short amount of time because they think the followers will get bored but what you often hear from the followers is that they prefer it if they continue something for a long time. Then when the leaders do that, they start to realise there is something there that can be developed. They also learn that if you repeat a sound or a movement over and over again, you start to learn what the emotion of that sound is.'* With patience, discoveries are made. And from this basic equation – one follows one – others are possible; for example, we can move into chorus work by making a four. One leader still, but now three followers. For co-ordination it needs to be a diamond shape; this way three can easily see one. Now the leader is told they can resign the leadership by simply turning inwards towards the others. This places someone else at the cutting edge of the diamond. As they practise, the players discover that leadership carries responsibilities. If they set off hurtling around the room, the complicity is destroyed. The point is to lead and *to be able to be followed*. Complicated hand movements in front of the body cannot be followed because they cannot be seen. So the leader is compelled to think dualistically, not just of self but of others, not just how it's fun to move but how the followers can stay in touch. Before long it's possible to use this technique secretly, within scenes. There's a group watching television: the tension of the match appears to be heightened because as the match prompts different reactions, the reactive gestures echo around the room. At the top of a high building someone is about to throw themselves to their death. Spectators gather; secretly they're playing the same copying game, only it isn't visible to an audience. The spectators observe good ensemble work, but the basic performative tasks are very simple.

Once the idea of copying is understood, it can be applied in different ways for different situations. For example, if a group feels uncomfortable with the exercise of individual leadership, an exercise like FRENCH TELEPHONE subtracts the element of leadership, relying instead on amplification of peripheral movements within a group situation. The group stands in a circle, two arms lengths between each. Then the facilitator has to work out where the telephone lines will run. We need for everyone in the group to be linked (see over). Either this can be worked out mathematically – or if you want a quicker way, then each player points to another who must point to someone else across the circle, but this needs monitoring to ensure the copiers are far enough apart from the copied.

The facilitator might be in or outside the game. If inside, they have to play by the same rules, in which case when instructions are fed in, the words used to give these instructions are not to be repeated. However the instructions *are* to be acted on. After the game has run a few minutes, movements are being echoed and amplified around the circle. Then different instructions might be fed in. For example, 'Exaggerate the copying – copy every movement you see, only copy it bigger!' Or: 'Make it rhythmic!' After it's been running a while, an optional strategy is to tailor instructions to capitalise on what's already happening within the group. For example, there might be qualities bubbling under the surface which can be expressed more consciously. The instruction might be: 'Make the copying more grotesque' or 'Make the copying more sexual.' Once the exercise has a momentum, there's the option of transferring it laterally away from its starting point. For example, the group movement suggests witches at a coven. So the instruction comes: 'You are now witches . . . ' and we break away from the formality of the exercise to consciously develop a physical-isation of coven life. Or the group turns into Nazi stormtroopers, or lost children at a rock festival or . . .

Phelim McDermott and Guy Dartnell have worked together exten-sively to explore the potential of copying. Exercises are used: a kind of crucible within which to 'cook up' characters, group scenes or storylines. If strands do emerge, they can always be extrapolated for other purposes. One central exercise is called THE GAME which *'is basically where you get up on stage, two people might get up or ten people might. And a movement might start. And then everyone does that movement. You're aiming for a place where no one is leading. Or everyone is leading and simultaneously everyone is following. It's like trying to get on some kind of surfboard where you're being carried along. And you play where it appears the movement, or the sound and movement, goes to. Now within that, you have to give that out to the audience. The very act of look-ing out to the audience, while you're simultaneously aware of everyone else in a group of ten, involves an awareness of the development of peripheral vision.'* As described here, there are watchers as well as performers. Perhaps the easiest way to start would be, assuming the group to be five strong, for one person to lead at the outset, while others follow. Then the leadership shifts to others in turn. Then at a certain point, no one

FRENCH TELEPHONE

The group stands in a circle. Players are to focus on another individual across the circle from themselves. We need to get to the point where e.g. A points at D, D at B, B at E, E at C and C at A. Everyone is linked. Then the group is instructed to 'do nothing' – however, *if* the person you're watching does any kind of movement, however small or involuntary, it *must* be copied. What happens is, all movements will become echoed around the circle.

Extension: The facilitator can feed in instructions which inform how the copying is carried out. For example by asking for the copying to be bigger or more grotesque or more rhythmic or more sexual.

THE (COPYING) GAME

The game starts by a group of people coming out from the audience and beginning movements which involve them copying each other. The aim is to establish a physical momentum which allows for there to be no evident leadership. It might begin by deliberately passing the leadership amongst the group – or by going straight away to shared leadership. The group might start sitting or standing, facing the audience, or facing in towards each other. The facilitator may periodically encourage the participants to share what's happening between them, with the audience.

leads. Or alternatively, the group starts as a circle facing inwards and all copy from each other straight away. With the audience element in place, they may be asked to *"give it to the audience" so they might look out to the audience, then come back to each other. There might be moments when you find yourself at the front of the group and you've got eight people behind you. You don't really know what they're doing. So part of you has to guess or be intuitive about what's happening . . . And also ultimately it's about opening up the emotional centre. What tends to happen is people get stuck doing things at the edge of their body, doing sounds with their hands or feet. Unemotional, a little bit safer. So in terms of training you would say, "Fill in the centre, let the sound come from the centre more, use your spine more."* ' Phelim McDermott.

MIRRORS is a well established copying game, which is normally played in pairs. There are different ways to play it. Perhaps the mistake is to play it like a mime, with people brushing their teeth, hair etc.

When this happens, the players have to work overtime to 'think up' good ideas which soon become exhausted. Better to play it either (1) with each player co-ordinating the movements so the mirroring player keeps more-or-less the exact same pace as the leader, or (2) with the mirror player echoing the 'emotional spirit' of the other's movement but not worrying about mirroring movements exactly. Instead, the player concentrates on reproducing the quality of feeling and the general physical shape. It's useful to be clear with the instructions at the outset what is required. With the second approach, the leaders are asked to project an emotional quality on to their mirror. 'Whatever you feel at this moment' – the facilitator might say – 'show it. And if your feeling changes – show that new feeling.' After all, emotion never stays consistent. So if the player becomes bored or anxious or frightened during the exercise, they should project those feelings of boredom or anxiety. Whatever they feel, in other words, they bring into play. This helps to encourage the idea that feelings belong *inside* the exercises not outside of them. There is no such thing as an inappropriate feeling – everything is fine as long as it's actively projected. In playing the exercise, you might argue that the projecting player is merely communing with themselves, because they are looking at their own reflection. They project a movement, then react to that movement as they observe it. What is felt subjectively returns objectively. 'How does it make you feel to see yourself? Show what you feel about yourself.' Again, the facilitator may wish to inject commands encouraging concentration, suggesting more energy, going deeper with the exercise. Boal's use of this exercise involves a set sequence of commands which must be followed in a certain pattern – the mirrors become rhythmic, they shatter, each player finds a new partner and so on. But each facilitator may prefer to conduct their own journey, tailoring it to the needs of their particular group.

The exercise can be extended into GROUP MIRRORS. Here one player faces a multiple image of themselves. It's as if their personality were divided into several parts – and they confront all those parts. If played in the second, 'free' version (see above), the exercise increases this sense of the player exploring a dialogue with the (multiple) self, especially when the movements are fast and the mirror movements are slightly 'behind'. So by the time a movement is reflected back, the leader can see those movements *as if* they were were generated outside of themselves. They can react to them as they choose, with disgust,

MIRRORS

Players stand opposite each other, forming two facing lines. At first, players down one line will be the leaders/projectors, their opposite partners will be mirrors. The mirror function involves reproducing the other's movement 'as if' they were the image in a mirror. In the second stage, they will change roles. The third stage involves neither leading, but each 'taking' from the other – so the leadership function is shared between them.

Version One: Involves the leader doing movements which allow for quite exact mirroring.

Version Two: Involves the leader projecting movement with a stronger emphasis on emotional qualities, and less emphasis on movements which can be copied exactly.

GROUP MIRRORS

One player stands opposite a group of five or six, who assemble in a huddle. The exercise works best in the spirit of Version Two above, with the lead player developing a dialogue with the self image. Other players can then replace the first.

THE GROUP COPIES

The facilitator instructs the group that whatever he says, the group must say – and whatever he does, the group must do. However, the words and actions are 'answered' rather than copied simultaneously. The facilitator then moves the group around the room, dialoguing with them while the copying pattern is maintained.

Extension: the leadership function might be handed over – if it's accepted, or it might be seized.

pleasure, amazement or whatever. If the player can let themselves go sufficiently, the exercise becomes a naked self-examination through movement; a dialogue with the externalised self. It's also possible to give different instructions to each of the copyers so one is more timid, another more aggressive in their copying, and so on.

Jonathan Kay uses copying to take the group through an emotional landscape. He leads and everyone in the group follows. It might start in a circle then move to a line or a huddle, then to a swarm moving about the room. Kay explores the paradoxes which arise in the exercise. The paradoxes emerge because questions or statements made by him, return, and these he then answers. The answers also return. For example, if he as the facilitator has the group in a circle and he talks to the person on his left, the person on his right will also speak to him. Turning back to reprimand the person on the right for interrupting, the person on his left reprimands him. So we soon find ourselves in a territory which is beyond sense, which is foolish. If participants allow themselves to engage with this foolishness, the trip will be fun. Endless, and fun. *'Everybody copies . . . because once that's established, you get a tremendous sense of community.'* Some however may find this difficult. *'But underneath you get a sub-text going on – "How long is he going to be doing this for" or whatever – you can clearly define that sub-text. That's commentary. But the fool does not do that. The fool goes "I'm involved." When you're involved you're totally involved, you're just copying away . . . "What do you mean 'when am I going to stop?' What a question. "When am I going to die?" But if the dictator becomes stronger than the fool, then your arms begin to ache and you want to sit down.'* In Kay's approach, the exercise is one of several which are intended to release a foolish aspect within the performers. Through copying, we learn to take less interest in 'what happens', more interest in playing for its own sake. We begin to worry less about being 'correct', 'inventive', 'a good actor' and so on and instead, start to go with the flow. We give up monitoring our own behaviour so much; in this case, we have no need to do so because all decisions about how we move and what we say are taken by another. In this way we become less afraid of content, because all content begins to get looked at in the same light – simply as a varying challenge. What's important is to retain an attitude of 'not minding'. We care less being seen badly in this light, or ridiculous doing that. It's just more play.

The facilitator may pass the leadership to another – or sometimes the leadership is seized. And for the exercise to truly work the facilitator must be prepared to cede some control. Firstly, you must be willing to cede control to inner impulses. *'As the person taking it, you must go through as many emotional things as you possibly can. The group will always reflect you, but you are also reflecting them to an extent. (You must go) to the point of not wanting to do it – then wanting to do it again. You must be on a journey of self-discovery – because they will discover much more about themselves if you're prepared to discover yourself.'* As a facilitator you may be frightened to 'relinquish' control in this way. It may feel awkward to have no direction in mind. But if the group feels that you're too dictatorial in your leadership, they may be reluctant to enter into the spirit of the exercise. Your lack of spontaneity results in their lack of trust. Secondly, you may choose to cede control by allowing another leader to take over – hoping they will take the group on a different journey. However, this second leader must lead consciously or the game fragments.

Jonathan Kay uses copying in a further way; by placing one player within the circle, then having a dialogue with them. As he does this, others in the circle copy him vocally and physically. This technique removes the tendency of the individual to 'repeat back' what has been asked. 'How do you feel?' 'How do I feel?' and so on. Because the question has already been repeated back by the copiers, there's no impulse to repeat it again. This time the journey is made through the dialogue between the group and the self-elected individual. The focus of exploration, the territory of the journey, is the individual's experiences. The dialogue may be conducted in words or actions or both. It can move in many directions. However it goes, the central idea is to use the power of the chorus/audience/dictators to stimulate different feelings in the central player/fool. *'The dictators are around the circle and the unprotected fool is in the middle. And of course if I move, then the circle moves and as we move that makes you (the central player) feel different. It moulds you, makes you move differently. If we all get down on the floor, this makes you as an actor feel different. Because that's the audience doing that. It helps you realise that all the time the audience are moulding the way you feel. So you feel more relaxed. It liberates. And if you start feeling like you're falling off the edge, people can come and hold you and touch you. But that has to be taken sensitively.'*

IMAGE

Perhaps a better title than the often used 'imagework' would be 'imageplay'. After all, the essence is all about 'playing with' the images created. When working with movement, the starting point is the physical impulse, whereas in imagework, the starting point is the (imagined) picture. While movement is all fluidity, imagework recognises that much can be broken down into components. (However, we recognise that once a still image is animated, the performers enter a dimension of movement while movement itself can always be dismantled into separate images. It's in the starting points that there are differences.) Imagework lends itself to a more discursive, polemical process. There's more we can discuss and argue about. We can bring subject matter into the room, and work with that material quite precisely, looking for ways to encapsulate our feelings and ideas in images. If we wish we can even discuss the material solely 'within the language of image'.

Augusto Boal speaks of 'the language of image' as a territory with its own laws. This territory is distinct, there's scope within it to explore our feelings of loss, anger, difficulty and hopes for the future more concisely than we could in any other medium. Furthermore, we are closer here to understanding how these feelings can be linked to social conflicts outside ourselves. The language of this territory is quickly and easily learnt. It's accessible, which is particularly important for those who lack literary or linguistic skills. Once the rudiments are mastered – see below – we begin with our memories, our desires and our dreams, translating these into the aesthetic language. Then we play with these images in that territory; experimenting, hypothesising, juxtaposing before retranslating back into our everyday vocabulary. Hopefully the return is characterised by an enriched understanding both of our feelings – how they are generated – and our capacity for acting differently on them in the world outside. The aesthetic territory has served as a double for the social.

Yet the process is not prescriptive. The process is not about getting 'answers' or 'recipes for action' in any simplistic way as commentators on Boal's work occasionally assume. It's about using imagery to express what cannot be captured in other ways. An image may contain a paradox more dynamically than a spoken sentence. On the stage there's a man pinning another man down with a chair, there's a woman shouting on a riverbank, there's a man talking to a pig, there's a woman in a devil costume enticing some holiday-makers. These images are often ambiguous in meaning. It cannot be *assumed* that working with such images we will reach an enlightenment about our human predicament or know how to improve it. But we might feel more confident we have better stated that predicament. And in exploring the image, we might well be able to comment on the situation from which it's been extrapolated. It would be naive to assume that what exists within this 'language of image' cannot be extrapolated without some loss of the ambiguity which is so characteristic of the image. That would be like imagining, when you're dreaming, you could take the money you won from the dream into the real world. So in imagework, you just can't say 'It was the knife in her hand which made the man submit (in the improvisation) . . . therefore we must use knives to deal with aggressive men.' It may not be appropriate to draw that deduction. The knife may have represented a more ambiguous idea than simply violent revenge. Its aptness on stage cannot insist we take up arms. Imagework is not susceptible to reductionism in this literal way.

Once this relationship between the idea or theme – and its embodiment as image – is understood, there opens up considerable scope for risk-taking. For example, we can begin with one person's subjective experience and through 'pluralising' it, create group material. For example, someone has an image. It's my image – of when I was mugged or when my girlfriend rejected me. In putting it forward, I also give it up in some way. Obviously it's still 'mine' but as in all acts of giving, there's now a measure of responsibility on the group – the receivers – to respect it. It's probably good that I've given it away, especially if it's something I formerly held in secret. Now the group may react in a variety of ways. The image may provoke, surprise or animate them or it may provoke revelations from them – but in some way or other, it's become their property. This is especially true if they alter it. They may change the image, add new elements or perhaps refine it because there's something in there they recognise. We're operating therefore along the axis of the individual/collective polarities. We're moving from the individual experience towards the group experience and hoping to embody the result in an image, or in several images.

However, we don't have to work from one individual's personal experience. After all, with some groups it may be inappropriate to pursue these contributions. Group members may feel shy or nervous about coming forward. There's another way to work: by running exercises which generate content more abstractly. Perhaps it has the same end result, but the process doesn't put people on the spot so much. We can still arrive at key themes – bullying, sexuality, authority, fear of persecution – but we haven't gone directly via personal experiences. Nor have we made the assumption that everyone is 'oppressed' which is a kind of yardstick sometimes felt inappropriate. An alternative approach can involve talking more generally about difficulties in life, being mistreated or being disallowed from fulfilling oneself. This way, we can simply proceed 'blind'. Without any given subject matter at all, we work with a blank sheet of paper and light will always be shed on participants' personal situations. It's inevitable that this is so, even if they are consciously copying from films or plays.

In other words, we provide a different kind of focus, which is the form of the exercise itself. This approach – putting form before content – helps us from being too controlling or censoring of our own productivity. Instead, our inner impulses are allowed to make the decisions.

To summarise then, there are two different ways of generating dramatic imagery within a group (although they often overlap):

1. To deliberately render subject matter into an image, perhaps drawing from personal experiences. From there, to explore this subject matter through different techniques.

2. To create imagery without thought of subject matter; proceeding spontaneously, ignorantly. From there to identify the subject matter created.

An example of the first approach might be MY DILEMMA, in which a single actor makes an image expressing a personal dilemma. An example of the second might be THE MODEL SEES where an actor is sculpted into a position and then spontaneously 'discovers' who they are and what they're doing.

But first of all we need to learn the essential tools of imagework which are used in either process. This allows the group to start handling knives and heat before actually cooking. Then we can take any direction we choose. An easy way is to divide the group into pairs, and have each player 'sculpt' another. The basic technique of sculpting is easy to learn, it can be done in a matter of seconds. The sculptor's hands twist and shape the model's body, as if the model was plasticine. Those with limited dexterity can 'instruct' how they want the model to stand or sit. It's a matter of judgement how far you go into detail. Manipulation of the face is possible if the model is happy with that. A fallback position is to simply demonstrate the pose. Then the sculptor steps back to look at the effect created. Does it have a clarity? Is it human? Of course an idea can simply be described, and someone embody it – but sculpting is more tactile and instinctive, circumventing the cerebral.

Then the two players can swap roles and the former model becomes the sculptor. Once the exercise is completed, a variation might involve the sculptor lightly touching different parts of the model's body. On

MY DILEMMA

Someone in the group comes forward and chooses two or three others to be in her image. She sculpts them into an image which represents a current or recent dilemma. The image can be representational or symbolic.

THE MODEL SEES

In pairs. Partner A sculpts partner B into different shapes. The aim is to find a shape which triggers a certain imaginative quality of feeling. Once the shape is made, A asks B 'Do you feel anything?' If the answer is 'No', A moves them to a different shape and asks again. If the answer is 'yes', A then asks questions: 'What do you see?' 'Where are you?' 'What has just happened?' B may discover they are back inside a scene which they remember well, which they can describe – or they may discover they're a scarecrow or the Statue of Liberty; there is no pressure to be literal.

being touched, that body part moves with an impulse. Taking the exercise further into abstract movement, the model could 'remember' the touching and move of her own accord in the same pattern, with the sculptor watching. In doing any stage of this exercise, the models should be asked to become aware of different feelings within their bodies as their physical positions are altered. 'How do you feel in that shape?' They may be surprised to feel distinct emotions rise to the surface. (The more 'controlled' participants will resist those feelings, or deny their presence.) If a participant *can* acknowledge them, you'll see the body adjust slightly as the body 'accepts' the emotion. The sculptor will be pleased, because the model will be living the sculptor's idea – proving the theory that human bodies are better than stone for conveying expression! Different routes are possible from this point. For example, the model might begin to articulate an imaginative reality, as in THE MODEL SEES. Or the sculptor could shape the model to consciously resemble herself in a former moment of crisis. The sculptor could work with two models to create a scene.

If players have stayed together in pairs, and the group has sufficient numbers, all the models could be lined up for an exercise called THE WHEEL. In this, the group makes two concentric rings, an outer and an inner. Ali Campbell used this in Ford Open Prison to look at themes of fear and freedom: *'The outer ring made an image of freedom, without any discussion and then we could see the connections with the image of fear we had made earlier – hands outstretched (in openness or self-defence?) eyes wide and staring (in honesty or confrontation?) bodies extended and poised (for an embrace or flight?) Using what we actually saw, rather than the duller starting point of a discussion about the nature of freedom, we then looked for fragments of story which might be organised into a meaningful sequence.'*[29]

An alternative strategy to sculpting might be working collectively, group members placing themselves on stage. Perhaps a theme has been introduced for the group to work on; jealousy, betrayal, power, the outsider, fear, unemployment, money – in which case the facilitator calls out the theme and group members get up to place themselves in an image under that heading. This is sometimes called IMAGE OF THE WORD. Or the facilitator may call out a title of a scene such as 'The last straw', 'No escape', 'Reunion'. The work is necessarily illustrative at this stage, but it builds a vocabulary within the group. In fact there are a number of different ways of working collectively like this:

1. The group gets up and spontaneously creates imagery by adding themselves into a single image, perhaps cued by a title from the facilitator.
2. A single individual sculpts a group piece. It might be a scene from memory, or an image to express a given idea.
3. A familiar image, perhaps an archetypal image, is created on the stage by the participants – Christ being nailed to the cross, Dionysus being torn apart.
4. Sub-groups can create imagery amongst themselves and bring them back for the main group to look at. Perhaps all the sub-groups are working on the same theme.
5. Images made by sub-groups can be joined together to make composite images.
6. Individuals make images of themselves in separate parts of the space, which are looked at as one image. An image made of oneself by oneself is sometimes called an autosculpture.

Sooner or later the group wants to see the images come to life. This allows us to 'get inside' the image, to discover the interior life of the imagery. Here the choice of technique is not always obvious; there are

THE WHEEL

After intensive pair work involving a lot of sculpting of one player by another, two concentric circles (the wheel) are formed. The outside ring are the sculptors and the inner ring are models, or sculptures. Then the wheel is turned so the sculptors are opposite others' models. It is their task now to sculpt themselves in response to what they see.

often safety considerations. Images of violence shouldn't be brought to life in a way that might endanger anyone. It may be a question of 'talking around' an image first. Maybe we should assess the group's response to this freeze frame first – why has it been put forward? If it's a moment in someone's story, is this the best point in the story to come in? Nic Fine uses fire imagery to discuss this question analogously. In a context where a participant has put forward an image of extreme violence, this is the fire 'out of control'. Perhaps we should see initially how that fire built to that point. What was happening when the fire was just smouldering? Could we look at the moment at which the fire was ignited? In this way, difficult imagery is always looked at in a context, perhaps a narrative context.

Once we've decided to animate the image, at this point it's irrelevant whether the actors 'know the story' or 'understand the image' because when it moves, they must interpret *as actors* not as directors or playwrights. So whatever they *feel* inside the picture must be their guide rather than what the image creator has told them. Otherwise we might as well ask the creator to write a play for them to speak! This process will allow a more instinctive animation of the image. It's about using actors as actors. Having said this, there are various ways for the actors to become animate. These are as valid for a sub-group working separately as they are for a large group working together:

1. The image may be brought to life by the protagonists finding a phrase or movement or both, from within the piece. The different phrase-movement sequences can be triggered by the facilitator.

2. The group move in slow motion to bring the image to life. There could be a second, desired image which they have to arrive at.

3. The group may improvise from this position. They break out into playing a scene without a conclusion being predetermined.

4. Individual protagonists may speak a commentary while holding their fixed position, as a stream of consciousness 'in character'.

5. Individual protagonists may move away from the image and speak – still in character – to others in the piece, who cannot move or reply.

These are some of the stratagems. A longer list might be created by the introduction of other elements; music, taped commentary, etc. Using them first in a demonstrative way helps the group perceive them as tools they can use later for themselves.

As soon as improvisation starts, the actors have to negotiate with each other to arrive at a shared sense of what is taking place, as they would do in any improvisation. According to how the impro develops, the facilitator may choose to give instructions, or simply let it run. It may be that the apparent reality of the image dissolves and another reality emerges – but unless the actors have been specifically briefed beforehand, this change of direction is their prerogative. What it feels like to be inside an image is often different to how one imagines it to feel, when looking at it from the outside.

Of course it's also possible to change the image not by animating it but by giving it a different *context*. This involves giving information to the spectators about the image, which alters their perception of it. If we have the image of a family relaxing at home, and then we inform the spectators that it's a family in London during the blitz, immediately the spectators take a different attitude towards it. Formerly we perceived the relaxation as contentment. Now perhaps it's escapism, tension or apprehension.

(One issue which invariably comes up during this – or in an exercise like COMPLETE THE IMAGE – concerns the type of images which are presented. I refer to three types, but these could be broken down again into further categories. I use 'abstract', 'representational' and 'projected'. All should be treated cautiously since categorisation can never be entirely clinical. But essentially 'abstract' is without intended meaning, 'representational' is intended to suggest a specific human or animal or inanimate shape or activity, while 'projected' imagery deals with deliberate exaggerations to accentuate a quality of feeling.)

Once a vocabulary is in place and the group is familiar with the basics – everyone has *made* images, *been placed within* images, *responded to* images and *animated* them – then we can use these tools to facilitate more elaborate constructions. Now may be the time to introduce key themes if they haven't been introduced before; crime, bullying, sexual relationships. Or group members may want to introduce personal themes of their own. The role of the facilitator may also shift at this point; it may be necessary to become more challenging and more determined in pursuit of meaningful work. There's movement along the axis of the individual / the collective, and also surface / depth. 'Who can relate to this picture?' 'Do we understand it?' 'If we do, what does it make us think of?' (This is perhaps more useful than, 'So what do you think it is?' which suggests there's an answer we need to 'get right'.) 'Do we all recognise / feel angry about what's happening here?'

Other pictures may be equally clear, we understand their content but they don't speak to us profoundly. We simply recognise them – that's all. I recognise the postman but I don't feel anything about his situation. He inspires nothing in me. Other times a picture is graphic from the first, and perhaps quite moving. 'Do we recognise that picture?' 'Yes, we do.' 'Do we identify with that picture?' 'Yes, we do. It's something a lot of us have felt.' So maybe we can travel somewhere from that picture. People invariably project their experiences on to the imagery placed before them – which is a clear case for allowing and encouraging ambiguity. Sometimes a mistake or a misunderstanding creates an image and everyone goes 'That's the one!' It's emerged quite unintentionally. Perhaps the image-creator intended a swimming scene but the audience saw people drowning. Maybe we then ask 'Could these people be drowning?' Perhaps the observation will stimulate the next exercise. We've moved sideways into a more productive area, albeit we got there accidentally. Ali Campbell suggests that *'the real trick is to know when a particular activity, however simple, has exposed something that resonates on a deeper level – and to stay with it and dig a little deeper rather than hurry on through a desire to fill up every minute with activity.'*

If a *projected* image speaks to all of us – that is, we identify it despite the projection and it moves us then we know the subject matter is important. A projected image might be an unemployment office projected as a trench war between two tired sets of troops. It might be a court room in which the defendant is slowly stripped of his clothes. It might be a woman thinking about her career, standing on the bank of a rushing river – to use three examples I've seen. The facilitator is picking a way through these images, facilitating dialogue and trying to promote some mutual understanding but *also* hunting down the big game; the major themes, the key images.

As the work progresses, more sophisticated techniques can be used. An obvious technique is sequences of images. These function like film frames or cartoons. For example, a personal story can be told through a sequence, or a sub-group prepares a sequence then the other watches it. The initial receiving of the other sub-group's pictures is an important moment; you want the benefit of first impressions – so it's good if preparations are not watched too closely. To help the presentations, Boal has developed what he calls the 'stroboscopic' image which involves the audience closing their eyes while the actors move from one frame to another. So they're in the dark until the actors are in the first image then they open them. Then they close again allowing the actors to move into their second picture, and so on. This helps to eliminate the imagery-which-is-not-part-of-the-imagery; i.e. the actors being themselves, getting into position. The audience only see the essentials.

NARRATIVE IMAGES is a sequencing exercise which makes no prior assumption about content. The group is starting work from a blank sheet of paper. By contrast to the more traditional technique of the sub-group getting together to 'translate' a story into pictures, this operates in reverse. It asks the sub-group to devise a story without knowing what that story is. It's the audience who discovers what the story is, and it tells those who created it. The exercise works because of the audience's inbuilt tendency to piece together stories from fragments, to 'make sense out of things' for themselves. Even where no sense is intended, they cannot help speculating and making assumptions that sense is there. (*L'Ascensore – The Lift* – a show by Pete Brooks discussed later, began life as an exploration of this precise question: how few pieces of information does an audience need to construct a coherent narrative?) Participants are sometimes sceptical about this so they cheat and 'fix' a story in advance. This robs the audience of its gainful employment. Such an exercise is particularly helpful in identifying the key themes for a group, it can mean bypassing some laboured discussions.

NARRATIVE IMAGES

The group divides into sub-groups of roughly equal numbers.
The exercise is explained; the first member of each sub-group will
sculpt the first image in the story. They have an idea in their head,
but they don't explain it to anyone; they merely sculpt. They should
aim towards creating a picture which has a certain momentum. They
sculpt all the other members of their sub-group into the picture,
then they put themselves in the picture. Now everyone has been
given their character – they keep this till the end. Next, the second
sub-group member takes over. They sculpt the second picture in the
story – again, there is no discussion and no consultation over the
content of the story. But they should aim to portray what they
imagine 'would happen next'. As before, they put themselves in the
picture last. This continues for each member of the sub-group.
If there are three or four in the sub-group, they could all do two
pictures each. So, for example, member A does picture 1 and 4
(or 5). Then the sequence is rehearsed.

When it's ready, the sequence is performed for the other group.
The other group, the audience, is asked to make some decisions
about the content of the story, and to say 'what is happening'.
The audience members may also be asked what they think is the
principle theme of the story. So 'interpretation' has happened on
two levels; the narrative and the thematic.

Extension: One way to extend the process, perhaps immediately after
the staging, is for someone to stand up and tell the story as if it was
one they've known for a long time. It's a folk tale, a true story, a
legend, a story in the newspaper.

To conclude this section, here are three further examples of image
exercises, each one serving a different function. MOVING IMAGES
is about encouraging relatedness within the group, IMAGE OF THE
HOURS is about bringing to life the living patterns and rituals of the
group while THE IDENTITY ZONE is about dramatising inner,
archetypal energies. The first of these is useful for learning about
group integration – the images created show how the group is working
together – or not. Playing it straight off, individuals can't help giving
themselves away. If they avoid each others' eyes and move within their
own personal orbit, distrust is evident. If they're always on the edge of

the circle, it's perhaps symptomatic of their refusal to take risks. Whatever is displayed, the facilitator can give instructions. She might encourage the participant to 'come into the centre more' or 'respond to the others more' or 'be aware of the whole picture, and your part in the whole picture'. Problems which the group members may be having in relating to each other will be reflected in this exercise and so we can go some way towards addressing them 'within the language of image'.

IMAGE OF THE HOURS allows the generation of content by prompting participants to share their daily routines. Ali Campbell describes how he used this Boalian exercise within Ford Prison, in the UK. It proved particularly effective in this context because the group participants all had shared experiences. With a different group, the effect might have been full of contrasts. As it was everyone's story was the same: *'What we found in that territory was very simple, and yet so moving that it instantly opened up a whole series of possibilities for a week's work. I asked the first group to make first the hours of a 'banged up' prison, and then to do the same hours a second time for Ford (an open prison). "Banged up" was what you would expect: for every single hour of twenty four the majority of the group just lay on the floor and slept. It is hard to describe the power of this image as hour after hour was called out, with only a few men moving at any one time, and then only in tiny circles. Despair, anger and a sense of the waste of human lives filled the room in an instant, and deepened through the simple repetition of the exercise.'*[30]

THE IDENTITY ZONE gives participants a chance to look at their inner passions. It begins by participants being asked to theatricalise their 'inner selves', to separate these out and cast them as if in a play. The times I've used it, I've found that stock or archetypal characters have emerged: the lover, the warrior, the guardian. Once these roles have been cast, there are opportunities to explore the imagery further through generating improvisations between the different characters. For example, one might set different inner characters against each other, asking the protagonist/creator to experience playing different roles at different times. What you usually find is an inherent paradox about the relations between these inner characters, so improvising becomes an exercise in elaborating this paradox. For example, the 'lover' might be far back down the line, and is trapped from coming forward by a 'guardian' or 'censor' character who – we discover through improvisation – is 'protecting the lover from getting hurt'. So we might ask 'What can the lover do to escape from the

MOVING IMAGES

A group of four or five make an image, abstract preferably. The facilitator slowly claps out ten – or twenty. As she does so, the group must move to a different image. They must move only in slow motion and they must keep moving all the time. On the final clap, they would hope to arrive at a new image which in some way 'makes sense'.

IMAGE OF THE HOURS

'The technique is simple: all I do is call out times of the day, and the entire group, each working in their own space in the room but alongside the others, mime the activity they associate with that time of the day. We end up with a kind of living clock, the purpose of which is . . . to build a co-operative group picture of the day.' Ali Campbell.

THE IDENTITY ZONE

A volunteer is asked for, who will sculpt her 'inner personalities'. She is asked to cast individuals from the rest of the group into these roles. She is asked to present these personalities in a line, with those nearest the audience who are closest to the surface and those at the back who are the most hidden. Clear instructions should be given to the players about their characters by the person doing the exercise. Once this still image is created, the volunteer can be questioned about the line-up, and what happens between the different personalities within it; what conflicts exist. The different personalities may be brought to life through phrases, speech or movements. Maybe the volunteer/sculptor will tutor the other players in their parts. It may then be appropriate to move on to improvising encounters between the different characters, exploring strategies to address the difficulties which have been identified.

Extension: There is the option of introducing the multiple personality to a single, external personality in order to see how she responds.

guardian's entrapment, in order to express the love quality?' The protagonist/creator can explore different strategies, both as the lover and the guardian.

Moving the work on further, it might be possible to introduce this 'multiple personality' to an external character, to see what impact this has internally on the balance of inner characters. At this point a number of quite sophisticated techniques are being employed, and the facilitator must judge the group's readiness for work which is more directly therapeutic.

PLOT

This section is about improvisational work which is character or plot-driven. Of course some kind of dramatic development of any scene is desirable: things need to happen. Students know this, and feel an enormous obligation to 'make things happen' all the time. So there may be value in not coming to this area too early – spending time instead getting the group feeling comfortable with just being on stage. Then we can come to the point of discussing how dramatic action evolves through *impulse, conflict and transformation*. And because actors aren't playwrights, the key to enabling this process is becoming aware of feeling – using emotions to trigger imaginative fictionalising. If the performers are able to do this – and can avoid being swallowed up by feeling, which at first they often are – then they can develop vivid and entertaining scenes. If inner feeling is lacking or they can't translate their feelings imaginatively, then the improvisational work is less likely to take off. Of course impros often *don't* take off even with good improvisers but the difference is, good improvisers may know how to 'rescue' a scene by other means.

If two players start improvising, they need to agree terms. They have to accept each others' inventions because they need to create the theatrical world of the impro together. It's a simple rule, applicable in most cases. Once this is happening, they can make all kinds of decisions about that world. We're penguins on the ice, we're bank robbers looking at plans, we're lovers facing separation, we're tourists at the Chelsea Hotel, we're two friends in a park. Either they've created that world themselves or it's been given to them by the facilitator. But it must be established first, before it can advance. If neither actor is in agreement with the other, unless they're quite brilliant at coming back on themselves, then they're going to get in trouble. If one actor thinks they're penguins and the other, tourists, they could fall through the ice. Once they agree however, things can happen. One penguin can discover that the hole in the ice leads into a secret chamber, one of the bank robbers is revealed as a police spy, one of the lovers has brought a list of financial demands, and so on. Then we need some dramatic action. Without any development of the scene, the players will start to feel trapped. They'll talk a lot, look around wildly and finally throw up their hands as if to say 'It's not going anywhere'. If this happens, it may be valuable to ask the audience what opportunities for development they can see. This may help to 'unblock' the actors – it may transpire the actors had the same ideas but self-censored them. Or the facilitator can give certain instructions to help the situation unblock: 'Take a piece of paper from your pocket and read out what's written there.' 'Go to the cupboard and open it.' 'Now make your confession.' 'Kiss her'. Or just 'Get into the car and drive!'

If development comes organically, it comes because the improvisers are able to translate what they feel into imaginative impulses. This might involve an increase of pressure to induce qualitative change. On the park bench for example, one of the two friends a) declares a hidden passion for the other, b) tells them they've accepted a contract on their life, c) announces they have a fatal disease and will be dead in two days, d) asks the other to throw a stick for them, then fetches it. In other words, one of the actors tilts the scene towards action which is playable. It's even better if that action was not predicted. If *nothing* arises between them, one or other may be able to rescue the scene by changing the *context* of the dramatic action. For example, they may alert the other to the presence of several approaching gunmen, or make references to 'having to get back to the cockpit to fly the plane'. (This is a bit of a cheat really, but if it kickstarts the action again, may be justified.)

In an impro of this type we want to see dramatic development which carries us forward, but the secret to this may be what lies in the past. The improviser always has the past, the present and the future at their disposal. Sometimes the potential of the past or future is ignored, such is the anxiety about creating a present. In relatively 'open' impros of this type, the facilitator must judge how much they intervene to guide or instruct the players. Minimum interference is probably desirable but none at all assumes a degree of expertise quite rare in community drama. Some of these issues were discussed earlier under 'Spontaneity'.

In such situations, improvisers will be working with a degree of inexperience, making these open impros extremely challenging. It may be more appropriate to look at structures which provide a degree of sup-port for their creativity, at the same time creating a kind of schooling for impro in general. Much will depend on the improviser's ability to relax on stage and allow a responsiveness to their inner impulses. If this is difficult, an exercise like EMOTIONAL REPETITION may help the players to realise how much variety of feeling they have and how these feelings can provide the motor for individual expression. This exercise deliberately halts dramatic action in order to generate awareness of *inner emotion*. Perhaps it should be called Groundhog Day after its isolation of – and focus on – feelings generated by the 'freezing up' of narrative development. Just as the central character in the film goes through emotional changes while everyone around him stays fixed (it's always Groundhog Day), so here the participants move forward in action-time very, very slowly, but experience a great deal emotionally. They only move the action forward when emotionally compelled to do so, ensuring an emotional honesty to the playing. Players subsequently discover there's a range to their emotions which surprises them. They're reminded that emotional momentum has its own logic, even though you can't necessarily describe that logic in words. Once the player engages with a quality of emotional momentum, it's like riding the surf; having found a strong wave, all you have to do is stay on it. It feels as if you're carried along by something greater than yourself.

A quite different way to provoke emotion in improvisers, and so cultivate an awareness about dramatic development, is to use *music*. Wolfgang Stange finds this an effective way of working with learning disabled participants. Music circumvents the verbal. The qualitative changes of mood in the music trigger imaginative ideas in the actors; it gives a source of inspiration to them as well as a structure to the exercise. It starts, it continues, it ends; allowing the participants to create material which will fill out that structure. *'Individuals having Downs Syndrome are extraordinary. When they get a cue from the music, they won't come back to the exact movement but the specific feeling will be recaptured. And I can then put it back into a piece if they wish to do so . . . This is what happens with improvisation. For example, one young man – I asked people to pretend they were down and outs. "You are in a place that doesn't exist, but just for now put these blankets on. And when the music starts, you slowly wake up. And then when I tap you on the shoulder, you either dance it or you tell me who you are or what you want to be – at that moment. And the others freeze." That's what happened. One of the women suddenly stood up and said "I want a lover". And one had forgotten to bring that kind of sexuality into it. Then she went on "I need a man close to my*

EMOTIONAL REPETITION

This exercise is played in pairs, with or without an audience. Player A begins by making an observation – which contains a value judgement – about the other person's appearance: 'I like your shoes'. Player B responds rhetorically by turning that statement into a question: 'You like my shoes?' Player A repeats the statement and Player B repeats the question. They continue the dialogue, allowing different feelings to inform the inflections. They're free to move around the space and physicalise the dialogue, but not to change the words. When Player B feels driven to do so, she may change the statement – but it mustn't happen too quickly: 'Your shoes are rubbish' or 'That shirt makes you look sexy' or 'Your hair is filthy' – and Player A turns that statement into a rhetorical question. The process continues in the same way. There is scope as the exercise progresses for the statements about the other person to become progressively more intimate or challenging.

body, I want a man . . . " and that turned into a whole dance: the Rejection Dance. It went on . . . and she was rejected by the man.'

The music helps the actors by creating a particular mood – with that mood prevailing, there's a certain trance quality which is induced. The performer becomes more open to inner suggestion. Emotion informs physicality which creates behaviour which makes dramatic action. Alternatively one might help the improvisers by giving them more information about the *narrative structure* of the situation which they're in. They're relieved of the task of 'creating the story', they can simply 'be in it' and allow the story to travel along its own tramlines. But it's important to put emphasis on the relationships and the dilemmas rather than on the sequence of events, otherwise the playing can become stilted. Different facilitators will have their own choice of STOCK SCENES which they can draw from. For example they may simply be scenes with stock beginnings: someone climbs through the window of someone else's bedroom. Another character is given the sack. So it's for the actors to find their own resolution from the given beginning. Alternatively, the story might be given to them, beginning, middle and end. It's not about taking their power away, but giving them a narrative structure to operate within. I might use TEMPTATION. This is based on the Garden of Eden story. Two improvisers are led into an environment in which there are many pleasures available to them. I simply provide two pairs of dark glasses which allow them to 'see' whatever they want to see; hologram projectors. When wearing the glasses, to all intents and purposes the actors are transported to the place they want to be. First however, the characters are introduced to the space by an authority figure who explains how the glasses work. The authority encourages their use. However, there is also a box on the table which the authority *forbids* them to open. The authority figure leaves. The players then explore 1) the pleasures of imaginative fantasy using the glasses, transporting themselves all over the world, then 2) a growing curiosity about what the box contains. Then 3) a difference of opinion over whether to open it. It moves on to 4) opening the box and discovering the contents – perhaps something enjoyable to eat. They eat it. Then 5) there's the guilt over having broken the single rule, and 6) the return of the authority figure. Now we discover how the two characters cope with their guilty truth. Finally 7) the authority takes away their glasses and chucks them out.

Drawing from plays and literature, it's possible to devise your own scenes. I've used CYRANO based on the scene where Cyrano instructs the tongue-tied lover how to seduce his beloved, and HELL based on the play by Sartre, *Huis Clos*. I devised this when only three participants came for a workshop. We established that Hell was this room. I as the butler/doorman introduced the characters into it, one by one. Each actor had previously decided the manner of their death. Each had different instructions: Woman A was to pursue Woman B, Woman B was to pursue The Man while The Man pursued Woman A. Everything was permissible but no one could leave. The doorman was available to answer any questions they might have. As in the written play, this mutually conflicting combination of desires generated endless variations of foreplay and no consummation. It ran effortlessly for over an hour.

A folktale like *Little Red Riding Hood* offers the possibility of working not just with a storyline but with archetypal characters as well. The value of the exercise lies in each participant exploring the different character qualities. There is a trickster figure – the Wolf, a virgin figure – Little Red, a Mother figure and a Hero – the Woodcutter. The story and the sequence of events are well known. This leaves us free to explore character and extemporise around the story.

THE ROUND PLAY

This exercise takes place in the round, with actors able to enter and exit on all sides. When they're not acting, they are spectators. The exercise involves an exploration through drama of a particular geographical context, the 'world' of the play. This might be a beach, a park, a hospital foyer, a courtroom foyer, a street – anywhere where people are likely to pass, or stay for a while, or meet. Actors are encouraged to enter and exit as they wish but to collectively build up an image and an atmosphere which is characteristic of that place. They are encouraged not to initiate critical incidents, such as arrests or alien landings, but instead to find a truthfulness in the everyday passage of a variety of characters. They may meet each other, explore or create relationships, but the emphasis remains on small moments rather than large. Actors are encouraged to try out a range of different characters for themselves, taking a different character most times they re-enter. If action begins in different parts of the space simultaneously, they should be aware of focus, complementarity and working together as an ensemble.

However, it's important to remain true to the essential narrative drive or the crystal clarity of the individual archetypes starts to diminish. Some participants will find certain characters easy to play, and others hard. Pete may do an excellent wolf but finds the 'open yearning for experience' of Little Red almost impossible. *But* if the players can perceive others finding those qualities they may get closer to accessing them in their own hearts and minds. Since the characters are archetypal – each embodiments of a different human essence – we should have within us the possibility of playing all the different characters. Role theory in dramatherapy utilises such folktales consciously to aid personal development.

Another way to help improvisers understand their art is to reduce the narrative element to an absolute minimum. In other words, have them focus on the *world* of the improvisation. THE ROUND PLAY creates a world, and disallows anyone from creating any critical incidents within it. The emphasis is on mood and character, and playing together as a team. Because the players are consistently changing roles they see more easily how different interventions complement or upset the stage action. 'Where is the focus at this point?' 'If there are two focus points, are you communicating which has precedence at any one time?' 'Should you be, or can they function simultaneously?' Additionally, once the exercise has run for a while, the facilitator can pick out moments to revisit. Characters and relationships can be selected for further exploration, perhaps in a different setting. Maybe the old man and the young boy who made friends in the hospital foyer can meet again at the scene of a crime. The questions which the players should think about while they're offstage might be 'What does the scene need?' 'Which characters need to enter, to fulfil the potential of this situation?' After the exercise has run for a while, feedback will be important. We need to look at what worked and why, and what failed and why.

WHAT DOES THE SCENE NEED? simply asks for one player to start a scene, and then freeze. The question 'What does the scene need?' is then put to the audience, and anyone is invited to enter the space. The second actor's task is to help the first actor develop the action. For example: the first actor enters, and lies down. Evidently, she's ill. The second actor introduces a nurse or a relative or a doctor. Now there can be action. *Building situations gradually* helps the improvisers to accumulate the information they require as and when they need it. We begin with a simple idea and slowly move towards a complex realisation. For example, an exercise like QUESTION AND ANSWER begins from abstract movement. The spectators ask questions of the improviser in the centre, and that player finds answers to 'explain' their (initially abstract) actions. Say the first actor moves around shrugging their shoulders. A question from a spectator might be 'Where are you?' The answer comes 'Outside the exam room.' (The actor has made that up spontaneously – it 'feels right'). 'Are you nervous?' 'Yes.' 'Why?' 'I'm trying to convince myself it doesn't matter that I failed, that I left early, that I've got time to kill before going home to mother.' Subsequent questions and answers elaborate the fictional reality further. Once we have sufficient information, the second actor's task is to enter and *develop the action*, by introducing a problem or conflict element. For example, the second actor is the student's girl-friend who has brought flowers (hastily assembled from available materials) to congratulate the student. This allows the improvisers to explore their relationship while simultaneously generating a predicament. The third actor has the task of moving the improvisation towards a possible conclusion.

QUESTION AND ANSWER

The group creates a stage area by sitting on four sides in a rectangle. Three players are nominated to be the first, second and third actor. The first actor comes into the centre and begins to make a repetitive movement, without any conscious intent to make it 'into' anything. The spectators then ask the actor a series of questions, and in answering the actor builds up a picture of who their character is, where they are and what they're doing. When answering, the actor should say the first thing that comes to mind – all the time conscious of how they're moving. So we might discover that the woman played by this actress is a housewife, hoovering and dreaming of being a rich man's mistress – or a tobacco planter in India, worried about her health. The spectators should ask questions which help to build up a picture of this woman, her situation and her relationships. When the second actor feels they have sufficient information, they enter – perhaps as one of the characters already mentioned by the first, or another character who has a connection with the first. Through their intervention, the scene will develop a measure of conflict or generate development. The third actor also comes in at their own impulse, thinking to develop further or conclude the action.

Let's say the girlfriend is so disappointed and shocked by his exit from the exam, that she starts to break it off with him. He realises in consequence that her affection was solely based on admiration for his scholarship. Now this illusion has been shattered. So the third actor might appear as the teacher who congratulates the boy on coming first in the exam, despite having left early. (This is the third actor's decision made while watching the scene.) Then the improvisers have to find a resolution to the scene. Can the girl get out of the mess she's placed herself in? Whether she does or not will be the concluding part of the impro. I remember a playing of this when the first actor was a woman. She was trying to decide whether or not to run away from her husband – with her lover. Her early decisions made it easy for the two subsequent actors to choose their roles. The first to arrive was the lover, the second was the husband – just in time to see the errant couple packing to leave . . .

THE GATE also shares responsibility for dramatic action between audience and actors. It's particularly useful when there's a theme which the group wants to explore such as 'parent-children relationships', 'identity' or 'crime'. It's important to place – and have understood – all the rules at the outset otherwise you have to stop and restart, which may destroy momentum. When it's run successfully, it throws up a multitude of plot lines and characters which can subsequently be teased apart. And because of this element of shared responsibility, it can run for ages. If a block is reached and the actors can't break through, the spectators have strategies to rescue them. But *hopefully* the actors will be left alone if they do enter meaningful exploration. And actors can bring to it whatever style of playing they wish. If they want to act a dog or a picture on the wall, and other actors can recognise what they're about, then that's fine. In feedback, the different plotlines can be separated out and selected for further work. It's an exercise which tests the ensemble skills of the group, so probably needs sufficient preparatory work.

Using exercises such as these, improvisers are able to gain an increased fluency with character, plot and incident – so are then able to return to more 'open-ended' impros where less information is provided by the facilitator.

Finally, here are Keith Johnstone's guidelines for improvisers, reproduced from an Impro newsletter distributed out of Calgary University. The advice is particularly valuable for open-ended impros – the use of Red Riding Hood as an example simply illustrates the unwisdom of impro crimes; the story loses all its power if the essentials are neglected. Clearly this advice places considerable emphasis on 'mistakes' – which can be dispiriting for newcomers. However, it's a useful checklist which may help actors understand why improvisations are snarling up, if they are. He writes:

Train the players to avoid:
1. Cancelling. Little Red Riding Hood was about to leave the house when Grandma phoned up and said 'Don't come.'
2. Sidetracking. She sets out with a basket of cookies and stops to throw stones in the river. Soon a raft came by and she hopped on . . . etc. (anything rather than meet the wolf!)
3. Being Original. (Originality is used as a way of sidetracking.) Little Red noticed something through the trees. At that moment she entered a time warp, which took her back to the sixteenth century.

THE GATE

Again the participants form a rectangular stage. A theme or question is agreed on, to be the focus of the exercise. One player volunteers an image to begin the action. That player selects two or three actors and sculpts them into an image, which expresses the chosen theme. The sculptor does not describe what is happening but tries to sculpt them with as much detail as possible. Then the sculptor sits down. These actors are asked by the facilitator to 'feel' the truth of the situation. At a given instruction, the actors begin to improvise. Their task is to continue to improvise, negotiating between them to find the reality of the situation. They are not allowed to exit the scene. The spectators at any time have three options open to them:

1. A spectator can call 'freeze' and replace one of the actors. They inherit that actor's character with all the information already acquired about that character, but now they can shift the action in a different direction. When they've replaced that actor in the freeze, they call 'begin'.

2. They can call 'freeze' and add themselves as a third character to the situation. In which case they call 'begin' when they have placed themselves within the scene.

3. They can call 'freeze' and alter the positions of the actors already on stage. This means that the spectator resculpts those actors and then calls 'begin'. It is for those actors to continue playing the scene, but informed by their new position. For example, the sculptor might wish to 'move the scene forward' by resculpting them to heighten the conflict.

4. They can call 'freeze' and take one of the actors present, out of the scene. Again, they call 'begin' once this has been completed. The facilitator will decide when the play comes to a conclusion. In feedback, there can be assessment of how the theme was tackled, and what plot lines emerged.

4. Wimping. This is usually a refusal to define – i.e. Little Red met a big, huge, hairy, grey, friendly, animal . . . in the forest.
5. Conflict. (when used to freeze the action).
 'What big teeth you have, Granma.'

'What's wrong with my teeth?'

'Well, they're big.'

'Let me see the mirror. My teeth are fine.'

'They're ugly.'

'Rubbish.'

6. Instant Trouble. Little Red stepped out of the door and the wolf gobbled her up.

7. Games. (Agreed activities). Little Red gets to the cottage and she and Grannie play table tennis all afternoon.

8. Hedging.

> 'Now you know Grandma's not been well, and she lives on her own. I've told her it's silly but she won't listen.'

And so on. She may never get to the point of giving Little Red the basket.

9. Gossip.

> 'Do you remember when I sent you with that basket of cookies to Grandma?'
>
> 'Oh yes, and I met the Wolf!'
>
> 'Yes. That was before we had his head hung over the mantelpiece.'

Here gossip is used as a substitute for action.

10. Blocking.

> 'Are you going to see your Grandma, little girl?'
>
> 'I don't have a Grandma.'

11. Negativity.

> 'All the better to gobble you up with.'
>
> 'Oh well, if you must. God! Wolves are so boring.'
>
> (This response is also a Gag.)

12. Gagging. (See above.) Little Red is a Black Belt and hurls the Wolf all over the room i.e. she stays out of trouble.[31]

NARRATIVE

This section is concerned with developing stories and acting them out. 'Stories' in this context assume an elaboration of narrative prior or separate to, dramatic action. In other words there is always a storyteller role involved in some way, either filled by an individual or by the group. I therefore include in this section, pre-existing stories. In terms of the

---

WORD-AT-A-TIME STORIES

The group sits in a circle. A story will be told, but each player will only contribute one word at a time. It may be that the first four words will be prescribed, for example: 'once' – 'upon' – 'a' – 'time' – at which point each player will contribute a new word: 'there' – 'was' – 'a' – 'giant' – 'called' etc. The facilitator might find it useful to put in full stops herself, or establish a convention in which a player says 'full stop' to mark a sentence end.

---

learning dimension, we're asking 'What makes a story effective?' 'What are the elements which give it narrative drive?' 'When acting out narrative, what are the necessary qualities of ensemble playing?'

An exercise like WORD-AT-A-TIME STORIES quickly brings the group up against the difficulties. We want a story which flows imaginatively from start to finish incorporating characters, tension, surprise and a sense of completion. It occasionally happens. When it does it seems effortless, the group can't believe their achievement. They need it to go wrong a few times to appreciate that. It's a useful exercise to tackle early precisely because of the discussion it tends to generate about these questions of what makes narrative. So the mistakes when they come, become a learning point. Some of the common mistakes made with this exercise are: *blocking* (dispensing with the central character, for example), *introducing too many characters*, *not listening* (and so forgetting the story), *being clever* (Peter – was – married – to . . . Superfrogperson), and *going off at incredible tangents* which leaves the central character back at first base. It was once pointed out to me (by a blind participant, interestingly) that the secret of story-making was to think of yourself sitting in a car, driving backwards along a dark road so your headlights pointed over an area you'd already passed. So what was illuminated was all the story-elements you had *already* created. The metaphor usefully pinpoints how good stories are all about incorporation. 'What happens next' is effective only if it acknowledges 'what happened before.' Participants often forget this, and plan more and more devious and wacky plot developments in a vain effort to make the story take off. So facilitators may well be advised to encourage them to be banal, prosaic and ordinary in their choice of story-elements, at least till they've got the hang of the process.

Another way to build stories, but using a questioner role, is INSTANT STORYTELLING. This works on building all answers given into a single narrative thread. The process accepts that there will be tangents, digressions and stylistically mixed contributions, but the questioner plays an anchor role in holding the story together. This doesn't mean asking 'leading' questions – they should be 'neutral' or 'open' questions – but it does mean retaining a keen eye on who the central character is and how that character develops. If the story is about a ghost, then that ghost has to maintain a centrality. At the outset there are certain fixed questions, which establish the building blocks. For example, they might concern themselves with: who, when, where, the weather, what next? Similarly they retain an awareness of what the genre is, if that's been decided. (This technique of questioning is discussed more fully in Chapter Six under INSTANT THEATRE.) Once the story has been created – and has been written down by a scribe during its creation – it can be used as source material for devising scenes, drawings, poetry, written dialogues or other exercises.

Working from pre-existing stories, it's always possible just to ask for contributions. If this is the preferred strategy, then the request will need to carry a focus, for example THE MOST EMBARRASSING THING. Katina Noble observes that *'the advantage of an exercise like this is you quite quickly get into an interesting area for discussion, and it gives you material for theatre. The material is always revealing in some way or other because it's about mistakes, being caught out, things not going right.'*

Simultaneously, there may be emphasis placed on *how* the story is presented to the group. The African tradition of storytelling offers a model which is rooted in performance itself. When Peter Badejo facilitates a group, he will ask for a story or even just a line from a story, to be presented through rhythm and movement. If appropriate the storyteller can work with a drummer. So *'it's enacting, having the feeling of what you are saying through the body. I believe you are able to communicate, to transmit much better without depending on the verbal. This is the way to get people to act in a community way.'* What happens is a reductive process, the words become fewer as the bodies and sounds do more. And the performances begin to have a wild, explosive quality never possible without having moved from the verbal.

But the value of anecdotal reminiscence may not be fully utilised by simply moving from telling to dramatisation. It might be that a creative

> ## THE MOST EMBARRASSING THING
> Everyone in the group is asked to think of a moment which was embarassing for them, but which they are happy to bring into the group. Decisions are made about how this could be acted out – but it should involve the person whose story it is, in a storytelling role.

manipulation of the story will aid the process of pluralisation. We established earlier how the bringer of any story needs to be happy for this to happen. Once handed over, even if the group consciously 'respects' that story, the group can never be completely 'true' to it; the very act of working on it, changes it. Even the act of the teller re-telling it is a selective and filtering process. If there's any doubt, simply ask the group to move the furniture round the room – and then straight away get someone to 'tell the story' of that event – there will always be different interpretations. We have to accept that recall is subjective and imperfect. But *pivotal* moments and feelings may be remembered very clearly – and these can be used as the armatural structure around which an interpretation can be built. A technique like PILOT/CO-PILOT can be used where the story teller tells their story not to the whole group, but privately to another group member in private. Then the co-pilot interprets that story back to the group, perhaps as an image, a piece of movement, a monologue or an improvisation. What we hope to capture is a truthful essence. The co-pilot has to get to the core feeling and empathetically construct imagery around it. Once presented, the pilot can assess it and say 'Yes, that captures something' or 'No, I don't recognise it.' Very often what you find is that something *is* captured *and* recognised, but from another point of view. For example the co-pilot might have concentrated on the perspective of a *different* player in the story, or a less obviously dramatic moment, but one which still has feeling attached to it.

It is important that the teller gives licence to the group to adapt their story. Jonathan Kay devised an exercise called THE EMOTIONAL MAP which specifically invites an interpreter to 'play with' elements in the teller's story. One player recalls the scene, the feelings, the colours, the events. The other takes this raw material and 'fools' with it, takes liberties with it, hoping to show back to the teller something of themselves. It marks a step on from the PILOT/CO-PILOT technique.

The initial story doesn't have to be especially dramatic or interesting, the teller simply responds to the memory which comes to mind when they 'draw the curtain aside', then the recall follows its own tempo. Memory is intensely selective and the dramatiser instinctively recognises this. So in 'inventing around' the recollection they may illuminate what the teller no longer sees. While the teller has told it from their point of view, the dramatiser may play any number of parts in their acting-out. They may be the carpet on the floor, the bed or a poster on the wall which witnesses everything. They may choose to be the teller's father or daughter or the teller's thoughts. In feedback, the teller can comment on what they recognised. What aspects of the memory were picked up on? Did they see themselves in this interpretation? Or did they feel disappointed that important aspects were ignored? Could more risks, more licence have been taken? At this point, the teller is speaking as an audience at the play of their own life. They can ask for *more* of whatever they choose – after all, it's their material. In some ways the relationship between teller and dramatiser is analogous to that between the community and its theatre company. The community provides the stock material for theatre. It's for the company to listen to those stories and dramatise them in such a way that illuminates deeper concerns. The truthfulness of the depiction must lie in the company's emotional understandings, less in the photographic accuracy of depiction.

Fictional stories can be devised and acted out simultaneously in IMMEDIATE STORIES. Two or three story-tellers are nominated while the remainder of the group divide between audience and performers. The storytellers sit with the audience in the front row, while the performers sit both sides of a thrust staging. There's a back wall. The storytellers will share the storytelling between them, and the performers act it out as it develops. Despite the apparent simplicity of the exercise's structure, the acting-out is particularly challenging. The storytellers have to plot a story which is *actable*. What is a good story to listen to, is not necessarily a good story to act out. The task is to anchor the story in character actions which are playable. There's a key difference between 'Tommy thought hard and decided he ought to visit his mother after all' and 'Tommy dressed quickly, realising he was late' – or between 'The giantess grew angry' and 'The giantess beat her playmate into submission'. Often it's hard to explain or understand the difference intellectually but *seeing* the actors behaviour on-stage, makes the points vividly.

THE EMOTIONAL MAP

The exercise is done in pairs. There is one teller and one listener. The teller takes the listener by the hand and they walk into their own space. The teller does not plan ahead what they are going to tell about, but simply does the action of drawing aside an imaginary curtain and 'seeing what they see.' From this seeing, they find a memory from their own life. They describe what is happening, but from outside themselves: 'That's me, sitting at my desk . . . over there is the teacher . . .' They can move around the image, leading their partner by the hand. The partner stays silent. They should aim to tell as much about what they 'see' as they can, even going 'inside the head' to see further memories, if necessary. Then the roles reverse, and the listener becomes a teller, taking their partner around a memory of theirs. Once the memories are told, the listener sits the teller down on the floor and performs, drawing on the teller's story. Then they reverse roles. Perhaps each player will get two or three chances to perform, in which case they alternate performing until the end of the exercise.

IMMEDIATE STORIES

The group divides between story-tellers, performers and audience. Each of the story-tellers takes it in turn to articulate a story. They make it up in the moment. At a given signal, the story-telling function is passed to another story-teller. Meanwhile the performers, sat at the stage edge, come into the middle and act out the story as it is told. They sit down and get up according to the demands of the story.

As with most story-based exercises, key narrative decisions will need to be made along the way. Steve Mitchell summarises these when describing his own dramatherapeutic work on stories: *'When I make up a story with a group, the questions I ask are both the playwrights' and the actors' questions: where does the scene take place; what time is the scene set; what is the geography of the location and where are they in the location, are they seated or standing, close or distant; what are their moods and what are their attitudes to one another; what happens between them, what is the next action; finally, why does it happen and what are the consequences of what happens to the characters in their story?'*[32] Decisions can be made beforehand about genre – folktale, horror story, soap opera or Hollywood

THE BRIDGE

It's important to have the right number of players for this exercise; four, eight or sixteen. A theme is predetermined for the exercise. Each player goes separately into their own space in the room. They decide who they are, where they are and what they're doing – in relation to the theme. For example if the theme is 'work' their character's action must connect in some way, be working or avoiding work. They then 'rehearse' a short moment of action. After this, each player pairs up with another and each shows the other what they've created. Then they discuss how the two moments could be bridged. They have to link them into the same short play. The bridge piece could come between the moments or before both or after both. But each initial moment should be kept 'as it was' – not corrupted. (If the second player is an aircraft pilot looking for his black box after a crash, then this moment has to be bridged with that of the unemployed woman counting invoices). When each pair has joined their pieces, they team up with another pair and the process is repeated. Finally, a group of four or eight can 'show' to another group of four or eight.

Variation: There is no theme, but each team of four is given character instructions. For example, one character has lost something, one has found something, one is searching for something and one is about to lose something.

action film, and about rules – actions only, speech permissible, performers play objects or whatever. Further complexities can be added, for example by having two of the offstage actors provide all the dialogue for those who are performing (in synch of course!). At the conclusion of the piece, actors can say what was hard to act out and what was helpful. The exercise tests the ensemble skills of the company: working together, thinking about others, using minimum material to create maximum effect.

To conclude, THE BRIDGE offers a different challenge. It's about devising a short play on a strictly democratic basis. The participants have to use narrative to thread together individually created elements. There's an enforced democracy. Those with loud voices are disallowed from taking more decisions than those with quiet voices. In fact it's more important to maintain this egalitarian structure than to produce a completely 'coherent' narrative result. The point being, an audience can look at the result and provide their own coherence. At that point of completion, elements or themes can be selected out for further exploration.

CHALLENGE EXERCISES

These have a special focus of nurturing social and communication skills. They usually involve tasks to be fulfilled by the participants. The challenge element lies in how well each individual can complete the task. The exercise might be repeated several times, giving different participants more opportunities to meet the challenge, perhaps drawing on lessons learned earlier. FORUM THEATRE is a sophisticated example of a challenge exercise. In Forum, a scene containing a problem is presented before the group, and spectators are invited to explore solutions-in-action. There's rarely any assumption there is one solution. Rather, the learning involved is around the *effects* generated by *different* interventions.

At the other end of the spectrum, perhaps the simplest challenge game is one like BANDLEADER which does involve finding a solution. In this case it lies in identifying who in the group is 'leading' the action. It's a simple exercise using observation skills. When the leader is identified, the exercise is replayed with someone else taking the challenge.

Most of the exercises given here were devised for working with probation clients or prison inmates, but they would be useful for working with any group where individuals were hoping to extend their social and communication skills. A good example is WHERE'S MY RADIO? given earlier. This tests an ability to demonstrate humility and low status playing. The facilitator can decide to what extent the participant is displaying these qualities, and whether or not the challenge needs be taken again. THE ANGRY NEIGHBOUR and THE FORGOTTEN JACKET involve setting up scenes where the challenger is required to play a certain role in order to overcome a given problem. Certain qualities are called for: diplomacy, tact, economy of expression and emotion management. In the first of these exercises, a not untypical social situation is established. The 'neighbour' is an awkward character who is refusing to return personal letters which have been misdirected to his door. The challenge for the actor is to

BANDLEADER

The group sits in a circle on the floor. One participant volunteers to go out. While they're out of the room, the rest appoint a (band)leader. That leader is going to lead the movements, or sounds and movement. These might involve anything from finger-clicking to moving the arms around, tapping the floor or shifting the body. The leader leads and all the others follow, trying to disguise who the leader is. The challenger comes back into the room, and sits in the middle of the circle. They have to try and guess who the bandleader is. Perhaps they are given three or four guesses. When the bandleader is correctly identified, that person goes outside and the exercise repeats.

THE ANGRY NEIGHBOUR

One player volunteers to play the neighbour, another to play the challenger. The situation is: the postman has been delivering mail to the neighbour by mistake over several weeks. That neighbour has become particularly irate over the situation, especially as he never gets any mail himself. He recently said that if he got any more mail wrongly addressed, he would tear it up. He also has a very aggressive pitbull terrier. The challenger has to go round to the neighbour and get the post back. Can this be done with tact and persuasiveness? Will the dog be unleashed?

go to this neighbour and – displaying sufficient patience and tact – encourage him to give them over. The actor playing the neighbour therefore, has to present the right level of resistance. They have to be angry and difficult, but *as the character only*. They have to mediate their resistance so as not to completely discourage the challenger. Yet at the same time, they can't make it all too easy. If they themselves – as the actor – get angry, then the intervention cannot be truly tested. So it calls for both detachment and sensitivity in the playing. Perhaps one of the facilitators could play this role. The exercise is typical of many such role plays which might be set up to anticipate social situations facing participants outside the rehearsal room; interviews, court cases, getting redress for complaints, arguing for rights to be granted, etc.

THE FORGOTTEN JACKET is more complex, and the facilitator needs to determine in advance what the truth of the situation is: has the jacket been lost or stolen? Probably the truth of the situation needs to be withheld from the challenger. Then it becomes more life-like in that they genuinely *don't know* how far it is reasonable to pursue the jacket's return. The challenge concerns how well the situation is played, not whether or not the jacket comes back. I've noticed how prison inmates, for example, find the idea of 'accepting a loss' very hard, especially if someone else is due to profit from it. Role plays of this kind can be set up to test very particular social skills. Here, the test involves patience, negotiating skills and 'reading' a situation. GRIEVANCES involves a more open-ended situation where the challenger has to take the role of an advisor in a conflict which is not of their invention. This lends itself to situations where, for example, an individual with learning difficulties has met with prejudice or discriminatory treatment. By placing a learning disabled participant in the role of the challenger and giving the other character the 'difficulty' the learning disabled participant can have a crack at problem-solving 'at a distance'.

Nic Fine and Fiona Macbeth developed a more formulaic model which allows for a range of different situations to be explored. Taking the format of a BOXING RING, an individual within the group will be invited to take a challenge which is based on a real-life challenge they may shortly face. For example, a prison inmate will soon leave a Young Offenders Institution. Once out he can expect to meet his friends again, and once again be invited to join in a robbery. How can he avoid getting drawn in? The exercise echoes the work of both Boal and John Bergman. The participant may feel, for example, that the very first day he gets out will be the toughest. He'll go back to the same streets and his friends are there. They'll want to pull him into their own schemes. They'll assume he's back on the street to continue the old stuff. So part of the challenge will involve dealing with these friends. Maybe what's at stake for him is his longer-term goal of getting an education.

The physical structure of a boxing ring is set up, using chairs. *'We start assembling teams. We need an opponent for him . . . then we need coaching teams so this guy doesn't get ripped apart. We want to give him an affirmative experience so that at the end he really feels some of those options he could try. We also want to give him the experience of getting real support. So we'll assemble a coaching team around that guy, and we need suitable people in the room to do that. It's quite nice to get a prison officer in that corner. Often a guy might have one or two mates in that corner. We'll also need support for the other guy. We'll create a name for them. One*

THE FORGOTTEN JACKET

Last night there was a brilliant party. However, the challenger has left his jacket behind at the party. It's his favourite jacket. His task is to go round there and get it back. However, the party host did a big clear out very late last night of all the accumulated rubbish in the flat. He thinks this included the jacket. Everything was bagged up and the dustmen have since collected the rubbish. But this character is noted as a shifty character who would not hesitate at taking advantage of others' forgetfulness. How can the challenger find out the true destination of the jacket? If it's truly gone, can he resign himself to that? If it's still present, can he persuade the other to give it up?

GRIEVANCES

The challenger is on stage, not knowing the challenge which is coming. The first actor and the second actor have agreed a dispute between them. The first actor then enters, to complain about the behaviour of the character played by the second actor. The challenger has the task of resolving the dispute.

Variation: The grievance is decided alone by the first actor, and the second actor has to improvise whichever character features in the grievance story. The emphasis here for the challenger is to help the first actor get redress.

might be called Dirty Dan – might use their own name but put an adjective in front, which they choose.' Nic Fine.

Once teams are assembled, they play rounds. It's an improvisation, but tightly structured. The opponent is testing the protagonist's determination to get an education. Each round is like a short scene where the outcome is uncertain. If the protagonist gets into trouble, he can call for time out and get more advice from his coaches. Maybe he has a weak spot, he's a recovering addict and the opponent will try hard to upset him on that. These are his danger zones which he needs to learn about, the aspects of his personality which are vulnerable to being preyed on by those who want to use him.

'The first round we'll try and see what's it's normally like. So there's probably no coaching in the first round . . . So everyone can look at what approaches the guy uses, what language he uses. That's when the coaches

will do the head work in their corners. Is he using a lot of low blows? We use a lot of fighting imagery that young guys will relate to . . . With expert coaching, they'll give him maybe only one small idea to take into the next round.' The ref's role is important. She has to ensure that the opposition is effective and sustained. She also has to ensure the protagonist is taking the coaching ideas – she retains the power to send them back for more coaching if necessary. At the end there can be assessment of how the protagonist felt during the encounters. Did what he *say* he would do match what he *actually did?* Often there's a reality gap between what he thinks he's doing – saying no – and actually doing – giving yes signals. And which strategies were most effective? Maybe those which he put less trust in, worked the best. In evaluation, lessons can be drawn on how best to plan ahead to events outside in the real world.

Geese Theatre UK have also evolved an exercise which draws on ritual elements to create an arena of challenge. This is called THE CORRIDA. It necessarily comes towards the closing point of a longer programme in a prison, as does THE BOXING RING, when participating individuals are ready for a more serious, personal challenge. It involves the team doing considerable preparation, looking at inmates' personal situations, piecing together very personalised exercises. *'Basically it's an arena, and a ritual. What happens is (the participant) comes in from the wasteland and makes a declaration. In the corrida there are three or four judges which comprise a Geese member, a staff member and one or two inmates. And he makes a declaration about why he wants to take a challenge. And what he wants to leave behind in the wasteland. And he might have his inner man with him there. (The "inner man" would be a representation on paper – a cut-out – of what he had achieved during the week). And he's given a challenge. The thing about the challenge is they're highly specific to the individual. Basically it's a high-risk situation and we don't say to him what it is. We just say he must deal with this situation. Examples of that: I did one with a guy – the situation was, he was a wing cleaner. Another guy had had something nicked from his cell and he and his friend think it's the wing cleaner. He has to deal with it in a non-violent way.'* So a considerable amount has to be in place for this exercise, in particular the participant's prior commitment to take such a challenge. Earlier exercises need to have been completed well. The facilitators need to have accumulated a sufficiently detailed assessment of the inmate.

DEVISING

'It is a community on stage. Part of the process is about meeting people. And within that, even if the workshop is not going to end up with a performance, there needs to be awareness of performance. Because there can be a safety in the workshop where it never actually leads to performance. I'm wary of that. Ultimately, for me, it's important that the work goes out in a more public way. If theatre is going to survive.' Phelim McDermott.

Often there's a legitimate and inevitable momentum towards performance. But how to judge readiness for an external audience? Many shows are begun and abandoned because the decision to mount a production is taken for the wrong reasons. It's taken to paper over the cracks of a group in trouble or because it's *assumed* you must perform to validate the exercise, or because the staff of the institution expect it. In any of these cases it may be better to stay within the workshop confines because a production which fails, wrecking the confidence of the actors, is hard to justify. Sometimes it's a difficult decision because a state of unreadiness *in itself* is no reason not to perform. It's par for the course in any theatre context. There's no such thing as complete readiness. A better question is: will the challenge of performance lift the group into a higher gear or will it put unhelpful stress on them? It's a decision to be taken with reference to the group, the challenge, the available resources, time restrictions and the likely availability of a supportive audience.

None of this should be taken to diminish the tremendous opportunity of production. Public performance lifts creative practice into a higher gear. The act of presenting the work and having it witnessed is a qualitatively different exercise from simply sharing it privately. The presence of an audience changes everything; it's not that a high technical standard is necessary, the audience may be merely friends and supporters, but doing a show makes a different kind of statement. For in it we make a gift of ourselves without expectation of equal return from the audience. We act, they watch. Additionally, the actors are demonstrating a mastery of role. Irrespective of any content, the play is about showing that emotions, impulses and physicality have been brought under control to a degree that allows coherence and articulacy. It is often this, rather than the fact we've 'made a statement' about this theme or that, which generates pride and self-esteem. The audience can therefore, through their applause, play a key role themselves within a rehabilitative or group empowerment process.

Once the decision to perform publicly is supported by the whole company – an obvious precondition – there come the questions of *the process*, *the content* and *the administration*. In this chapter we're concerned largely with the process only, and how it might begin. We're concerned with starting points, for often these are led into from workshop processes. Decisions about process will inform those about content, the assumption being we're not starting with a prewritten text. Administration and rehearsal issues we have to leave aside. Devising a play is rather like travelling round a golf course, only you get to choose your order of holes. Let's imagine there are certain holes you *have* to go round, in the same way there are always certain essential challenges; plot, character, style, theme, the world of the play but you can choose where to start and how you travel. If you start with theme, you come to character later. If you start with character, you at some time have to address the question 'So what is this play really about?'

At the beginning, there are potential pitfalls. For example, it's probably a mistake to start conjuring an unhelpfully narrow idea of what the play will be about, too early. 'Let's create a jazz age musical' or 'Let's create a thriller set in an abattoir' are ideas which may sound innovative but this is starting with an image of the end of the process rather than with the process itself, trusting it will deliver. Having said that, the abattoir thriller just *may* be the perfect idea if previous work has been leading to it.

Any process begins with the creation of a team if it doesn't exist already. This sounds self-evident but can be ignored: if the group is fractious at the outset, the difficulties of production will be exaggerated several times over before the end. The facilitator needs to feel sure there is sufficient teamwork to underpin the move to performance. Issues such as regularity and punctuality of attendance become critical. Similarly, the facilitator needs sufficient confidence in their own leadership to take the group from the beginning of the process to the end. The different challenges at different points need to be anticipated.

There must be reasonable knowledge of and confidence in, appropriate strategies. Put at their simplest, these will be the key stages:

- creating teamwork
- generating raw material
- assembling that material into a structure
- rehearsing that material

Perhaps the most problematic area will be assembling the raw material that has been generated. When we get there, who will make the key authorial decisions? Will there have been a careful record made of the improvisations? Who will take the decisions around structure? Will there be a professional writer appointed to assist the group? If the group decides all this democratically, mutual respect must be in place; anything less may be damaging. Perhaps the director/facilitator should make it clear from the outset that she will make the final decisions about narrative structure. Perhaps it should be made clear that other responsibilities such as casting and the work timetable are also hers. The group should agree to this strategy. They, for their part, have the task of creating the material.

Devising is a process of widening and narrowing at different times. At the outset, if we haven't already agreed on content, we begin a process which is wide open. From a blank sheet of paper we generate various ideas and possibilities. We accumulate a mass of shapes, of different colours and character. Then we start to discriminate, deciding to *include* certain possibilities and *exclude* others. We finally get down to just one or two which will be the lodestars of the project. We reduce down to 'friendship and betrayal' or Harry the butcher or the story of Chernobyl. Now we have an essence, and out of this it's possible to unwind a story. So we go on to invent Harry's shop, research nuclear power or devise acts of betrayal. The next stage will involve the facilitator/director cutting that material down to size. We throw out these scenes, but keep those scenes. Narrowing at this point is a savage but necessary task as Roger Hill observes: *'One of the less successful pieces I made was for Hull Truck Youth Theatre. We had two weeks to do it. I let the process get too discursive. So by about day eight, I realised we had this mountain of potential organic material and I would not compromise the process of putting it down. I would not go out there and say "While you were in bed last night I cut the play down to size."* . . . *We eventually laid so much food on the table no one was able to eat it.'* If I was challenged on the secret of devising, it would be about knowing when to be ruthless and 'cut down to size' and when to say 'right now – anything goes'.

Here are some different starting points for devising.

1. Using the locality and group memories. Examples from David Slater and Roger Hill.
2. Working from a predetermined theme. Examples from Spare Tyre Theatre Company.
3. Using character as a starting point. Examples from Lois Weaver.
4. Working from documentary material. Examples: *Guernica* and *Material Unaccounted For* by Third Theatre.
5. Working conceptually. Examples: *L'Ascensore* by Insomniac Productions, *People Show 100* by the People Show.
6. Using image techniques. Examples: *The Anger Dyes* by Insight Theatre.

WORKING FROM GROUP MEMORY

This approach draws from what the group can recall. For example, the group members might all live in a particular neighbourhood. Maybe they're teenagers attending a youth centre or pensioners visiting a drop-in. So they share interests in common through their familiarity with an environment. There's a local bridge with stories attached to it or a wasteground which attracts vagrants. Or they might be members of the same trades union, sharing an affinity of craft. So they all remember specific disputes, they share a sense of labour history. A successful picket or industrial dispute is recalled with particular affection.

There's an assumption that the group members all hold different corners of the same cloth. Their individual relationships may be more or less strong, but what links them is a subjective, collective, perhaps mythologised experience of a shared situation. In this section, we'll look briefly at two examples of strategic development with such groups: Roger Hill's approach to building plays with a neighbourhood youth theatre, and David Slater's work with retired people in South East London.

Roger Hill's starting point is . . . '*the Mental Map. It's the idea that the place you live in, is a construct of everybody's mental ideas about it. Therefore it's essentially a soft city as Jonathan Raban said. I rarely do a project now without using it. You establish what geographical area everybody lives in. You give them all several pieces of paper. You say, "Thinking about this area, choose six places, specific like bus stops or general like estates, and I want you to write the name of it. And put something about it under one of these headings: Hearsay, Fact, Personal Connection or History and Tradition."'* Each participant then draws one local land-mark on each piece of paper. So each paper has perhaps a drawing, a description and a heading. For example, there's the swimming pool, and on the paper is the story of when somebody drowned. The heading for that is 'Hearsay.' When this is completed, the facilitator establishes the points of north, south, east and west on the floor. Then he asks the group members to take their pieces of paper and lay them down to create the geography of the area. What is created therefore, is a kind of 'mythological' map. It won't pass a geography test. It's a portrait of the area with all the mental and emotional bias that is a feature of subjective memory.

'*Then you say "Go to any piece of paper that you agree with, and put a tick against it. And put a cross against anything you disagree with." So you enhance the truths of the thing. So if all the scruffs of the area hang around Safeways supermarket, then the ticks start going on there – that's become an image of life for them. So you can pull away from that and start to read it as a painting. Everyone conjoins in this – you ask questions. The map starts to throw up the imagery, the agenda and the preoccupations of that group. Now whatever you tackle thereafter, you've got that as a kind of underpinning of what you do.*' The process allows for the group to detach themselves from their area – to objectify it as well as mythologise it. They can be encouraged into discussion or perhaps into making tableaux. For example, the facilitator may split the group into threes and get the sub-groups to walk around the map, and make tableaux or scenes based on those parts of the map which are thought interesting. Where the youth club was burnt down, a tableau is made of someone with a match and a can of petrol. In this way the imagery starts to lift off from the ground into drama. The participants are asked to 'actively prefer' parts of the map. Hill points out there's an important task for the facilitator here – to see where the group is most animated. For example, the town square leaves everyone cold, but whenever anyone comes to the 'wasteground', there always seem to be arguments. Energy, dissent or interest is stimulated by this part of the map. Maybe that wasteland is worth exploring in more depth.

Even if the group has already committed to doing a play based on, for example, *Macbeth* or *The Trial*, this process may have pertinence. For example, where do you think Macbeth would meet the witches if he lived in this area? Who would those witches be? What could be the wood that comes to Dunsinane? Or with the Kafka story, where would K live? What crimes could he be accused of? Could the investigating committee be exploring the burning down of the youth club? So work on classic texts, which can so easily just drift off, unharnessed, is now anchored in the immediate preoccupations of the group, identified through the Mental Map.

Once this stage is concluded, Roger Hill will bring in a number of 'story archetypes' for the group to choose from. So to complement the decisions about the world of the play, there are now decisions made about the plot to be explored. *'I've got a set of story archetypes – they're completely neutral – but they all describe elements of story. When I go into a group I read out the list. It starts for example,* A GROUP OF PEOPLE WHO ARE LOST, A GROUP OF PEOPLE WHO KNOW SOMETHING THAT NO ONE ELSE DOES, A GROUP OF PEOPLE WHO GO ON A JOURNEY. *I've honed them down over the years to the most useful. And then there's* A SMALL GROUP OF PEOPLE WHO OPPRESS A LARGE GROUP OF PEOPLE, A LARGE GROUP OF PEOPLE WHO OPPRESS A SMALL GROUP OF PEOPLE. *Or I might use the term "make life difficult for".'* After reading out the list twice, Hill will then encourage the group to positively *prefer* one or two of the options. If necessary, there's a voting procedure. The three most favoured options will go forward for further exploration. That however leaves the problem of those who have voted for unfavoured options. Hill advises keeping a note of these personal decisions, because there may be some way for these to be brought in later. But now the purpose is to find the macro view. Could the favoured plot lines be represented pictorially, using large pieces of paper? Would it be possible for the two storylines to be combined? For example, A LARGE GROUP OF PEOPLE OPPRESSES A SMALL GROUP OF PEOPLE and A GROUP GOES ON A JOURNEY? This stage of the process is characterised by discussion, experimentation and a search for common agreement. But what if the group has split and no amount of negotiations mitigates that conflict? Then the facilitator could take that 'disagreement about the truth' as another element in the story. *'Because if we're talking about two different views of reality, that is essentially what drama is about . . . It's like Catholics and Protestants. A death happens. Did it happen this way or did it happen that way? But I won't try and integrate the two opposites. Because obviously part of the dynamism of the group exists around those two views.'*

Once a storyline is agreed, it's written up on the wall. Then Hill will divide the group and send each sub-group off to brainstorm around the plotline. He encourages them to think of as many different scenarios as possible, in whatever place or time is appropriate. They can draw from films, personal experience, history or literature. They all get written up on the wall. This stock of material provides a source for the improvisational work which follows and which takes up most of the devising process.

David Slater's work with retired people was stimulated by going on journeys with a group of pensioners to the South Coast. They would pile out of the minibus and take over one of the local pubs, regaling all and sundry with a cocktail of jokes, anecdotes and songs. Could such vivacity and inventiveness be channelled into theatre-making at the home base? Some years later at Rotherhithe in London, there is a pool of retired people who perform as community actors in a project called Time and Talents. These individuals include several who have learning difficulties or a mental handicap. Slater describes the role of the group as being 'chroniclers of the age'. The creative process is very much a get-together; it's a chance to get out of the house, have a cup of tea and chat. There's emphasis on the meeting-place atmosphere. The process of theatre-making often begins with an invitation: maybe a primary school has asked for a performance to commemorate an anniversary, or a conference would welcome a short play on pensioners' lives. With the commitment to devising in place, there begins a search for narrative. But to get to narrative, we need a central character. *'Because we're trying to locate a new story that exists "within the group", so as a group we have to find it. So sometimes the approach is to do with . . . creating a fictional person, looking at their situation and looking at a moment. We're always trying to find an individual on the edge, as it were. Finding the place and the time which allows the group to have a take on that moment, a belief in that predicament. It might be someone of, say, 75, and from there on, invariably, it's just been a question of moving time forward and back, unravelling.'*

The KEY MOMENT might be relatively banal – an old woman decides she wants a cup of tea. But by speculating around it, a web of relationships is established. The zoom lens, having started in close, widens out. Why is that character alone? Has she ever been married? Who would be likely to visit her? The group speak from a sympathy with that character. They hope to see their own predicaments acted out. Layers are peeled away until we see that beneath the apparent ordinariness there are great, perhaps heroic struggles. *'It's a spontaneous way of allowing (older) people to make their own theatre, using their own skills. I don't think that anything I've done has involved imparting theatre skills. It's all there already . . . Because of all the negotiation you have to do. If you're ninety you have to do so much negotiation and bartering, so many sleights of hand with all the people that pass you by all those years. It's survival techniques. You bring those to the stage.'*

The facilitator teases out a story through asking questions. 'Who does the central character talk to most frequently?' 'Always to a neighbour.' 'That neighbour has a mother herself who likes to . . .' etc. Once other characters are invented, group members are asked to assume those roles. And then the improvisations begin. Because in this kind of group ideas 'tumble out' and members may not be skilled in collaborating over sharing ideas. There's a balance to be found. After all, with the learning disabled especially, it's necessary to create open space which will allow them to contribute. *'It's a question of finding the fictions which people can throw their own experiences on to. Without prejudice. So it frees people up to talk about their own problems, but within the disguise of the fiction.'* Once a compendium of moments is compiled, then the shape of the play starts to emerge. *'One play called "The Decision" dealt with the question of responsibilities which arose when a man was no longer able to support himself in his own flat. Should he go to a residential home, should he go to the children, live with them? Narrative then took us to situations which we wanted to explore.'*

And then there are songs. As situations are discussed, song titles are remembered: Let's All Go Down The Strand, It's A Great Big Shame, Suffragette songs. A moment later, the song may be sung. The final play will be *'shot through with songs from the 20s, 30s and 40s.'* There's no determination to arrive at a finished script. Slater hones down the dramatic material, but improvisation is maintained into performance, despite what are sometimes unpredicted moments.

WORKING FROM A THEME

Some facilitators prefer to introduce a theme at the outset. The choice is vital, if it's the wrong choice, the work may never gather momentum. Sometimes staff members encourage the adoption of a particular theme. This may even be a precondition to the work; that it deals with health, drugs or safe sex. The danger here lies in working to the staff agenda when it doesn't chime with the group's agenda. The group don't want to feel a topic is being forced on them. Harriet Powell and Clair Chapwell of Spare Tyre Theatre Company work predominantly with youth groups. Harriet Powell: *'We always go in with a theme and that can be very broad. Sometimes it's been suggested by teachers. Our next project is, we've been commissioned to do a show about "the future", that will be our general theme . . . and we see no harm in that . . . we don't push things on the group, we are entirely about the experiences that are relevant to them.'*

It may be a matter of negotiating with the teachers. Clair Chapwell: *'And after (a piece about AIDS) the teachers said, what about drugs because drugs is the theme we want to hear about, but we chose to do a show about addictions . . . '* In fact, the couple observe, this theme did prove problematic because although relevant, the young people found it hard to admit their addictions. So the task of realising material from personal experience became partially thwarted. Where a theme has worked best is where a group is able to look back on issues in their lives from a position of some distance. So a successful theme was 'sexism in schools' with a group which was on the edge of leaving school. Despite the theme generating enormous tensions, the project was successful because it was able to find some measure of resolution for these within the group. The understandings which resulted from that resolution, contributed a wealth of material.

What the company aims to achieve is a process whereby group members are gently provoked into becoming the creative authors of the material, even though the facilitators may write the script. The script is closely based on improvisations. In that sense, the use of a preselected theme is seen as saving time – it allows the group to get on quickly with inventing sketches, improvising and writing songs. Music is always an integral part of the process. Early games use music to get the group easy with the traditions of singing, making rhythms and performing musically. Individuals who already have instrument skills will be encouraged to bring their instruments in. *'Sometimes people play a bit of flute, a bit of guitar – we had a cello in the last show – however small the talents, we build on that. And with singing, we do a lot of vocal exercises. We work on confidence-building for singing. It's a question of getting used to the sound of your own voice and just enjoying doing it.'*

So the company's pattern goes: initial drama games and exercises, discussion around the theme to provoke ideas, then selection of threads which can be woven into dramatic or musical material. Group members may be encouraged to take home ideas to work on, and return with material to try out the next day. For example, in one show, the young women were asked to make two lists. Firstly, a list of 3 good things about being a woman, secondly, 3 bad things. The subject matter on the lists was then used as starting points for both songs and sketches. Another exercise involved drawing a picture of a situation where one felt oneself to be most distinctively 'different' from others – again, impros were created from this. Working with older people, the process was not dissimilar, only slower. Clair and Harriet used objects to stimulate memories. Phrases used by the older people, which encapsulated aspects of their past, were written down and worked into poems.

The sketch show is a commonly used format by Spare Tyre, evolving from their own work as a professional women's touring company. It allows a relatively swift transition from initial idea to performance material. In one youth theatre project, prohibitions against smoking are satirised by drawing on the television style of *The Twilight Zone*, and with the addition of an invented rap song, the idea soon feels complete. The finished show will likely conclude as a series of both comic and serious sketches, interlaced with songs. This allows for material to be added to, or subtracted from, right up to the last minute.

WORKING FROM CHARACTER

Often people come to theatre workshops imagining that character work will be primary. And in drama school it's often true, this work comes early. I prefer to see it come late. Too early a concentration on character can mean the individual losing sight of group objectives. Participants become so involved with character that all you hear is 'My character would . . . ' or 'My character wouldn't . . . ' A sense of shared responsibility for the group project starts to be lost. However, Mike Leigh, Lois Weaver and others place an exploration of character early in the process. Leigh's process, now well known, involves each actor choosing an individual known personally to them, then building a character around that perception. The actor will initially present several such characters, then Leigh will choose one to be concentrated on, or ask for two to be merged. This character-building may even take place separately from other actors, perhaps the actor going out into the streets of the city *as* that character. So by the time characters 'meet' in improvisation, they are already grounded within their subjective worlds. Such techniques probably need to be used discerningly within community drama as they can mitigate against group solidarity. (Leigh's practice, to my knowledge, is used exclusively with professional actors). However, the technique of holding back information from actors *about* the other actors (i.e. the other actors' characters) until the moment of staged inter-action, can stimulate powerful improvisations.

A more collaborative route to character work is offered through movement. It's only when physical personae have been developed that personal biographies get considered. This process might begin by actors simply walking the room, exploring how emphasis can be placed on different parts of the body. Every individual carries stress and tension differently. One person is all shoulders, another all hips or stomach. In deliberately switching the emphasised part of the body while walking, participants experience a range of different sensations. Characters can begin life this way. A particular way of walking starts to generate an embryonic, interior life for a character with its own moods and impulses. The actor begins to imagine phrases their character might use. The actor discovers whether their character is extrovert or introvert, and how they respond to provocation.

Lois Weaver uses fantasy to stimulate ideas for characters' movement. This process might begin by thinking extravagantly: who would you like to be? Don't be too narrow or restricted in your answer. Napoleon, Madonna, James Dean – if these characters work for us at a fantasy level, maybe we could begin there. Why not aim for a character who is very, very different from who I am – but has a quality I envy? Weaver encourages participants to draw from current and popular iconography. But the admired figure doesn't have to be Beyoncé or Brad Pitt, it could be an imaginary character, an emperor, a dancer or a prostitute. Then using the image of that person, participants explore how they can transform physically. So the questioning goes: 'Where is James Dean in your body?' The task is to find that quality of James Dean and exaggerate it, to move with that essence. We're not trying to mimic or impersonate but to find where in the body that person seems to exist; in the hips, the legs, the chest, where? Then the actor works with that physical quality to develop their own individual and unique persona. Which is you . . . but at the same time, not you. *'I'm not training actors but creating the independent artist. People who come into that situation often think about what it means to be an actor. But what we're thinking about is what it takes to be a creative person. And therefore a creative artist.'*

Lois often works within the gay and lesbian community. When the work is not anchored to performance, there's more emphasis on working with people separately, on their own but still within the group context, looking at how they might move their characterisation forward. Following this one-to-one work, there might be a coming back to the circle where characters are introduced to each other. Character work is extended through inter-action. Dean meets Madonna meets the Emperor. Clothes provide another route: 'These shoes are butch, those shoes are femme'. Using word associations helps to break up traditional ideas about what makes something masculine or feminine. Concepts and ideas are selected which cut against the way that gender and sexuality is traditionally understood. *'There's another route, too. I guide them into two possible characters. Sometimes those two possible characters come from my perfect body and my imperfect body. Or my butch body and my femme body. And I bring them back to the circle and have them do a one-line story. For example, "One day I am so and so, and another day someone else. I am Jack and sometimes I am Jill". So it's a one line story. Then I get them to take one of those and to develop a life and a text for that character alone . . . I prefer to use association exercises to create biography rather than having them sit down and write a literal biography. For example saying "I remember" from Jack's point of view. Or "I don't remember" – then writing a list of what you don't remember.'* What is not remembered is then incorporated. So by a process of association we generate rough material, then take one fragment of that and generate further associations around it. For example, in the list of what is not remembered is the fact that the father disappeared for six months. So that fact, denied by the character, can then be 'associated around.' Although some elements of personal biography might have been the starting point, we're moving away from any accurate recollection and towards a random, unpredictable set of resonances which can establish a fictional character. Then characters meet and the work moves forward through their meetings. By this time, the characters are embodying desires and fantasies which lift the work away from naturalism into a heightened, exaggerated theatricality, perhaps incorporating costume. Then the process leads off towards a show or remains more reflectively within the workshop parameters.

WORKING FROM DOCUMENTARY MATERIAL

In our fourth example, Phil Knight, Director of Third Theatre, begins with documentary material. The company's approach might use diaries, documents from a court case, or a sheaf of letters as a starting point. The company's production of *Guernica* took diaries and other records from the town, prior to and following the bombing. *Material Unaccounted For* took a news report about a nuclear accident in Brazil. The Guernica diaries were so rich in emotional incident and personal anecdotage that stimulating character work was easy. With the Brazilian tale however, there were no character sketches, only the bald report, so all had to be worked up from the ground imaginatively.

The devising process begins by participants bringing in material which might connect with the story. That material might be literary, photographic or visual, associating directly or indirectly with the story. This material will be used to trigger initial improvisations. With *Guernica*, as indicated, there was more than sufficient; characters were described in the diaries in some detail. So the work began with exercises to explore these characters. *'Because of the way the material was presented, we took bits of what was written and filled out a character for each actor. Everybody played everybody. We played about with these people. . . . We'd improvise a boss and a servant. Then we'd swap it (the casting) around, and in the end we'd choose the best relationship (which the casting offered).'*

Working with documentary material, decisions inevitably have to be made about allegiance to the truth of the documents. The group was committed to respecting the accounts as they were written; there was no intention to rewrite history. So when improvising, Knight had to set imagined events against what was already known. He didn't want to improvise *in spite of* known events. So when imaginary scenes were created, 'decisions' about these characters had to be set against the knowledge of what happened when the town was bombed. Can what we have created imaginatively, remain consistent with what we know of the character's behaviour *as reported?* And the other question alongside this is, how can we guess at what they would do, given what we know of them already? If one creates a complete coward out of Pablo, but we know for a fact he is brave at the bomb's impact, can this prior characterisation be justified? *'If we're working on a real event – and we want a character in there, and there's an argument about how they'd react – what we tend to do, is just improvise it through. At this stage the character is fixed in a certain way, and the answer comes immediately from the improvisation. Should the soldier, for example, shoot this particular person because he's obviously very political, and hated the arms manufacturer? So perhaps he should. But we're stuck within various constrictions – and he didn't shoot him in the book. But the actor was saying, "Well, he'd shoot him." But we acted the scene out, and he didn't shoot him. He couldn't shoot him. He knew it would have broken all the rules of his character. And that answered a question that could have been discussed for days.'*

While this character work is going on, the group will also be generating physical images of key incidents. It's as if a photograph album was being compiled – so there's a store of photos to draw from when the narrative is assembled. The group might spend up to about a third of the time available simply playing with the material in these different ways. The next priority becomes the work of creating 'the skeleton of the piece', *'which is like saying "those two people are going to have that conversation then" and "that argument will be in the play" and "that incident where all the soldiers rush off is also going to be in it".'* It's an editing process, splicing together improvisational material and linking it with other phantom scenes as yet undevised which history or dramaturgical sense suggests ought to be present. Such scenes might call for soldiers, mayors or housewives to be introduced or might involve tying up of ends, e.g. after the bombing. Constantly the aim is to adhere to historical accuracy. Where there are accounts of individual behaviour, these are cornerstones.

With *Material Unaccounted For*, the process was more reliant upon imagining particulars out of the general. The story is not so well

known. Some students in Brazil, needing money, broke into a disused
radiation treatment clinic. They stole the equipment before selling it
on to a scrap dealer. The dealer, a gypsy, not understanding its significance, broke it up for sale again. But he retained some capsules of
pretty blue powder. He and his family had a party, and family members
all painted themselves with this pretty blue powder. They were particularly impressed by the way the powder glowed in the dark. When
people started growing sick, and some died, they thought it must be
cursed powder. But they couldn't find a remedy. Eventually modern
science offered a diagnosis through the local doctor. This doctor
advised them to take the substance to a clinic. On the bus journey, the
gypsy accidentally dropped a trail of powder over twenty five miles, all
along the route. The paper bag was thrown away and was recycled as
toilet paper. The ghastly saga led finally to 25 miles of territory being
cordoned off and every single inhabitant expelled from it.

Here there was considerable scope for interpretation, albeit any loss
of the story's central thread would destroy the authenticity of the exercise. As in the other example, speculations about particular characters
were found to be more useful onstage than off. Or if they originated offstage in discussion, they had to be tested through a process of acting out.

In both the Guernica and the radiation story projects, as the period
of playing drew to an end, the director took on the responsibility of
editing the material down to create a *mise en scène*. A storyboard for the
play is brought into rehearsal, having been worked out privately,
consisting of scenes based on improvisations, images created earlier
and scenes yet to be devised. Then a process of rehearsal begins. As to
style, Third Theatre place stress on movement, choreography and
heightened characterisations *'using the body rather than words – this
process is fundamental'*. There is neither script nor props – the scene-
by-scene action provides the armatural structure. Other characteristics
of an ensemble style develop organically, for example, actors playing
several characters, and the use of physical tableaux which move and
shift, creating alternative realities.

Knight stresses that the facilitator/director's role is largely about
maintaining disciplines which are unalterable; ensuring actors attend
warm-ups and monitoring character development with each member.
The same applies whether the context is professional, community or
student. He also talks about not falling victim to the need to 'entertain'
the actors. They are there to find pleasure *within* the work, not to judge

success around whether the process feels entertaining. Finally, the director's job is to ensure the founding idea is adhered to – even though it may change, its essence has defined the character of the project. You may begin *'with a triangle and end up with a square, but what's important is you retain the quality of the triangle you started with . . . In the end you want everybody to be happy and play, and use their imaginations in a free way . . . But it's important to keep a very firm idea of where you want to go, that is totally changeable. I know it sounds like a paradox, but that's what it is.'*

WORKING CONCEPTUALLY

This approach is more commonly found within a professional theatre context where company members share working conventions. It's less of a methodological process since it relies more on imaginative hypotheses. There is less a sense of starting here and moving through these points to there, than pragmatically switching direction according to a constantly reassessed order of priorities. However, there are features of this approach which are transferable into a community context, not least the democratic nature of the working processes and the determination to devise work which springs from the collective imagination of the devisers. The two practitioners quoted are Mark Long of the People Show and Pete Brooks of Insomniac Productions.

Mark Long argues that for the People Show, *'it's not absolutely necessary for someone to come along with some deeply thought-out notion or criteria or idea. Devising can be down to a group of people from day one. Usually people are very inhibited if they don't have the big idea – they feel that there should be something of enormous importance here. Something we're going to dedicate our lives to, for the next X weeks. Having said that, I do think it's important that* during the process *of creation, the group* does *start to realise that notion and does start to dedicate its life to it. And if you've got the right kind of trust, the big idea does evolve.'*

So the People Show begin with just a 'flicker'. The 'flicker' in previous shows has been a musical score (number 97), the idea of doing a show in a ballroom (number 99) and the information that Chet Baker died falling out of an Amsterdam window which was only 8 feet off the ground (number 100). Clearly, when you have one hundred or so devised shows under your belt, you've experimented around a bit. In the Chet Baker show, the group began the devising process by listening to Baker's music. It then moved to creating a set. In previous shows the set-building might have preceded even the music. The business of actually building something together stimulates discussion, ideas and plot lines. And it's important for people coming into the People Show to realise that this is expected of everyone. In the Chet Baker show, the set was to represent part of a hotel. Which, as well as connecting with the fragmentary theme, also had poignancy for the group. *'When we looked at his touring schedules, and our touring schedules, we saw a lot in common. A lot of one-night stands, two-night stands and an enormous amount of travelling times. He obviously lived the hotel life . . . '* Once built, the sculpture inevitably imposes itself on the thinking of the group. Certain ideas can now be tried out, others simply won't fit. Certain kinds of movement and certain scenarios suggest themselves. This approach might feel a bit like boxing yourself into a corner. However there's an expansiveness to the People Show's approach which is reflected in the way they perceive theatre as able to draw on several media at once especially sound and visual sources. The work of devising is seen as operating within a number of related disciplines – in turn this implies that company members need to feel happy to work away from their chosen discipline. Individuals are brought in who have only limited experience of performing but have expertise in lighting, music or video. Wherever they come from, it's expected they'll bring a commitment to the process and will contribute to it from the base of their own skill area. The challenge lies in learning from others.

Rather than these different individual orientations proving problematic, Long argues they're a positive benefit once the group starts to synthesise. *'When a group is working well, a "collective group consciousness" does start to appear. The track starts to get narrower. You all start to travel down the same line. Purely because of working in all the areas together, I think. Because even if you're not a musician, you should have ideas and notions about those other areas of the work and be able to make demands of those areas, and criticisms of those areas. In so many groups this doesn't happen, this compartmentalisation still does occur.'* So having begun with a fragment, built a set, played with scenarios, perhaps three-quarters of the way through rehearsals, the group starts editing down. By which time, some notion of a central idea is in place. However, there is deliberately no director in any of this. *'The People Show is very bad at telling people what to do. But we are very good at telling you how to do something. If you have an idea you want to achieve, we can help you realise it. We also tell people from day one that in many ways this is a chance to realise a fantasy they have about themselves or they've had artistically that they've never been able to achieve before . . . people do appreciate that freedom.'*

The second example draws from the approach of Pete Brooks. While Impact Theatre Co-operative was active during the 1980s, Brooks was influenced by the People Show's emphasis on a visual theatre language. Within Insomniac Theatre's trajectory the influence is still evident albeit the stamp of originality is distinct. Brooks also works with the National Youth Theatre and other similar non-professional companies. Like Mark Long, there are no key exercises you could pinpoint as essential to any 'method'. *'My work is not methodological . . . It's much more conceptual. The devising work I do is very much about devising ideas and then pragmatically realising them.'* Within what Brooks calls a kind of 'pre-devising devising' there are intellectual speculations around ideas, which can then be tried out. He looks for the kind of ideas which naturally offer themselves for theatrical rather than literary or filmic treatment – although, paradoxically, this does not exclude ideas 'about film.' *'There is an idea for a show which might be more or less worked through in terms of characterisation, narrative and, if you like, thematic. Privately, in my head or in conversation with other actors. . . . What we all understand is there are three processes. One is, in a sense, having an idea for a show. A second sense is visualising that idea as theatre. The third is realising that visualisation on stage.'*

As with the People Show, the kind of participants involved will be those who feel comfortable working with quite cerebral ideas. *'Improvisation is not a technique we use a lot . . . we work out how the scene should be . . . We don't do a lot of fumbling around. We don't do hours of improvisation . . . it's more cerebral than that . . . I've no time for actors who stand up and say "I'm sick of sitting around, let's do something." You have to work out what you're going to do. What does takes time (in terms of character work) is resolving internal paradoxes.'* The germinating idea for *L'Ascensore* was quite theoretical. It was initially worked out with students. It concerned this question: how far can you go in deconstructing a story into fragments and still have the audience able to reconstruct it? Brooks points out how we as readers happily accept the task of reconstruction in a novel, for example by Raymond Chandler. We're given certain fragments and the writer expects the reader to build a picture from them. The second germinating idea for

L'Ascensore was the traditional idea of the 'heart of darkness' – man's or woman's journey into the private self. (The show was done initially with a woman at the centre, then with a man.) Once these ideas were in place, then it was a question of discussing how they could be realised on stage through movement, image and design. During this stage of experimentation there occurred the kind of creative leap that every deviser hopes for – when the image appears which embodies, contains and illustrates the essence of the themes being conjured with. In this case it was the idea of putting a lift on stage. No more than that. So the river journey became a journey of a lift travelling between floors. At each floor, different events occurred. Each sequence helped the audience reconstruct the background narrative.

'When you make a piece, you ask every possible question you can ask of the piece, and answer it, and if you're looking for an idea, you ask every possible question of what that idea has to do. And what you do is eliminate lots and lots of stuff until that creative part of your brain that's looking for ideas is looking in a smaller and smaller area so it's not grasping at anything – you're not saying it could be a rock musical or the answer could be Cliff Richard – no the answer is a lift . . . and that process is shared with the group.' Once the concept of the lift was in place, it became possible for the team of students to exploit the creative freedom offered by it. Having narrowed down, now the process opened out. *'What I tend to try and do within a teaching process is to create a structure within which the students have total creative freedom in the hope that the armatural structure will hold together their disparate creativity. So in L'Ascensore you have fundamentally an episodic structure. So what happens on each floor, or level, is left to the students to input as they want. So I would say "The lift is going to stop on certain floors, there are certain performative climaxes we look for . . . certain rhythmic structures, we need to contrast for example, interior and exterior, small numbers of people, large numbers of people", all the kind of textual juxtapositions that make a show, then I'm able to say "Make some scenes".'*

Pete Brooks draws on the jazz analogy, as Jeff Nuttal did when referring to People Shows as jazz-like constructions, to explain the notions of boundaries and freedom. He argues that what gives jazz musicians their enormous creative freedom is the constraints provided by the key signature they're working in. In the same way, the world of a piece of theatre can contain anything, but it too has boundaries. It may contain only what rightfully belongs within that world. This idea belongs in the show, that doesn't. *'The secret to devising work is . . . about creating a language – a visual, physical, textual language which everyone speaks, and if anyone speaks outside that language, it's not acceptable within the piece. (The key signature represents) a theatrical world, it's a world with rules and logic, it's a parallel universe and you know immediately if something doesn't belong in that world. If everyone agrees about how that world defines itself, then the only problem at that point is, creating the material and editing it.'*

WORKING FROM IMAGE

In this section, we look at a process which starts with a blank piece of paper and uses imagework techniques to build the play. The advantage of this approach is that it can be used with almost any group, irrespective of previous experience. The contemporary master of imagework is Augusto Boal – followers have borrowed from his extensive wardrobe of techniques, and applied them everywhere from Shakespeare to theatre-in-education. Here the example is a play devising process which I led with a mixed company of ex-offenders and professional performers. The play, *The Anger Dyes*, was devised for touring into prison and criminal justice venues. The process moved methodically through different stages: definition of theme, definition of theatrical world, exploration of that world, determination of plot, rehearsal.

Finding the theme   There is an assumption made here which is that although we haven't predetermined a theme, there are themes already in place, albeit below the surface of the group's consciousness. These might take the form of dilemmas, preoccupations or shared dreams. We're not aware of them in the sense that we can easily articulate them, but they do reveal themselves through the drama work and we are able to recognise their significance when they emerge. Hence the need to hunt down the themes afresh each time. So in a project like this we begin ignorantly, without preconceptions; it's a research project on ourselves. It might begin for example by running some simple image exercises like MY DILEMMA, IMAGE OF A JOURNEY, NARRATIVE IMAGES or MONOLOGUES. These allow individuals to bring forward their personal experiences. MY DILEMMA simply asks a participant to construct a sculpted image using others from the group, which represents a current or recent dilemma. A woman sculpted an image of herself sitting in a park while close by a man and a woman were playing – or were they fighting? If she intervened on the woman's behalf and they were only playing, her intervention would be resented. In another, a woman stands on the side of a river. In the water, there's a man, drowning. By her side another man stands whispering 'If you try to save him, you'll drown.'

IMAGE OF A JOURNEY asks participants to find a dramatic metaphor for their current life journey. A volunteer instructs other group members on their roles. One participant set up his metaphorical world as a jukebox in which he was the ball. Propelled into a maze of moving objects, each actor pushed him away with a line. 'Don't come near me!' 'You're not allowed in here!' 'You can't afford it!' 'Get back where you came from!' MONOLOGUES also starts with the individual. Actors are each asked to create a character for themselves. They decide where that character is and what they're doing. Then the task is simply to speak directly to the audience, unheard by other characters. An example: a woman sits on her bed and talks about how her boyfriend beats her. But this time when he comes home, she says, it'll be different. She produces a knife from under her pillow.

My approach at this stage is to take copious notes of the imagery generated. To these I add notes of how participants responded to the different images as they appeared. These responses are important since they cue us in to the most resonant images. Even off-the-cuff comments are useful. Before long my notebook is a mass of drawings (matchstick men) and phrases stuck alongside. (Janet's image. A man holds out a hand to a woman but she recoils. 'He's an abuser', said one spectator. 'It's her father and she doesn't trust him', said another. 'He represents temptation', says a third.) Other facilitators I know use a polaroid camera at this point, which ensures a more exact record. While the work is being created, there's little discussion of themes, it's important not to descend into the kind of psychologising which makes people nervous about revealing personal details. And the work *is* revealing, no doubt about that, but there's considerable room for choice as to *what* to reveal and *how* to reveal it.

The process of discerning themes from the imagery and their interpretations might be done with the group or I might take all the notes away and study them at home. Perhaps the key theme doesn't leap up immediately. It's more buried, or there are several key themes. It's like the shape hidden within those 'magic eye' pictures. you have to look from the right angle and with a degree of indifference, or you miss it. But usually the primary theme leaps to the front – in which case you propose it back at the next session. If the analysis is correct, the group will recognise that. They may be surprised to have hit upon such a profound theme without intending to do so.

This facilitative task of discovering and proposing a theme is divinatory. It involves consciously looking below the surface. Using the term 'divination' is not casual, there is a real sense of getting the material to 'speak to you'. It calls for receptivity, being careful not to impose your own preferred interpretation. At the same time, instinct *can* be combined with a more methodological approach. You ask questions of the imagery: 'Where does the power lie in these pictures? Are the characters the same status or do they have unequal status?' 'Are there any recurring motifs?' 'Where is the primary conflict and who is it between?' 'Within the pictures, are there observers? Is there anything distinctive about all the characters who are experiencing difficulty? And so on.

Preferably the theme should be expressed as a paradox. A theme expressed only as a word – 'bullying' or 'drugs' – may be inadequate. Paradox implies conflict and conflict implies action. So conceptualising the theme as paradox can help lift us into improvisation. Besides, we're not making a statement to the audience but asking a question of them, one which genuinely preoccupies us. Working on *The Anger Dyes* we arrived at the theme of identity. It shone through from our early imagework. But then we asked, could this theme be expressed more dynamically? Could we be more specific? We arrived at this question: *'Who am I if I'm not who you say I am?'* which was both paradoxical and implied a conflict. It suggested a central character who, in a search for identity, met stereotyping. This in turn caused self-doubt. With this question in place, it was possible to set up improvisations quite easily. We had a central character, we had a conflict. There also emerged a secondary theme concerning male violence and female revenge. Rather than abandon this element, we were able to draw it in to create a sub-plot. This balance between plot and sub-plot reflected the fact that some of the cast had it as a priority theme, others didn't.

Finding the world   Once the theme is in place, we have to determine the world of the play. This will give us a theatrical language which is appropriate for kicking the theme around in. If the company has limited performing experience, probably we'll use a rough naturalism, stretching it at different moments to incorporate rhythm, movement or tableaux. If the company is more experienced there's scope for a less orthodox theatrical language in which case we may bring in different directors to help define the style. To arrive at a decision about the world, we needed to ask some questions. Have any ideas been thrown up by early impros? How diverse are our options? Could the play be set in a playground, a nightclub, the inside of someone's head, a desert, a castle in the 13th century? What kind of theatrical world would give us the most scope? An exercise like THE BRIDGE or Q and A might be used to throw up ideas. Once suggestions are written up, we can try them out by running INSTANT IMAGES. We determine the stage as one of our possible ideas, say a nightclub or a park. Any actor can go into the space and begin moving as a character from that world. Others who recognise what's happening, also get up to join in. They make a scene quickly and sit down. Then another actor gets up to start another scene. Quite simply, if people get to their feet and create characters and situations which work, we know that world has potential. Then we must ask, are these scenes connected with the theme? Do they help us dramatise the theme? Working on *The Anger Dyes*, we discovered that the world of a South London housing estate gave us an almost unlimited supply of characters: restless teenagers, cheerful gossips, mothers under pressure, crack dealers, social workers, upbeat local politicians and anguished vicars. This was a world in which our central characters might seek their identity. Of course we retained the option of going outside this world, i.e. moving to another location, but if we did this, we did it knowing it to be a geographical digression to be returned from.

Finding the plot   With a world selected, it's time to pursue a narrative line. The group might be divided into sub-groups, given one aspect of the theme and asked to devise short scenes. An instruction might be: 'Within a couple relationship, one partner experiences identity denial. How is this possible? Show, in a scene'. Or 'Devise a movement sequence which shows in a series of images the impact of external prejudice on the individual body'. Or again: 'Devise a chorus line routine which draws from gestures which are associated with the expression of prejudice'. Alternatively, THE GATE will allow for quite an exhaustive exploration of the theme. It can be allowed to run for half an hour or so, generating characters and storylines faster than any discussion.

We had already decided that our central character would be a man. We now needed a narrative line which would allow this character to meet with assumptions about his identity which he felt were wrong. After exploring several ideas, we hit on the following: this man had been in prison and was now returning to his former home, the estate. People there had known him as a bully, a hard man who built relationships on fear and violence. But now we wanted him to reject this identity. This would create the kind of inner and outer conflicts we were looking for. But why, credibly, would he want to reject his former self-image? Simply having a conversion was too implausible – it'd be a kind of magic solution, therefore false. We needed a device. We came up with the following image – a prison brawl had left him suffering from partial amnesia only he'd covered it up because he didn't want it to affect his release plans. This enabled him, when he met former associates, to be confused about their assumptions of him. He simply couldn't remember the earlier vendettas, the drug deals, the rivalries. He no longer felt like the hard man who used violence to get results. Now he wanted a different kind of life.

So he rejected what others projected on to him. But if he wasn't this hard man, who was he? *'Who Am I If I'm Not Who You Say I Am?'* To answer the question we decided it was necessary for him to revisit the crime which had led him to prison. He simply couldn't remember it. In this crime and the events surrounding it, lay the key to understanding. So he became, as it were, a detective on his own crime. This journey of detection would provide the central plot thread. And to sharpen the conflict, while he played detective, others pursued him for unfinished business. None of this he fathomed. Least of all could he understand why the gossips were muttering that he'd lost his bottle.

Once this narrative was there, it became a question of experimenting with scenarios to get the best from the story's potential. Once improvisations had been tried, the director/facilitator became authorial, selecting out scenes to form the scenography. The actors for their part, having been involved in all key decisions regarding casting as well as theme and storyline, were now sufficiently anchored in the production to trust the process to the end.

THE SUN SHINES AT MIDNIGHT:
MODELS OF PARTICIPATORY THEATRE

I. INSTANT THEATRE

While the better-known Forum Theatre is combative, Instant Theatre is celebratory. It celebrates narrative and the power of an audience to create narrative. While seemingly operating in wilful ignorance of conventional theatre wisdom, Instant Theatre has in fact its own carefully constructed conventions which facilitate a unique actor–audience relationship. It was developed by R.G. Gregory whose experiments in participatory theatre language in Europe and Africa led towards a theatre form which puts the actors at the service of the audience. Gregory had worked with Stephen Joseph, many of whose ideas about the round he adopted. He also visited Dorothy Heathcote's training programme, but ended up moving away from, rather than towards, her ideas of actors-in-role. What was required, he decided, was a form which *'placed the control of the story in the hands of the audience, rather than having it controlled by the teacher.'* For him, this meant a search for a series of conventions which governed both the creation of the story and its acting out. In turn this changed the emphasis of the actor's role from 'doer' to 'receiver'.

INSTANT THEATRE begins with the assembling of the audience on four sides of a rectangle. It's important that the audience should be evenly spread with good sight lines and easy access to the enclosed stage area. The ideal number is around 100. Congregated blocks of either sex are avoided – especially with younger audiences. If necessary, spectators are asked to move seats. The questioner enters the stage area and having introduced the company – which usually numbers two other actors beside the questioner – begins the programme. There are several different kinds of INSTANT THEATRE programmes, but formally three different ways of beginning. The simplest starts with a series of neutral, open questions. The programme Detectives, for example, begins in this way. There is no initial scene or use of props. The questioner merely begins the questioning about the central character. A second way to begin uses cards. Here, large-scale playing cards are produced which might, for example, feature a range of folktale characters. Members of the audience are invited to pick three different cards. The first card will give us the central character, the second, two subsidiary characters. Once selected, the questioning will begin. A third way to begin involves the company acting out a short scene. For example, in *The Survivor*, an old wo/man is thrown out of a hostel for setting light to a bed. The Survivor renounces all further help from the Social Services and vows to go off alone. The questioning would pick up from this point to find an articulation of this character's subsequent journey.

There are now fixed guidelines for how the questioning in INSTANT THEATRE develops. Firstly, if we haven't already defined our central character, this must be established. In Detectives for example, the questioner might ask whether the Detective will be a man, a woman, a boy or a girl. A key feature of Instant Theatre is that all answers heard must be accepted. If contradictory answers are heard, the ensuing paradox is fed back to the audience: they must resolve it. For example, if two answers to this first question are 'a man' and 'a woman', the audience is asked how that might be possible. It could emerge that the detective is a man but dresses in women's clothing or that the detective is a woman, but works with a male partner. Once this has been sorted out and the 'who' is established, subsequent questions tease out a narrative. R. G. Gregory: *'When we started going abroad in the eighties, teachers became interested in the system . . . so I devised the system of the five 'W's: Who, When, Where, the Weather, What happens next . . . First you ask about the who. You establish enough about the who so you've got a thumbnail sketch of the (central) character. Then you say "When does this story start about this woman?" So you ask about the season, then the day of the week, then about the time of day. Then you ask where, and people may say "in bed" or "in America", two different concepts. Both of them are not enough. It's like a film. If it's in bed, you have to take the camera back. If it's in America you have to take it in. So intermediate questions are asked in order to develop the Where more clearly. Once you've got the Where, you can't ask about the What until you ask about the weather. If it's a bright, sunny day in winter, that's different from a snowy day in winter. It's not different from the kind of information you'd ask about to build any play. Then you ask, given the weather, what is the who doing? Then you ask what happens next?'*

There is no censorship of answers. No audience member is told their contribution is unacceptable – if it contradicts in some way with information already held then the contradiction is offered back for resolution. So the medium deliberately incorporates both paradoxes and imperfections. 'What's the name of the king . . . ? 'Um . . . ' 'George'. 'King Um George.' So for the rest of the story, the man who lives in a castle whose slippers are the size of a lake, is known as King Um George. *'I was working in a school in Sweden. Potatoes came into the answer. It was necessary to ask about the type of potato, so I did. Some boy behind me made a joke that I didn't hear and everybody around him laughed. So I turned to him and said "Come on, tell us. Put it into the story." And he said "Nie, nie" meaning no, no. So I took what he said. And then I asked "What kind of potato is that?" And this same voice said "It's a Nine Eye Potato".'* What emerges is a story whose fabric is rich in colours, incidents and contradictions. It must however, be actable. Just as a playwright would, the questioner is looking to create a story which will make good theatre not just a good story.

At a point where sufficient information has been gathered, the questioner retells the story to the audience. There's often an audible shift in the audience's perception of the exercise at this point. Perhaps they hadn't quite believed that all answers would be taken. Perhaps they're surprised that the questioner can remember so much. (But it's always easier to remember a story when it's you that asked the questions.) Perhaps too, they're surprised the story can develop such a conceptual unity given the apparent randomness of the process.

Next the questioner invites the audience to act out its story. It can only take place *with* the audience – the company will not act out the audience's story on their behalf. However the central character is always played by a company member while the second actor will play a number of smaller parts. Gregory likens these two functions to the poles and pegs which keep up a tent. The first actor provides the central pole while the second harnesses the necessary tension by supplying pegs around the edges. Once the story has been recapitulated, the questioner names the parts which need playing. There's no coercion and no direct invitations. Audience members have to come forward – if they don't, there's no play. *All the parts – including the inanimate objects, the weather, key material objects, in fact all elements of*

the story, are played by people. There are no material props and no set.
If Dracula has a cloak, someone plays the cloak, assuming it has a
function in the story. If the saucepan on the boil contains Margaret
Thatcher, Barbara Windsor and a pound of plums, people must play
these separate parts. If the wind has a smile on its face, someone may
have to play the smile. *'You have to work out which are the important
parts to be played. There are stock ways of representing rain, mist, sun. It's
stock theatre. The actors are not acting out particular, peculiar characters.
They are like commedia dell'arte figures. For example, if you're playing an
evil king, you play the evil king, you don't try and make him particular to
that occasion. You play the archetypal representation of that figure . . . And
they do not have to sustain the characterisation right the way through. They
give a few broad brush strokes to begin with and later on, drop from that.'*
Once there are sufficient volunteers, the questioner becomes a kind of
stage manager, setting out and preparing for the acting out. Volunteers
are directed where to stand initially. The first actor character may have
one or two audience members alongside because, for example, the
detective begins the story with a magnifying glass and a gun. When all
is ready, the first actor kickstarts the action.

*'Quite often when I've been the first actor, the character is in bed
asleep. The audience look around for the character in bed asleep and
they can't find anyone. Because I always make a point of starting from
outside the round. Whatever role I'm in, I try and surprise the audience
from the outside. I suddenly jump up in character and address the
person next to me. To give that moment of shock. Which is like this whole
business of acting in the round. Suddenly you're going to play a role and
you switch on this electric bar which runs down through you. Not a bar
which sends the heat in one direction. It radiates heat all round you.'*
Acting in Instant Theatre calls for the ability to 'radiate' rather than
'project' energy, and yield to, rather than dominate an audience.
It means giving yourself up to the audience's agenda. It's unlike
conventional impro in that the story is pre-given and cannot be
significantly moved away from. It's unlike scripted theatre because of
the need to be consistently engaging and interacting with the audience-
as-actors. You also need to hold them to the essential elements while
encouraging them to invent around those essentials. They're perfectly
at liberty to send the story up if they wish to, make jokes about it or use
any style of performance which fits with the form. The atmosphere is
usually boisterous. Meanwhile the questioner remains the controlling

influence, calling on audience members to play their parts, keeping the story on track.

After the initial piece of acting out, the audience return to their seats and a second set of questioning begins. This picks up the story where it left off. Now the audience has seen how the form works, they're familiar with the characters, perhaps they've been entertained by particular performances. So the answers come more quickly. It's like moving from the early days of photography when subjects stared unknowingly into the camera to today, when subjects knowingly exploit the medium. There is a second acting out, then a final questioning and a final acting out. It usually concludes within the hour.

Often when this process is described, the assumption is – this process is valueless because it's not controlled. There is no censorship or selection of material. It can be nothing but a jumble, a surreal pick-and-mix of diverse narrative elements which have a surface jokiness, but no more. In fact the company's experience of performing in countries over some twenty years suggests a different picture. The process creates a narrative fabric which is akin to a folktale or a myth, and can claim comparable resonance. The story represents a snapshot of the inner life of that group, at that moment in time. Gregory argues that this process allows it to function not only as an exercise in language and a raucous release of shared energies, but also as a signalling of the inner understandings of that group through a paradoxical, mythical, consistently ambiguous language.

2. FORUM THEATRE

Forum Theatre was developed by Augusto Boal and his collaborators, initially in Latin America in a period during the 60s and 70s. The dictatorship in Brazil had made it impossible any more to do popular or agitational theatre in the old way. As a result, his group developed Newspaper Theatre and later Forum Theatre. The latter allowed groups of peasants and workers to meet together to explore possible solutions to their problems through theatre. The form has since become popularised within Europe through his establishment of a Centre for Theatre of the Oppressed in Paris, set up in 1978. His arsenal of techniques have become increasingly familiar to theatre practitioners throughout the world. This is not least because of his books which have been translated into several languages.

Forum Theatre is one strategy, albeit perhaps the most influential, within the Theatre of the Oppressed system. Other principle forms include Image Theatre, Invisible Theatre and the techniques of the Rainbow of Desires. Given the current availability of published works on and by Augusto Boal, the purpose here is to do no more than summarise the essentials of the Forum Theatre model; its founding principles, its mechanics and its rules.

A key aspect of Forum Theatre is the re-positioning of the actor-audience relationship. The typically Boalian concept of 'spectactors' itself summarises the proactive role Boal has in mind for those who watch. They may be sitting in a seat watching, but they can and should be mobilised to cross the lights. Crossing the footlights means engaging in a theatricalised debate, being proactive in seeking solutions to social problems. In effect, what is being asked of the audience is that they should join in rehearsing strategies for life. This makes it sound a rather joyless and academic exercise, but those who have experienced the Boal touch will know that Forum Theatre is most effective when it's playful, non-coercive and humorous. It relies far more on humour and the spirit of collaborative play than it does on any ideas about political correctness.

While summarising the essentials of Forum, it may be useful to remember that it emerged initially from situations where people were familiar with each other. They shared a situation – as fellow-workers or rural labourers – so there wasn't the inevitable frostiness you find in many European theatres between spectators. There was less sense of 'us' the actors and 'them' the spectators. The context was a lot closer to what we traditionally view today as a theatre workshop situation.

One starting point is: those who feel themselves oppressed, become artists. The term 'oppressed' is often altered to a vernacular more familiar to different communities – 'done badly by' 'experienced injustice' 'unfairly treated'. As artists, the participants will use the language of art, of theatre, to express their concerns. A deliberately fictional world is then constructed in order to look at this reality. The intention is to fictionalise and theatricalise a problem and present it to an audience, to have them address it. Through this process, there can be a shared exploration of possible solutions.

The Forum Theatre play itself needs to be constructed according to specific guidelines. It's worth recapitulating the story which Boal tells, which led him to propose the founding concept. At the time his touring group was presenting short plays – stories of oppression – which allowed spectators to propose solutions to problems and then the actors would act these out. The technique was called Simultaneous Playwrighting. So a short play would lead to a moment of decision, then suggestions canvassed. The actors would take the suggestion, act it out and there would be discussion. This is how Boal told the story to Chris Vine in an interview in 1984. The setting was a community in Peru. *'But there was one occasion when I was doing this Simultaneous Playwrighting when suddenly a spectator told us something that we should do and I asked the actors to do what he had said. Then another spectator said "That doesn't work", and I was about to pass on to this second one when the first one said, "It didn't work because you didn't do what I told you to do, you did it differently." And then I said "OK, I'm sorry, so explain again what you want." and he explained a second time and I said, "Well, I thought that I had understood what you wanted but we are going to try again." Then we tried the same man's version a second time and then he said at the end – he was nervous – he said, "No, it's not like that, I didn't say that", and I said, "Well, explain to me again; what do you want?" And he explained for a third time and for the third time we tried it. We tried exactly what we had heard, exactly what we had understood, and we asked him, "Do you agree?" and he was very nervous and he said, "No, it's nothing like that." And then I was nervous myself and I said, "Well, if it's not like that, you come here and do it yourself" and he was very happy and said, "Yes, I am going to do it." And the extraordinary thing was that he came on stage and did it himself and he did exactly what we had done; it was the same thing but when he did it, it was completely different. We were* interpreting *somebody and he was* living *what he wanted. . . . When he did it he crossed the line and though he was in the fiction of the theatre, he was living completely that fiction. . . . We could not because we were* representing *his problems which were not our problems. We did our best, but there was a difference.'*[33]

So Forum Theatre moves this process one step on. It invites spectators to contribute by getting up themselves and trying out their own ideas. Therefore the play needs to be constructed as a provocation to the audience: we see a character, we see their problem, we see them defeated by the problem. And there's a question explicitly made. 'Can you accept this unsatisfactory ending?' 'Does anyone have an idea how the protagonist might avoid this fate?' 'What could she or he do?' I remember Boal talking about those films where the victim is about to go down into a dark cellar and you just *know* that down there lies the most terrible danger. *But* if the hero goes into that cellar knowingly – and prepared – he may live. While watching the film, you can do nothing about it, you can't help him. But in Forum, you can. You can leap up and say 'Stop!' and take over that part. So the play must be constructed with that provocation in mind. This has led to criticism; some have said the plays are too pessimistic because they inevitably end with defeat for the protagonist. But the play is not intended purely for a passive presentation. So here is a rough summary of the guidelines for creating Forum Theatre, based on my own interpretation of Boal's expressed determinants. The scenario must have:

i. A central idea. For example, 'how a family forces one to remain a child'. This has been arrived at by the group through a process of using Image Theatre or other techniques. It embodies the problem they want the audience to address.

ii. A conflict of wills between the protagonist (the oppressed character) and the antagonist (oppressor/s). Each has a clear motivation. It's not a case of black v. white but of conflicting desires, the desire of the protagonist being a legitimate desire for self-expression or the the fulfilment of natural rights.

iii. A sequence of physicalised (perhaps also verbalised) actions which show how the protagonist begins the story in a strong, positive position – seemingly unassailable – but due to the tactics of the oppressor and on account of making various 'mistakes' in dealing with those tactics, ends up defeated by the antagonist.

Any theatrical style is permissible if it serves the objective of the exercise while Boal himself has expressed a preference for 'objective expressionism'. Once the play is rehearsed, it is introduced to its audience. In a workshop context this might even be the remainder of the group. The sequence of events at point of performance (following a 'conventional' Forum practice) would be as follows:

The joker introduces the company and the theme at the centre of the play. The joker's function has clear parallels with that of the facilitator, it's to mediate between the actors and the audience, perhaps occasionally acting, putting challenges to the audience, fielding their interventions and summarising the strategies attempted. Secondly, the play is presented. Let us imagine a scene where a woman is being given notice by her landlord because of neighbours' complaints. In fact, the landlord is responding to local prejudice against her colour. The scene ends with her eviction. Now the joker explains that the scene will be run again. Only this time, the audience are invited to address the protagonist's problem. If they can see an error on her part in dealing with the landlord, or how her case could be handled better, they should put up a hand or shout 'Stop!' At that point the joker will invite them to replace the actress and act out what they think the woman might do differently. Men or women may get up. Once the spectactor enters the stage, we're improvising. One spectactor wants to fight the landlord, another wants to threaten him, another wants to use blackmail. The actors remaining on stage have to improvise with the spectactors, testing the new idea, not squashing it flat, but genuinely testing it. The model is a fight, a contest, a combat albeit one conducted in a spirit of play.

The joker explains that the purpose is not necessarily to find a correct solution but to look at as many alternative courses of action as there are time for. When one spectator has intervened, another may try. If no one comes, the play may revert to its original course or it may get picked up at another point. The joker may always cajole the audience again – 'Are these events inevitable?' 'What else can the woman do?' If the play has been correctly constructed and there is sympathy for the protagonist, there will be interventions. The joker acknowledges both weak and strong interventions without judgement – after all, it is for the audience themselves to make their own assessments. An apparently weak strategy may still be successful in eliciting something from the landlord – for example about his source of information – which proves to be vital knowledge. So it cannot be discounted. Much depends on the joker for a successful Forum. Here are some outlines for Joker Behaviour, given in Boal's Games for Actors and Non-Actors:

1. Jokers must avoid all actions which could manipulate or influence the audience. They must not draw conclusions which are self-evident. They must always open the possible conclusions to debate, stating them in an interrogative rather than an affirmative form ...

2. *Jokers decide nothing personally. They spell out the rules of the game, but in complete acceptance from the outset that the audience may alter them, if it is deemed necessary for the study of the proposed subject.*

3. *The joker must constantly be relaying doubts back to the audience so that it is they who make the decisions. Does this particular solution work or not? Is this right or wrong? And this principle applies most of all in relation to the spectactor's interventions. Often a spectactor will say 'Stop!' before the preceding spectactor has finished their intervention. The joker must then tactfully persuade the the newly intervening spectactor to exercise patience, while also trying to sense what the audience wants; they may well have understood the intervention and want to move on . . . Jokers must watch out for all 'magic' solutions. They can interrupt the spectactor/protagonist's action if they consider this action to be magic, not ruling that it is magic, but rather asking the audience to decide.*

5. *The physical stance of the joker is extremely important. Some jokers are tempted to mix with the audience, to sit with them; this can be completely demobilising. Others allow their own doubts, indecision or timidity to show through . . . If the joker on stage is tired or confused, he or she will transmit a tired and disorientated image to the audience . . .*

6. *Finally . . . the joker must be Socratic – dialectically – and, by means of questions and doubts, must help the spectators to gather their thoughts, to prepare their actions. Maieutics – the joker is a midwife . . . The joker must assist the birth of all ideas, of all actions.*[34]

Once interventions begin, the role of the other actors who are not replaced becomes important. This is one area of expertise where European actors have sometimes underestimated the degree of skill required. Perhaps it seems a relatively innocent function – after all, it's merely improvising. In fact it calls for tact, sensitivity, imaginative skill and a firm eye on the central concerns of the piece. It's important neither to accord the intervention more success than it deserves – the landlord may simply call the police if you suggest arson – nor to beat down the idea before it's been tried. If the actors' preparatory work has been sufficiently intensive, they will know their character's likely response to different interventions. Boal talks about the iceberg effect. On the sea, only 10% of the iceberg is visible – that's what we show of the character. However, there is 90% of the iceberg below – that's the larger part of the character which is only shown as necessary. The actor playing this part must know that 90% of what he *might do* if pressed. The landlord might be extremely friendly with the only other landlord in the village. But this isn't stated. But it will emerge if the actor thinks it necessary. To hide it would be to exaggerate unrealistically the strengths of the tenant. As in the exercise PUSHING which Boal refers to as a metaphor, the company actor must use the minimum of force to bring out the strengths of the spectator. If the actor playing the landlord meets a particularly forceful and imaginative intervention, then he may have to draw out all his hidden resources.

Since the introduction of Forum Theatre to Europe in the 1980s, it has undergone revision and adaptation in the hands of different practitioners. These are just a few examples of projects which have borrowed or adapted techniques:

THE LAWNMOWERS is a company of individuals with learning disabilities which was established with support from Them Wifies, based in Newcastle. They have been touring Forum Theatre pieces which deal with issues of contraception and the rights of the disabled.

THEM WIFIES is a women's collective which uses a practice they call 'Rhythm n' Role'. This draws equally on the ideas of Dorothy Heathcote, Augusto Boal and John Chernoff whose work is rooted in African music.

THE CARDBOARD CITIZENS is a company formerly based at the Bubble Theatre in South London which presents forum pieces on issues relating to homelessness. The company consists of formerly homeless individuals whose negative experiences of street living provoked them into searching for strategies which would publicise their situation. Their shows, often performed to groups of homeless, centre around practical ideas for dealing with life on the streets.

AGE EXCHANGE is a theatre company creating plays based on the memories and concerns of older people in the London area. The company has run several Boal-influenced projects including Many Happy Retirements which explored the challenges of leaving work for the last time. Other Forum pieces have looked at the different expectations of men and women when reaching retirement.

3. PLAYBACK THEATRE

Founded twenty years ago in the US, Playback Theatre draws preexisting stories from the audience as its performance material. Its founder, Jonathan Fox, reputedly developed the techniques while observing his own children. The company is made up of a Conductor, several actors and often a musician. In a performance setting, the actors invite stories from the audience then literally 'play them back', provide a dramatic interpretation, more often than not in a metaphorically imaginative way. There are some parallels with Keith Johnstone's Lifegame in which a performance is improvised around the telling of stories from one person's life. Playback also shares certain characteristics with psychodrama – yet there are key distinctions as well. Veronica Needa, who leads the English company, points out: *'Psychodrama has tremendous associations and affiliations with Playback Theatre, but they are not the same entities at all. Jonathan is very keen to distinguish Playback Theatre as a theatrical experience which has therapeutic impact, and psychodrama which is very clearly a form of therapy. They share certain things – for example, psychodrama works very much through authenticity and spontaneity . . . The important thing for Jonathan is that we're working through art as a transformative and healing tool.'*

The most common setting for Playback, at least in this country, is a community one. The company occasionally stages public shows, but relies particularly on commissions to perform with different groups. In all cases, and companies work now throughout the globe, the format is standardised: the audience having been seated (the English company tends to work in the round but there are no restrictions on this), the Conductor introduces the programme. Behind them may be a number of milk crates for use as furniture, the Conductor's chair, the Teller's chair and the actors – probably accompanied by a musician. There may also be some cloths for use as props. The actors may also introduce themselves, perhaps with a one-line story. The Conductor will then talk to the audience, *'using one of several techniques – one of which is sociometry – asking how many have seen one of these performances before, asking how many have come from outside London, asking for example how many are over the age of 40 – it's beginning to enable the audience to know each other, get a sense of each other . . . And then gradually, or quite quickly, we will engage the audience to describe a feeling they have – and will immediately play that back.'*

A spectator will offer a word to describe a current feeling. The actors interpret this in a short sketch or 'Fluid Sculpture'. There are a number of such short forms to either begin or end a programme, another is 'Pairs' where two actors play two feelings within the same person or 'Chorus' where a group represents a single quality. At the beginning, these techniques have the function of warming the audience to the exercise, and engaging them at a feeling level. Then the Conductor moves to asking for stories. *'There are many different ways of doing that. Invocation is our formal way. The Conductor may say a few words which may enable the audience to tap into a story which is present, and which enables them to want to share that story with a community of people. Some companies start with a theme, like some of the Australian companies. Or when you're working in a specific context like a business conference for example, or with medical students, your employers might wish you to address a theme they're interested in. But the classical, traditional way is to let the stories emerge.'*

If the Conductor announces a theme, 'Meetings', 'Time Stories' or 'Animal Farm', it's permissible for the audience to interpret the title as they will. The title is merely a hook, which triggers the audience imaginatively and allows them to contribute. When a spectator is ready to volunteer a story, the individual is invited to sit in the Teller's chair, and begin. The Conductor helps the Teller give their story concisely; avoiding vagueness, unrelated digressions and unclarity. Once told, the Teller is invited to choose an actor to play themselves. The story must in some way involve or relate to themselves – if the central character is another person, there must be a visceral link to their own life. As to content, the story may be light or dark, none is rejected or disparaged. What tends to happen is that *'when the right level of trust and safety is created, then the deeper stories will emerge. It's a tremendous gift to everyone when someone is prepared to tell a deep story, and it's played back.'* Once the story is told, the Conductor gives a signal. The musician may play a prelude as the actors set up, this may involve coming together in a silent circle then each moving to take up a position on the stage area, creating a tableau. When the tableau is felt to be complete, the musician stops and the action begins.

Performances aim to capture the truthfulness of the story rather than adhere to any strict idea of realism. *'Some of the less theatrically skilled companies tend to perform in a naturalistic way, and it's still powerful but the more you increase your theatrical vocabulary, the more you can offer . . . Our preference is to move into more metaphorical and physical work.'* This latter approach tends to be less character or plot driven than harnessed to images which sequence together to create the story. There's a prevailing mood to each scene which echoes the emotional qualities within the tale. Generally the only props are the scarves, which can be used in a variety of ways – in one performance a scarf is an umbilical cord, in another the water from a fire hose, or fire itself. The Conductor may intervene, for example to bring a scene to a conclusion but will tend to stay out of the action as far as possible during the several scenes which make up the interpretation of a story. If the Conductor feels however, at the end of an interpretation, that the essence has been missed, they may refer back to the Teller: 'Is that how it was?' There is an option of a further enactment, or the Teller may add verbally what was lacking, or incorrect. *'Sometimes we offer the Teller the opportunity to change the ending – or some elements of it – particularly if it was a very painful story. It might have been about a funeral of a parent and they missed an opportunity to say something. I remember a story where a 13-year-old girl was put into a car going to the funeral of her father and instead of going with her mother she was put between two grizzly aunties . . . she was miserable . . . she told us she wished at 13 she'd had enough strength and presence of mind to tell those aunties I want to sit with my mother – and we did that.'*

Inevitably the success of the process much depends on the skills of the team. *'The actors need to have witnessed a lot of stories, so they can communicate with the audience in an engaging way. Everyone brings their own style, but they need to be able to see the larger picture – to hold the context of the evening but be present in the moment. To hold in mind the context of that community and even connecting what's told that night to the context of history.'* Their overall task is to interpret personal stories through an understanding of the emotional core of the tale. They aim for an essence while avoiding any inference that they should be factually truthful. Their role is essentially non-critical but this can change. If for example the Teller expresses pleasure in cruelty, the team might choose to focus their dramatisation more on the victim of the cruelty than the perpetrator.

As with the role of the Questioner and Joker, the Conductor is the bridge between the two worlds of spectators and actors. Many of the general facilitative obligations apply; giving attention, managing structures, troubleshooting and cultivating a harmonious event which brings people closer together. *'The Conductor literally takes the role of conducting the energies from the audience to the actors and back again . . . '*

CONCLUSION

NEW FUSIONS

Following the end of the twentieth century, a recurring characteristic of post-millennium tension can be identified as a growing distrust in the single art form. Whether this hunger to mix and match aesthetic traditions is merely a fashionable, passing exercise or the beginning of new hybrids which will achieve longevity, is perhaps too early to say. But as in music where bhangra and rock, reggae and Cajun, classical and pop meet and marry, so too drama and theatre traditions are being fused with photography, video, music and sculpture to knock accepted models of working into a back room. In the community arts field too, these processes are evident. Computer technology in particular is helping facilitators achieve in new ways the now well-established aim of realising the creative potential of groups of non-artists, through forms and structures which are comparable in impact with those of established artists. So too for the drama facilitator, the challenge is there: to work with artists from other disciplines and conspire with them to create new forms which will best reflect the shifting zeitgeist. Because theatre is one of our oldest and most powerful art forms and because our ancient plays still pack a punch, does not mean we are relieved of the obligation to invent new formal structures which are appropriate for a changing society. The responsibility, and the necessity to do so, however, can only be informed productively by awareness of what recent and current generations of practitioners have themselves devised. Indeed, these earlier paradigms will themselves contain the future, albeit they have to be turned upside down first. So if theatre is a house of games, it will need to be ransacked and refurbished periodically, but perhaps not at the expense of the foundations.

FURTHER GAMES AND EXERCISES

SPARKS — EARLY EXERCISES

A. ATTENTION

X CALLS Y

Sometimes referred to as a name game. The group stands in a circle and each player is asked to find a movement to accompany the giving of their name. So they give their name, with their movement. Then the facilitator, as part of the circle, gives their own name with movement, and 'calls' someone else. So they might say 'Chris-calls-Jan' doing their own movement with their name, and Jan's movement with hers. Then Jan has to call someone else, and so on.

YES AND NO

This game used to be the mainstay of a popular British game show in the sixties. In pairs, one player asks another questions to which any answer may be given except yes or no. If yes or no is given, a point is lost or the questioning passes to the other player.

CHANGE THREE THINGS

Another exercise which is run in pairs. First, Player A takes a good look at what Player B is wearing. Then Player A closes their eyes while player B makes three small adjustments to what they are wearing. Player A opens their eyes and has to identify the changes.

WRISTS

In pairs, one player leads another around the room by means only of a very light contact, wrist to wrist. The leader should vary the pace and height and dexterity of their leading.

GLASS COBRA

A further blind exercise involves the group coming to the centre of the room and forming a long line, each player facing the back of another. There will be someone at the front who has no one ahead of them. Then the facilitator/s ask for the players to touch the back of the person in front. They need to be able to identify this person again, but with their eyes closed. Then they close their eyes and the facilitator/s lead them separately around the room, leaving them in different parts of the room. When everyone has been led to a different position in this way, the players' task is to re-form the original line-up, the cobra, without opening their eyes. If possible they should find the exact point in the room as well as identifying the person they were behind, to achieve this.

MATTHEW, MARK, LUKE AND JOHN

A rhythm game with a competitive edge. Players stand in a circle. A hierarchy is established which reads Matthew, Mark, Luke, John, 1, 2, 3, 4 and so on. The lowest numbered player stands next to Matthew. The purpose of the game is to 'get to heaven', i.e. climb the hierarchy and become Matthew. The group stands in a circle and establishes a slow 2/2 rhythm using a combination of slaps, claps and finger clicks. The final two clicks are made simultaneously with the name of the player who is passing the focus on. For example, Matthew starts and the rhythm goes: 'Slap – clap – Matthew-to-4.' So then it's 4's responsibility to pass it on, on the next appropriate beat. So she goes '4-to-Mark' after the initial two beats. Then Mark has the focus. If anyone makes a mistake, they simply go down to the bottom of the pile, i.e. the lowest number and everyone else moves up one. The point is not to make any mistakes and to always get the words in time with the rhythm.

BLIND HUGS AND HANDS

An exercise for co-ordination and developing the non-visual senses. In pairs, the players walk towards each other – from several yards apart – and shake hands. Then they try it again immediately after, but with eyes closed this time.

Variation: Players walk towards and hug each other, then repeat with eyes closed.

WHAT'S MY ADDICTION?

Simply, a question and answer game, a corrupted version of 'What's My Line?' One player sits apart from the others and agrees to be asked questions. He or she has a secret addiction which is highly personal and unusual, for example smelling other peoples' socks or licking the condensation off car windows. Questions are asked by the rest of the group to establish the nature of the addiction. The only answers permitted are Yes, No and Maybe. The group have to expose the addiction.

B. ENERGY

LET'S!

This game operates in free space, with players moving around as they want, but following the instructions given. Initially the players just walk in the space. Anyone has the opportunity to say 'Let's . . . (do something/be something)!' For example, 'Let's jump as high as we can!' or 'Let's be assassins in a car park!' or 'Let's be electrocuted!' Everyone in the group must then shout 'Yes, let's . . . (be whatever)!' in response and immediately start acting out as per the instruction. They continue doing this action until someone else shouts out: 'Let's . . . !'

CHINESE PUSHING

There's probably nothing Chinese whatsoever about this, but it does have a hint of the martial arts. In pairs, the players stand with feet some eighteen inches apart. They put their hands out, palms facing the other person. Each has the same objective: to knock the other off balance without losing balance themselves. Players are not permitted to move their feet. The only permitted form of contact is palm to palm. But of course arms and hands can be moved out of the way, and so it becomes a game of tactics and skill, not strength. If a player moves their feet, they lose a point.

THE BEARS ARE COMING

This game works better in a larger group. Two or three individuals are nominated to be bears, and the majority of the group are lumberjacks. The bears are sent out of the room. The lumberjacks start chopping down trees and singing jolly lumberjack songs. However, there is a bear problem in this vicinity of the Californian redwoods. The bears come in and eat people. The only way to defeat the bears is by persuading them that you are not a person but a tree or a stone. So, at a given signal, the game begins with the bears starting to growl outside the door. When this happens, the lumberjacks initially run around, very frightened, shouting 'The Bears are Coming!' Then the door is opened and the bears come in, still growling. The lumberjacks immediately go very quiet and still. The bears then have to test to see if these are really are inanimate objects or just, lumberjacks, pretending. If they're lumberjacks of course, they will be eaten. The bears can use any means within their power to test the creatures, except actually touch them. Usually the bears try to get the lumberjacks to laugh. After a minute or two, one or two lumberjacks have been exposed, and the bears are sent out again with the exposed lumberjacks who now become bears. The surviving lumberjacks go back to chopping wood and singing songs. Again the bears start growling, again they rush in, again the lumberjacks pretend to be stone or trees. The game ends when there is only one lumberjack remaining who is pronounced the toughest lumberjack in the redwoods.

HANX
Every player is given a handkerchief or a rag to tuck into the back of their trousers. Players then have to try and steal as many hanx as they can from other players without having their own stolen. This exercise can also be played in pairs, perhaps as a prelude to the group game.

C. IMAGINATION

TWO LINES
Players form two lines, with each line facing the other. The lines are about 6 ft. apart. Every player has another opposite them. Players in one line close their eyes allowing their partners to take up a physical shape, one which they can hold for several minutes. The blind partner then has to identify this shape through touch, and reproduce it opposite, as if in a mirror. When they've finished, they open their eyes and compare the reproduction with the original.

SHOLA'S EXERCISE

Named after a theatre director who introduced it to me, this involves players each bringing to the workshop one or two objects each which have a personal association for them. They need to choose objects which they are happy for others to improvise with. The objects are set out on the stage area, and the group sits in the audience area. As and when they feel inspired, players come out one at a time on to the stage and select one or two objects. They simply improvise a short scene on their own, using the object/s. The scene can be as short or as long as they wish.

BLOWING UP A BALLOON

In pairs. One player folds over as if they were a limp balloon which has no air in it. Then the other player 'pumps up' the balloon until it's up to full size. This means probably that the first player is as large as they can make themselves, fully inflated. The facilitator might then ask these players to walk about the space and interact with each other, continuing to make themselves as large as possible. At a given moment, their partners take an imaginary pin and burst the balloons, which then fizz about the room and expire.

Extension: While they are walking about, scenes and interactions can be set up between these super-tense, aggressive, hostile – yet vulnerable – cartoon characters.

MY ROOM

A volunteer comes on to the stage and, questioned by the facilitator, describes his room at home. He walks about the stage, describing where particular items of furniture are placed. The facilitator may ask detailed questions about the contents of cupboards or the contents of letters.

Extension: The facilitator asks the player to allow fictional elements to be introduced into the room. For example, the facilitator might say 'Take out that small tin that's in the back of the cupboard and open it up' or 'Whose initials are carved on the end of that bed?'

D. COMMUNICATION

BLIND GROUP SCULPT

The group splits into two, and one half leaves the room. Those who remain inside, select a group image which they are going to build, using the other group members. For example, they select a scene at the gallows during the French Revolution or the moment when Kennedy was assassinated. Then they go out and tell the other players to close their eyes, and keep them closed until the exercise is finished. Then they bring the other players back into the space and sculpt them into appropriate positions, as per the image. When this stage is completed, the blind players must describe to each other the positions they're in, and so deduce collectively what the image is, which they're representing.

PRESENTS

The group stands in a circle, facing inwards. The facilitator asks someone in the group to give a present to someone else. The nominated player then walks across and 'gives a present', in effect miming a large or small parcel and handing it over. After appropriate remarks, the receiving player opens the package. In opening it, they define what is inside. They see what they see. The giver acknowledges whatever present the receiver says it is, and the dialogue continues accordingly. Then the receiver gives a present to someone else in the group.

Extension: The facilitator extends the scene by adding instructions or setting up a further scene. For example, it's one month after the gift has been made, and the giver is coming round to see how it now looks or how it's grown up. But unfortunately the gift has been accidentally destroyed . . .

ANTHROPOLOGISTS

Can be played as a group, or in pairs. The game is based on the understanding that each social group tends to have its own forms of gesture which are particular to that social group. We imagine that in a remote area of the world there is a group whose gestures are unique, and unknown. The anthropologist has to find out what these are, in order to strike up a dialogue. One player is nominated to be

the anthropologist, another is a leader of that tribe. The player
playing the leader privately defines two gestures, one which means
hullo and one which means 'here is my offering'. The player playing
the anthropologist has to work out what these are, in order to use
them. So when the anthropologist arrives and holds out a hand, the
tribal leader shrinks back. This is clearly not seen as a friendly
gesture. The anthropologist has to use trial and error to work out
the appropriate gestures; when the first is discovered, then the
second can be aimed for. Only then does an exchange of gifts
become possible.

RHYTHM GAMES
Here are just a few of the many different rhythm games.

CALL AND ANSWER   The group stands in a circle. The facilitator, on a rhythmic beat, establishes a call and answer pattern, either
using claps or voice. So a 'clap-clap' is echoed by the group. A 'heya,
heya, heya, ho' is echoed by the group. Once a pattern is established
using simple rhythms, more complex rhythms can be explored. The
leadership can also be passed to another member of the group at
which point the facilitator becomes part of the answering chorus.

Variation: Words can be introduced for the calling, which are then
answered.

HIGH AND LOW   Also in a circle, a rhythm is passed around the
circle in the form of a clap, so the two players standing next to each
other clap together, then one of these turns to their other partner
and claps with them. If one pair clap high, i.e. with hands above the
head, then the next pair should clap low, with hands down at knees.

RHYTHMS ON THE FLOOR   Players kneel on the floor, in a
circle, and all place hands on the floor. Each player then has their
left hand next to another's right hand. In this way there are pairs of
hands around the circle, each pair made by two different players.
A simple rhythm is given by the facilitator which has to be passed
around the circle by the different pairs of hands. This means that the
left hand of Player A needs to co-ordinate with the right of Player B,
and then the left of Player B with the right of Player C, and so on.

HUNTING THE LION   This is effectively a variation on FOLLOW-MY-LEADER coupled with CALL AND ANSWER. In this case, the leader remains consistently one person, perhaps the facilitator. The game was introduced to me by a Nigerian theatre practitioner and it's hard to imagine it without his level of energy and enthusiasm. He led the group on a hunt for a lion over African terrain, negotiating hills and rivers and invoking all the gods, before finally cornering the beast. Every speech and every action of his was echoed by the group. At different times we danced to a rhythm, swam through treacherous rivers and crawled like ants through the undergrowth.

SCAT SINGING   The group stands in a circle. One player begins by establishing a bass line rhythm, which should remain constant through the exercise. Another comes in with a rhythmic, repetitive sound which fits with the first, and complements it. Other players come in as appropriate. The last to come in, sings 'scat' over the rest, improvising sounds or words as they wish.

CLOSING RHYTHMS   Perhaps a closing exercise. The group stands or sits in a circle. The facilitator stands within the circle. At a constant rhythm, the facilitator starts a clap or some other sound. The player on their left copies this rhythm, and the person on their left then follows in turn. It's important that all players follow in this way, rather than copy the facilitator. This enables the facilitator to change the sounds or words of the rhythm and for these changes to filter round the group slowly.

BUILDING A GROUP: TEAMWORK

A. SUPPORTIVENESS

FALLING

The group move around in the space, which needs to be clearly marked out, if the room is not small. At any point, someone can call out 'Falling!' at which point they start to slowly topple over, as if they would fall like a leaning tower. All other players have to rush to them to ensure that they are caught safely before they reach the ground. As soon as that person is caught, the group can start walking again and the exercise repeats.

THE WAITER

A couple are sitting at a restaurant table to order their meal. The exercise is really a training exercise for the player in the role of the waiter, who must learn to be completely responsive to every small gesture or instruction.

THE VISITOR

Two volunteers go onto the stage area. One is to play a Visitor from another planet or remote part of the world, the other is to play an Interpreter. Let's imagine Kirsty is the Visitor and Bill is her Interpreter. Bill introduces her, let's say, as Habena Washroom from Planet Kettle. She has come to earth for a short stay and tonight is giving a short demonstration of some aspect of life back home. Kirsty then begins a mime, a physical presentation of, for example, how crops are grown or how cats are manufactured. Or she might describe some love-making rituals or demonstrate interplanetary fission. Bill then has to interpret to the audience what she is doing and why she is doing it. The two players should aim to feed off each other.

B. SPONTANEITY

TWO RUSH IN

The audience is assigned the role of a group of friends. Two other players rush in and one immediately starts describing an extraordinary event they both became embroiled in, while they were on the way over. They tell the story of what happened between them, without any pre-discussion. For example one starts 'This bus stopped and twenty-five gangsters got off. They started firing into the air – ' and the other continues ' – which brought the police running up at which point – ' and the first continues ' – the gangsters stripped off to their underwear and started dancing . . . ' and so on.

A to Z

Two players improvise a scene which is predetermined, for example, two cowboys are reminiscing or a drag artist is trying to buy a bra from a very conventional shop. The first player to speak must begin their sentence with the letter A. The second player must reply, beginning their sentence with the letter B and so on. The improvisation ends when the end of the alphabet is reached.

WHO, WHAT, WHERE

Two players go on to the stage area and begin an improvisation. Their task is to establish, without pre-discussion, who they are, where they and what they're doing. They must achieve this through actions and through co-operation. For example, one begins a mime of shoeing a horse. The other might ask 'Is it finished yet, Bob?' to which the other replies 'Almost, Boss'. So we know who they are and what they're doing, we only need to find out exactly where they are — in the country house of the owner or their own premises, where? When the facilitator is happy all questions have been answered, then it's the turn of another pair.

C. ADAPTATION

'I'VE FORGOTTEN MY ...'

This exercise is constructed to help a player experience embarrassment. An improvisation is played out between a secretary and a boss. The secretary is to come in and take a letter. However, each time the secretary comes in, he discovers he's forgotten something essential to the exercise. For example, the first time, it's a pen. So he apologises, goes out and returns with a pen but this time there's no paper. Next time he has nothing to rest on. Each time the actor must apologise and each time the boss must get more and more angry. Finally the secretary reveals that he can't write so he's sacked. It's only then the secretary realises this is the wrong room and the wrong boss ...

THE INTERROGATION

The group stands in a circle, representing the suspect. In the centre is the detective who is conducting an investigation into a crime. It's the detective's job to force the suspect into replying inconsistently to questions. The detective can turn to any member of the group, elicit information, then turn to another and ask the same questions again, requiring the same answer. It's for the group members to be aware of what everyone else has said, about the alibi for example, and always stick to it.

THE EXPERT

This game is one of a series which uses the word-at-a-time technique. Three players come out and sit facing the audience. They are announced as 'The Expert', in effect one person. Perhaps they are given a name. The facilitator, having introduced them and having established by agreement their area of expertise, asks questions of the Expert. The facilitator might ask how the Expert began to be interested in, for example, teaching ravens to fly underwater, or nude skiing. The three players answer as one, giving one-word-at-a-time answers. The effect can be amplified by the three players copying each other physically at the same time. Then questions can be taken from the audience.

GREEN GETS IT

This exercise has the quality of a social skills exercise in that it theatricalises what happens when individuals unconsciously transfer resentments caused in one area of life into another. The group stands in a circle. The facilitator asks one player to ask another across the circle if they would come out on a date. The reply comes back as a polite but firm rejection. It's for the rejected individual then to pick on another member of the group and express their resentment over this rejection, through the medium of a quite different subject. For example, the dialogue might go like this:

Beth: 'Dave, I wonder if you'd maybe like to go out with me tonight?'

'Dave: Sorry, Beth, I'm busy.'

Beth: 'How about next week then?'

Dave: 'Sorry, I really don't want to – ever.'

Beth: 'Jamie – where are my cds? I've told you time and again you're not allowed to borrow them!!'

At which point, Jamie would make the next request of someone else.

D. EMPOWERMENT

THE CHANGELING'S BALL

All the players write down on a piece of paper a quality they would like to embody more fully. For example one might write down 'self-confidence' or another 'outspoken-ness'. Then a role play is set up in which all are invited to a grand party. The host of the party, who might be the facilitator, dispenses drinks. There is also a wizard at the party, who has been secretly nominated by the facilitator beforehand. Once the guests have arrived and are socialising, the wizard – who is simply one of the guests – starts winking at people. When a player is winked at, he or she must immediately embody their desired attribute. They must play that quality to the full. It is for the facilitator to watch this playing and when it appears that a particular player has played that quality fully and for long enough, they are allowed to leave the party.

YOUR FANTASY

In small groups, one player in each group nominates a fantasy scene they would like to participate in. Sexual fantasies should normally be excluded, but fantasies of power or achievement or fame are permitted. The protagonist should describe to the players exactly what happens in the scene so they can play it out with the protagonist's participation. For example, in one scene a detective pursues a murder investigation and successfully gets one of the suspects to break down and confess. In another, a servant girl is recognised as being of greater worth than the Queen herself, who is deposed in the servant girl's favour ... The scenes are enacted, then the fantasist can be asked how well the enactment realised the dream, before performing again for the whole group.

SELLING

Two volunteers come forward. One is to be the seller and the other, the seller's assistant. Some props are required for this, to serve as objects which are sold. There is no necessity for these to be literally used, for example paper cups can be used as eyeglasses which reveal the future. The seller's task is to sell as many of these to the audience as possible, with the assistant providing back-up, as you might find on any street market in the world. The remainder of the group has a supportive role also in looking for opportunities to get a bargain, while testing the seller to be persuasive about the object's properties.

HOW DARE YOU! / I'M SORRY!

This is a dialogue exercise between two players which can be run in front of the group, or privately. Player A first advances on Player B and demands 'How dare you?' to which the other replies, 'I'm sorry!' The same lines are repeated, with each time a variation of tone or increase of energy. The dialogue should be physicalised as much as possible and pushed to the maximum point. So, for example, Player A ends up towering over Player B who is cowering on the ground. When it has gone as far as it can, the roles suddenly reverse and Player B, from that same cowering position, says 'How dare you?' The see-saw starts to tip the other way.

CLOWN FROM AMSTERDAM

This exercise is a variation on the copying exercise in which one player follows another, copying their movements. In this variation, the follower begins to send up the movements of the leader, who occasionally turns round and 'catches them at it'. The point for the follower is not to avoid capture but to be caught, and explore excuses and pretences to justify what they are doing.

Extension: The leader gives a lecture-demonstration to the audience (one of the best I ever saw was on the theme of 'Coins of the Realm') and the follower, now an assistant, proceeds to send up from behind, everything the leader does or says. Again, the objective is to be caught out and find imaginative justications for the behaviour. The player playing the leader should where possible try to accept these excuses. From here we move into the kind of double act popularised in England by Morecambe and Wise.

DEATH IN A MINUTE

Two players must perform an improvised scene lasting exactly sixty seconds. Nothing is predetermined about the scene. During the scene, one of the characters must die. The death can be by any means necessary; suicide, murder or natural causes. However, the scene must, by the time it has completed, reveal something about the death or the reasons for it. The scene must achieve a completeness, dramatically, within the sixty seconds.

JANUS

In pairs, players improvise a conflict between two characters embodying very opposite attitudes. For example, there's an argument between a brave person and a cowardly person over whether to get into a plane, and one between a licentious person and a censorious one about drug-taking. The improvisations are prepared, and each partner in each pair gets to play both roles. The next stage involves each partner playing both roles, moving between them at will. During this, the other partner can support and direct them. Then individuals come back to the main group and show their work, each player presenting a prepared improvisation during which they play both roles, switching quickly between them.

STEALING THE LOVER

This is for those who feel comfortable with more elaborate rhythm exercises. A circle is formed by the group members sitting on the floor. Two players come into the centre and build up a rhythmic sound and movement, in effect a dance between them. Preferably the movement should involve both hands and feet. The rhythmic patterns should be constant and clear. Outside the circle, a third player develops a quite contrasting sound and movement, then he or she comes into the circle and tries to steal away one of the two other players by 'seducing' them with the new rhythm. When this is accomplished, the player who has been ignored, and by implication rejected, leaves the circle. The stage is set for a further intervention.

THE TELEPHONE

This is an exercise for developing an ability with split focus. A single actor is given a telephone, and two relationships are set up. For example, a mother and a boyfriend. The actor is talking to the mother on the phone and has the boyfriend in the room. Both the mother and boyfriend roles are played by actors. The actor on the phone has to juggle both conversations. A third element can also be introduced, that of asides to the audience about the characters being spoken to, and how difficult they are as people!

HELLO AND GOODBYE

This exercise is to develop an ability to play feelings which are opposite to the words spoken. In pairs, the players rehearse scenes of leave-taking. First, the simple version. Two lovers say goodbye to each other and each expresses great fondness and regret. Then the same words are spoken, but each partner plays the scene with a feeling which is opposite, i.e. they really want to go. Then one player plays it with honesty, one with hypocrisy. Other scenes can be explored, for example, welcoming an old friend into the house or drinking a toast to Christmas.

SEXY, SILLY, STUPID

An improvised scene which works by endowing players with particular qualities, which they don't necessarily possess. For example, three friends go on a picnic. One is sexy, one silly, one stupid. But the three don't necessarily play these characteristics – the other two assume that person possesses them. So the sexy one doesn't play sexy, but the other two always want to get close to that person. The stupid one doesn't play stupid, but the other two behave as if everything that person says is dumb.

Variation: The characteristics can be changed, as well as the scene itself. For example, a mother, her daughter and her boyfriend go to a rifle range. The daughter is very good at making jokes – so everything she says, the others find funny. The mother is accident-prone – so the others are very careful with her. Finally, the boyfriend is vulgar – so the others have to correct his words all the time.

TV GAME

This exercise is for sharing and passing focus. A number of players are required; two to share the presenter's role, one to be a reporter in the field, two improvisers to be whatever interviewees are required and possibly an expert in the studio. First, the team decides a theme and a title for their documentary television programme, which is magazine-format. For example, the theme is adventure holidays and the title 'On the Rocks'. The premise is that the programme is recorded 'live' with no scope for retakes. After a countdown, one of the two presenters introduces the programme, then hands over to the fellow presenter for a – completely improvised – description of programme contents. Then they 'hand over' to the reporter in the field who is already in Newfoundland with, for example, a woman who likes to wrestle with penguins for sport. 'And I believe you have a penguin with you now . . . ?' After each brief report has been improvised, the reporter hands back to the studio for further commentary or a presentation from the expert, before the studio presenter goes back again for a different report from another part of the world.

If you would like to contribute games or exercises
to any future editions of the book,
please e-mail the author at

cj@fluxx.co.uk

CONTRIBUTING PRACTITIONERS

PETER BADEJO is a Nigerian performer and teacher, and Director of Badejo Arts. His productions, based in part upon African story-telling traditions, have been toured world-wide.

GERALDINE LING has been learning, using and developing drama since 1970. Since joining Them Wifies in 1983, she has spent time developing Theatre of the Oppressed work with groups in the North-East, especially girls, women and the disabled.

ALI CAMPBELL is a facilitator, formerly with Breakout T.I.E. He is now lecturer at Queen Mary and Westfield College in East London. He also runs community arts and theatre programmes with Glyndebourne Opera.

JON PALMER has worked in community theatre since 1981 as performer, musician and workshop leader. As artistic director of Interplay Theatre Company he developed 'inclusive theatre' – a methodology which works from the needs of young people with learning disabilities.

NIC FINE has worked extensively with LEAP Confronting Conflict, a community arts organisation based in North London, running projects with offenders and young people at risk. He has subsequently moved to South Africa.

PHELIM MCDERMOTT is a performer and director with Improbable Theatre, which tours internationally with shows such as *Coma*, *Sticky* and *Spirit*.

GUY DARTNELL is an actor working with Improbable Theatre Company who teaches widely in Europe and beyond. His particular interest lies in the possibilities of physical and vocal performance, as reflected in his one-man shows, which include the award-winning *Would Say Something*.

CLAIR CHAPWELL, formerly Clare Chapman, came to England in 1973. She is Artistic Director of Spare Tyre Theatre Co. Spare Tyre specialises in working with groups of young people in projects which lead to performance.

HARRIET POWELL is a musician and music tutor who has worked extensively with Spare Tyre Theatre Company.

KATINA NOBLE is a performer and facilitator based in Bristol, formerly with Spare Tyre Theatre Company.

ROGER HILL is a facilitator who has worked nationally and internationally with youth theatres. He was the President of the National Association of Youth Theatres for several years, and was instrumental in its growth and development.

LOIS WEAVER worked with Split Britches in the US and has since been Artistic Director of Gay Sweatshop Theatre Co. in England. She is currently lecturer at Queen Mary and Westfield College in East London.

FRANCES RIFKIN is a director and facilitator, and founder of Recreation Ground Theatre Co. She has worked with Clean Break and other theatre companies and currently runs Utopia Theatre.

JONATHAN KAY is a performer and teacher who has worked in Canada, Australia and Europe. His workshops focus on the art of fooling. His performances are entirely improvised.

WOLFGANG STANGE is the Director of Amici, a theatre company which combines able-bodied with disabled performers. The company's dance-theatre performances have toured on a number of occasions within Europe.

SAUL HEWISH was a founder member and former director of Geese Theatre Co. (UK) and has worked extensively in prisons and probation venues throughout theUK and USA. He is currently Co–Director with Chris Johnston of Rideout (Creative Arts for Rehabilitation).

JOHN BERGMAN founded Geese Theatre in 1980. He has worked in over 800 prisons around Romania, Australia, England and America. His current plans are focused on international versions of community/ restorative justice issues and the process of theatre.

DAVID SLATER is Artistic Director of a S-E London art company Entelechiy. He has a long and varied experience of working with theatre and communities.

CLIVE BARKER ran acting workshops in many parts of the world, using his own approach to actor training, the basis of which is set out in his book *Theatre Games* (pub. Methuen). He was Joint Editor of *New Theatre Quarterly*, and following his death in 2005 is mourned as a major influence on a whole generation of theatre-makers.

R.G. GREGORY was a teacher of English and Drama from 1953 to 1972 when he started Word and Action Theatre Company. He has been there ever since.

PHIL KNIGHT was Artistic Director of Third Theatre Ltd during its incarnation. The company's main area of research was to explore expression through actors' physicality. He has taught workshops on physical theatre throughout the UK, most particularly at Rose Bruford College. He is now based in France.

PETE BROOKS was a member of Impact Theatre Co-operative and then Artistic Director of Insomniac Theatre Company. Both companies toured internationally. He now teaches in the University of London.

MARK LONG was a founder member of the People Show which has been performing throughout the world since 1968.

VERONICA NEEDA was a founder member of London Playback Theatre.

NOTES

INTRODUCTION

1. Simon Callow, *Being an Actor*. Methuen. 1984.
2. Baz Kershaw, *The Politics of Performance*. Routledge. 1992.

PART ONE

3. Richard Schechner, *The Future of Ritual*. Routledge. 1996.
4. Sybil Thorndike, unidentified interview.
5. Simon Callow, *Shooting the Actor*. Vintage. 1992.
6. Richard Schechner, *The Future of Ritual*. Routledge. 1996.
7. Nic Fine and Fiona Macbeth, *Playing With Fire*. Leaveners Press.
8. Augusto Boal, *The Rainbow of Desire*. Routledge. 1992.
9. R.G. Gregory, *The World of Instant Theatre*. Wanda Publications.
10. Baz Kershaw, *The Politics of Performance*. Routledge. 1992.
11. Augusto Boal, *Games for Actors and Non-Actors*. Routledge. 1992.
12 Arthur Mindel, *Dreambody: the Body's Role in Revealing the Self*. Arkana. 1982.
13. Carl Jung, *Archetypes and the Collective Unconscious*. Routledge.
14. Ibid.
15. Viola Spolin, *Improvisation for the Theatre*. Pitman. 1963.
16. Clive Barker, *Games in Education and Theatre*, *New Theatre Quarterly*, Vol V, No 19.
17. Ibid.
18. Mark Long, Lecture at the ICA. 1995.
19. Keith Johnstone, *Impro*. Methuen. 1981.

PART TWO

20. Julian Beck, *The Life of the Theatre*. City Lights. 1972.
21. Clive Barker, letter to the author.
22. Chrissie Poulter, *Playing the Game*. Macmillan. 1987.

23. Keith Johnstone. *Theatresports and Life-Game Newsletter.* Issue No. 1, 1987.
24. Keith Johnstone, *Impro*. Methuen. 1981.

PART THREE

25. Clive Barker, letter to the author.
26. Keith Johnstone, *Impro*. Methuen. 1981.
27. Ibid.
28. Arthur Mindel, *Dreambody: the Body's Role in Revealing the Self*. Arkana. 1982.
29. Alistair Campbell, 'Falling or Flying? A Meeting Between Forum and Opera', in *Contemporary Theatre Review*, Vol. 3, 1995.
30. Ibid.
31. Keith Johnstone. *Theatresports and Life-Game Newsletter.* Issue No. 1, 1987.
32. Steve Mitchell, *The Handbook of Dramatherapy*. Routledge. 1994.
33. Interview with Boal, *Documents on Theatre of the Oppressed*. Red Letters. 1985
34. Augusto Boal, *Games for Actors and Non-Actors*. Routledge. 1992.

INDEX OF GAMES AND EXERCISES